Contemporary Directions in Asian American Dance

EDITED BY YUTIAN WONG

THE UNIVERSITY OF WISCONSIN PRESS

The University of Wisconsin Press
1930 Monroe Street, 3rd Floor
Madison, Wisconsin 53711-2059
uwpress.wisc.edu

3 Henrietta Street, Covent Garden
London WC2E 8LU, United Kingdom
eurospanbookstore.com

Printed in the United States of America

Library of Congress Cataloging-in-Publication Data

Names: Wong, Yutian, editor.
Title: Contemporary directions in Asian American dance /
edited by Yutian Wong.
Other titles: Studies in dance history (Unnumbered)
Description: Madison, Wisconsin : The University of Wisconsin Press, [2016] |
©2016 | Series: Studies in dance history | Includes bibliographical
references and index.
Identifiers: LCCN 2015036821 | ISBN 9780299308704 (cloth : alk. paper)
Subjects: LCSH: Asian American dance. | Dance—United States. |
Dance—Canada. | Asian Americans—Ethnic identity. |
Asians—Canada—Ethnic identity.
Classification: LCC GV1624.7.A85 C66 2016 | DDC 792.8—dc23
LC record available at http://lccn.loc.gov/2015036821

Contents

Preface and Acknowledgments

YUTIAN WONG

The idea for this book began as a conversation in 2001 at the Society of Dance History Scholars conference at Goucher College when Susan Manning suggested to Priya Srinivasan and me that there should be an anthology about Asian American dance. Given the nascent stage of Asian American dance studies at the time, Priya and I found ourselves working alongside our colleagues in Asian American theater studies to carve out an academic space to recognize the significance of performing arts as an expression of Asian American culture. Beginning with a series of fits and starts, the idea morphed into a proposed volume coedited with Esther Kim Lee, Ron West, and myself on Asian American performance in its broadest terms. The prodigious number of submissions we received in response to our Call for Papers was evidence of how much the field of Asian American performance studies had grown and compelled us to rethink the scope of the project. The number of essays we received on dance made for a compelling case that the time was right for a volume specifically about Asian American dance, and we decided to pursue separate projects. *Contemporary Directions in Asian American Dance* is the result of the conversation begun so many years ago.

I would like to thank Raphael Kadushin and Amber Rose at the University of Wisconsin Press and the members of the Studies in Dance History editorial board for their support of this project. Priya Srinivasan, Thomas DeFrantz, Jens Richard Giersdorf, Mimi T. Nguyen, Fiona Ngô, and Sarah Davies Cordova provided insightful feedback at different stages of the manuscript. To Susan Manning, Sherril Dodds, Ann Cooper Albright, Anthea Kraut, Lucy Mae San Pablo Burns, and Susan Rose, I am grateful for your counsel. Most of all, I would like to thank the authors who contributed their work to this book. It was a privilege to work with each of them. Wendy Diamond, Cathleen McCarthy, Ray Tadio, and our students at San Francisco State University have sustained my belief in the potential and resilience of dancing bodies. Last but not least, I want to thank Bruce for making everything possible, and Blake for reminding me what is not impossible.

*Contemporary
Directions in
Asian American
Dance*

Introduction

Issues in Asian American Dance Studies

YUTIAN WONG

Contemporary Directions in Asian American Dance argues that the study of work by Asian American dance artists, and the practice of Asian American critique, are central to nuanced analyses of dance as an artistic practice and dance studies as a disciplinary field. Asian American dance is a critical frame of engagement between dance studies and Asian American studies—two interdisciplinary fields concerned with the materiality of the body. Both legal and social questions of race, immigration history, and citizenship and the discursive parameters of cultural belonging raised by Asian American critique broaden analyses of dance, while attention to movement vocabularies, choreographic structures, and performance conventions pushes Asian American studies to attend to the significance of aesthetics in Asian American cultural production.

Ever since Chinese and Japanese indentured and contract laborers arrived on the West Coast of the United States during the nineteenth century to work agricultural fields and build railroads, Asian bodies in America have been racialized via the legal and social discourse of immigration. Asian Americans in the United States are assumed to be foreigners whose personal or ancestral arrivals to the country are marked on the body. Measures of Americanness, whether conferred via birthplace, citizenship status, or familial history, negotiate belonging for Asian American subjects as that which must nonetheless be proven rather than presumed. The intersection between race and citizenship shapes the way Asian American dance artists must navigate expectations of what their work should look like or what its function should be. Asian American critique as a mode of analysis gives form to Asian American dance studies as a field concerned with the diverse spectrum of responses to the racialization and positioning of dancing Asian bodies.

Asia has been present on the Western stage since Jean-Georges Noverre choreographed *Les Fêtes Chinoises* (ca. 1751). European and American choreographers have long staged scenes of dancing in an Orientalized Asia. Jean Coralli's *La Péri* (1843), Marius Petipa's *La Bayadère* (1877), Ruth St. Denis's *Radha* (1906), Michel Fokine's *Scheherazade* (1910), and Martha Graham's *Flute of Krishna* (1926) have all cited/sited the Orient as an imaginary space of sumptuous excess and aesthetic renewal, with white bodies performing Asian characters. Unlike theater and film, in which white actors don yellowface and speak in broken English, dancerly signifiers of Asianness are oftentimes a matter of décor or scenery. There is nothing particularly Indian about the "Entrance of the Shades" other than the fact that the viewer knows that the ballet is supposed to take place in India. If Asia is merely a visual referent in ballet, Merce Cunningham and John Cage's adoption of the *I-Ching*, Steve Paxton's training in *aikido*, and Laura Dean's kinetic citation of Sufi spinning have been translated into the minimalist forms and analytic procedures of postmodern dance. Yoga and belly dancing have provided Western bodies refuge from the perceived ills of modern life through the possibility of accessing alternative experiences and identities rooted in difference.[1]

The idea of Asia has long been a pool of inspirational possibility for American choreographic renewal since Ruth St. Denis premiered *Radha* in 1906, but the scholarly work of defining a body of Asian American dance has only begun to emerge in recent years. Unlike histories of African American, Native American, and Latino dance practices that must work against and problematize the essentializing narratives that naturalize assumed affinities between dance and black, Native, and Latino bodies, Asian Americans have been historically figured as nondancing bodies.[2]

Rooted in nineteenth-century stereotypes about the corrupt nature of the oriental as incompatible with American political and social life, and mid-twentieth-century Cold War stereotypes of Asian Americans as politically passive and imaginatively lacking, the place of Asian Americans within American creative life remains uncertain. The belief that Asian Americans are not artistically inclined continues to circulate in American culture. Amy Chua's *Battle Hymn of the Tiger Mother* (2011) provoked heated debate about the nature of "American" versus "Asian" parenting, and she was criticized for stifling her daughters' agency and ability to be creative subjects. Her self-described parenting style was cited as evidence that Asian Americans excel at math and science at the expense of arts and the humanities. Chua was criticized by other Asian Americans for buying into and perpetuating the most basic stereotype about Asian Americans as model minorities.[3]

In his 2012 *Wall Street Journal* article called "Rise of the Tiger Nation," Lee Siegel speculates whether his previously published resentment and criticism of Amy Chua's *Tiger Mother* is really a manifestation of his own fear that Asian Americans will become the new American Jews—assimilated and successful.[4] Rather than question the veracity of Chua's characterization of "Chinese parenting," as he did in his 2011 review of *Battle Hymn of the Tiger Mother*, Siegel accepts the stereotype of the Tiger Mother as an essential quality of Asian motherhood. From this position, Siegel attempts a comparative history of Asian American and Jewish American success stories and concludes that Asian Americans are in fact fundamentally different from American Jews. Siegel locates his evidence for this difference in his claim that American Jews excel in all areas of public life, especially in politics and the performing arts such as acting, singing, or dancing, whereas these are two areas in which Asian Americans are notably absent by either cultural choice or innate inability.

It is this perceived absence from the public stage, one that is decidedly political or performative, that Siegel posits as the reason for the instability of Asian American belonging within the larger idea of America as a conceptually unified abstract whole. Siegel gropes in the dark for an explanation of Asian American absence from the American stage and seems to forget that the acceptance of American Jews on American stages has been contingent on Jewish proximity to changing definitions of whiteness. He is remarkably color-blind to the discriminatory casting practices and the narrowly defined roles allotted Asian American performers with racially marked bodies.

The complex dynamics of American racial hierarchies do not figure in Siegel's conclusions about the nature of Asian Americans, and he reproduces the most widely circulated myths about Asian American achievement. Under the umbrella of model minority success, Siegel allows for classical music as the one arena in which Asian Americans can excel on-stage; however, he characterizes music as nonverbal, disembodied, and therefore suitable for Asian American sensibilities.[5] This is not surprising. Even within the world of classical music, the physicality of Asian musical virtuosity is framed as a matter of reproducible skill rather than that of artistic achievement.[6]

Any consideration of dance and choreography requires attentiveness to the bodies that Siegel claims are absent from American stages. Asian American dance refers to choreography that engages with dance practices brought to the United States by Asian artists, choreography that references Asian American history or experiences, or work choreographed or performed by Asian American dance artists. As a critical methodology, Asian American dance studies attends to the aesthetic and political transformations of Asian bodily practices in the United States, the politics of how Asian-based movement genres are situated within the larger American cultural landscape, and the effects of racial discourse on the perception and reception of Asian American choreographers and choreography.

Dance requires Asian American studies to recognize movement analysis and choreographic literacy as valuable tools for understanding the place of dancing within Asian American artistic life. Dance has been one of the last fields in the expressive arts to figure as a topic of scholarly inquiry within Asian American studies. Publications about Asian Americans as dance practitioners or choreographers represent a wide range of disparate practices from social and vernacular dance to classical forms. Asian American dance studies locates Asian American dance as a set of practices tied together by a constellation of investments and concerns over cultural belonging and otherness.

Historically, Asian American studies is an outgrowth of the Asian American movement in the 1960s and 1970s. Modeled after the Black Power movement, the Asian American movement emerged not out of shared cultural practices among Asian Americans but from political necessity. Whereas black cultural nationalism focused on African American cultural identification as a distinctive culture with shared African roots, Asian American cultural nationalism did not focus on Asia as a shared cultural foundation but on the commonalities of shared oppressions resulting from living within the geographic space of the United States. Asian American cultural nationalism and its focus on a racialized experience of living in the United States, rather than Asia as a source of cultural identification, runs counter to the impulse within dance studies to link racial minorities with traditional practices. The recognition of black cultural practices as rooted in Africanist aesthetics symbolized a progressive move to reclaim Africa in the context of slavery when enslaved Africans were forcibly disconnected from their linguistic, religious, and cultural practices. In contrast, Asian Americans whose historic arrival in the United States was governed by immigration law were viewed as essentially foreign.

Given the assumption that Asian Americans were first and foremost foreign and could at best be acculturated but never successfully assimilated, Asian American cultural nationalism provided a means to ground the Asian American presence within the borders of the United States.[7] Pan-Asian American identity was created to affirm Asian American subjects within their geographic location in America over shared linguistic, cultural, or national pasts. That some Asian ethnic groups might share overlapping traditions was secondary to the shared experience of enduring social or legal discrimination based on looking Asian.

Contemporary Directions in Asian American Dance is born out of queries from colleagues and students who have asked for resources to teach Asian American topics in dance courses and dance topics in Asian American studies courses. The literature on Asian American dance has grown over the last decade to represent a wide range of genres and disciplinary approaches to studying Asian American dance. Arthur Dong's award-winning documentary *Forbidden City, U.S.A.* (1989) is one of the earliest studies of dance situated within an Asian American historical context. The film chronicles the lives of Asian American dancers and singers working on the Chop Suey Circuit in the late 1930s and through the post–World War II era into the late 1940s. Much like the Cotton Club in Prohibition-era Harlem, featuring black entertainers performing for white patrons, the Chop Suey Circuit described a network of restaurants and nightclubs in San Francisco and New York's Chinatown featuring "Chinese" entertainers who performed vaudeville-style song and dance routines for white audiences.

While many of the "Chinese" entertainers were not actually Chinese but other Asian ethnicities, white audiences found the performance of American-style movement vocabulary—tap dance, ballroom dance, chorus lines, and strip tease—by "Chinese" bodies a considerable novelty. Of course, the novelty of performing Asian bodies was also coupled with their imminent danger. Japanese American performers passed as Chinese Americans in order to fulfill the circuit's promise of all-Chinese entertainment and to circumvent both pre- and postwar anti-Japanese sentiment.[8] At the same time, nightclub acts emphasized the ordinary Americanness of the mostly American-born performers to dispel the widespread belief that Asian bodies could never truly adopt these cultural forms. Though the racial politics of the Chop Suey Circuit for representing Asian bodies were problematic for these and other reasons, SanSan Kwan observes that the circuit was one of the few employment opportunities available to Asian American performers. The Chinese American–owned businesses on the circuit were also key to bringing non-Chinese patrons to Chinatown and establishing what once was deemed a dangerous ethnic ghetto as a popular tourist destination. Kwan thus identifies the Chop Suey Circuit—not just the boundaries around Chinatown in each particular city, but the network of nightclubs between cities—as Asian American space.[9]

The tension between granting representational agency to historical subjects (especially dancerly subjects) and contextualizing auto-orientalist moves haunts Asian American dance studies. Writing in the 1990s, Mary Jean Cowell and Shelley C. Berg sparked scholarly interest in the careers of Sada Yacco and Michio Ito. Dance historians unevenly acknowledge the impact of these two Japanese-born dancer/choreographers on the formation of American modern dance. Though Sada Yacco's place within American modern dance history is central to the mythologized origins of modern dance, she does not figure as an innovator. Instead, within this mythology ("mythology" used in the Barthian sense), Yacco gives Ruth St. Denis a dance lesson in Paris at Loie Fuller's theater. Yacco thus provides the exotic inspiration—as did the fabled poster advertisement for Egyptian Deities Cigarettes—to propel St. Denis into her historical place as the bridge between Isadora Duncan and Martha Graham. Berg fleshes out Yacco's tie to American modern dance history by focusing on her 1899–1900 American tour to New York City and San Francisco, during which Yacco introduced Kabuki theater to American audiences.[10] Yacco embraces the opportunity to modify Kabuki for American tastes, while Ruth St. Denis embraces Yacco as inspiration for envisioning her own career as a solo dance artist. This exchange between Yacco and St. Denis via Japan, France, and the United States speaks to the transnational origins of American modern dance history, in which the encounter between Asian and American dancing subjects in various locations dispels the discreteness between East and West as distinct categories.

Like Yacco, Michio Ito is often treated as an anomaly, as an exceptional Asian subject, within the historical record. Ito's rise to fame as a leading figure in American modern dance during the 1920s and 1930s was followed by his literal and figurative disappearance from U.S. soil and dance history after World War II. Cowell's work has been instrumental in establishing a resurgence of interest in Ito's career, culminating in the recent release of the Bonnie Oda Homsey's documentary film *Michio Ito: Pioneering Dancer-Choreographer* (2012).[11] Together Yacco and Ito make an interesting case for thinking through the politics of migration and orientalism for creating cosmopolitan Asian subjects, who can transcend the social registers of racism in controlled situations.

While the early literature on Yacco and Ito did not position their careers and choreography within the context of Asian American history, the early 2000s marked the beginnings of dance scholarship addressing the intersection between Asian American studies and dance/performance studies. For instance, situating Asian American participation in social or competitive ballroom dance scenes, Carolina San Juan's "Ballroom Dance as Indicator of Immigrant Identity in the Filipino Community" (2001) and George Russel Uba's "International Ballroom Dance and the Choreographies of Transnationalism" (2007) attend to ballroom dancing as a marker of class, assimilation, and performances of modernity.[12] In "Splendid Dancing: Filipino 'Exceptionalism' in Taxi Dance Halls" (2008), Lucy Burns historicizes taxi dancing, a key site for theorizing masculinity and labor in Filipino American studies, within American dance history.[13]

The cultural history of a Philippine folk repertoire and its assimilation into collegiate PCN (Philippine Culture Night) productions is treated in Theodore Gonzalves's *The Day the Dancers Stayed: Performing in the Filipino American Diaspora* (2009). Gonzalves refers to PCN productions as rituals whose formulaic programs are reproduced on college and university campuses across the country. The work has generated attention to the significance of extracurricular participation in collegiate dance productions and competitions that exist outside of academic dance departments and programs. Jessica Falcone's "Garba with Attitude: Creative Nostalgia in Competitive Collegiate Gujarati American Folk Dancing" (2013) examines how authenticity is codified through established criteria for judging competitions.[14]

Similar investigations into investments in authenticity and identity among second-generation Asian Americans can be found in Priya Srinivasan's *Sweating Saris* (2012). Srinivasan analyzes the ways in which Indian

dance has been shaped by U.S. immigration laws governing the importa-
tion of Indian labor in the United States. Using labor as an analytic framework, she argues that the dancing body labors physically in its execution
of movements and also culturally in performing ideal Indian femininity.
That is, in addition to locating Indian dance within its unacknowledged
appropriations in modern dance history, Srinivasan attends to post-1965
U.S. immigration laws that privilege white-collar professional labor and
thus shape Bharata Natyam as a marker of middle-class, second-generation,
Indian American femininity. The subject of a singular yet collective Asian
American experience is the topic of SanSan Kwan's "America's Chinatown:
Choreographing Illegible Collectivity" (2013). Kwan reads H. T. Chen's
racially diverse cast of Asian and non-Asian dancers in *Apple Dreams* (2007)
as a specifically Chinese American dance in the aftermath of 9/11.[15]

The transnational turn in Asian American studies emphasizes the movements of peoples, goods, and ideas between Asia and the United States,
making dance an exemplary marker of circulating bodies. The shift away
from cultural nationalism within Asian American studies follows from the
influx of increasingly diverse populations of Asian immigrants, requiring
new approaches to defining Asian American dance.[16] This includes the
dilemma of thinking through work by dance artists who vehemently deny
that their work is "Asian American." In this case, Asian American dance
studies is also useful for understanding the refusals of Asian Americanness
in favor of long-distance belongings to countries outside of the United
States, or a desire for a borderless universal subjectivity.[17]

SHEN YUN: AN ASIAN AMERICAN DANCE COMPANY

In the past ten years, a number of different friends and acquaintances have
forwarded to me promotional materials about the New York–based Shen
Yun Performing Arts. Most of them have no professional connection to
dance and yet received flyers and DVDs in the mail for having a Chinese-
seeming surname. The sincerity of Shen Yun's essentialized representation
of Chineseness did not appeal to my Asian American postmodern sensibilities and predilection for irony. Until now, I never gave the Shen Yun
Performing Arts much thought, since my research has dealt primarily with
artists who define themselves as Asian American and are forthright in their
engagement with race and national belonging.[18] To me, Shen Yun's self-
proclaimed mission of "reviving 5,000 years of [Chinese] civilization" and

"bringing the wonders of ancient Chinese civilization to millions across the globe" seemed overly invested in producing an auto-exoticized, ahistorical spectacle of Chineseness.[19]

Over the last few years, I began to notice the ubiquitous presence of Shen Yun posters papering storefronts in almost every major city in the United States and wondered if I should theorize Shen Yun Performing Arts as an Asian American dance company. The company's glossy posters feature Asian female dancers with impressively hyperflexible spines and joints. Wearing diaphanous robes, harem pants, or flowing tunics, the dancers are caught midflight with their legs fully extended in a 180-degree *jeté grand attitude*. The dancers' back legs are oftentimes parallel to their upper bodies. Other favored poses include *arabesque penchée* and *développés* in which a dancer holds a leg extension near or past vertical. Shen Yun dancers have the lean physique of ballet dancers with their 180-degree turnout, perfectly pointed toes, high in-steps, and hyperextended legs.

For the women, the choreography makes use of their flexible backs and fluid arms. They swirl long silk sleeves, fans, scarves, umbrellas about their bodies, or pretend to play small musical instruments like drums or flutes. The fluidity in their upper body movement is punctuated by virtuosic balletic jumps, turns, and poses. They can *jeté*, pirouette, and hold their *arabesque*. The men too can *jeté*, but they also barrel turn, hold their extensions with feet flexed, and do kung fu. The dancing is polished and ebullient; costumes favoring near-neon shades of pink, blue, green, and yellow offer a veritable explosion of color; the lighting makes the dancers appear luminous; and the accompaniment by a live full orchestra rivals that of any world-class ballet company. If the successes of the Jabbawockeez stage show in Las Vegas and Sheryl Murakami's award-winning choreography for Beyoncé signal the arrival of Asian American dancers and choreographers in the commercial dance industry, the institutionalization of Shen Yun Performing Arts signals another kind of arrival, but one that is not without its contradictions. I offer this discussion of Shen Yun Performing Arts as an entrée into the intellectual conversation of what constitutes the theoretical, methodological, aesthetic, and political contours of framing Asian American dance studies.

At the heart of Asian American dance studies lie negotiations between the multiple and oftentimes contradictory ways in which the term "Asian American" is used as a political operation for pan-ethnic coalition building, a shortcut for a racial designation, a short shortcut for a racially marked ethnic designation, a shared collective experience, a perceived collective history, or a mode of analysis. The fact that Shen Yun Performing Arts is based in the United States, and a growing percentage of its cast are composed of dancers trained in the company's U.S.-based dance academies, would seem to make Shen Yun an ideal Asian American subject. The cast of 180 performers that compose the three touring companies features an international roster, and yet the majority of performers are not from China but from its feeder schools. Since the company formed in 2006, Shen Yun Performing Arts has opened three branches of its Fei Tian Academy of the Arts in upstate New York, San Francisco, and Taiwan. The organization also has its own degree-granting conservatory called Fei Tian College, also located in upstate New York, offering a BFA degree in dance.

However, despite the organization's growing institutional base in the United States and the company's merging of Eastern and Western aesthetics, the organization does not identify itself as "Asian American." Instead, Shen Yun insists on the cultural purity of its Chineseness, arguing that ethnic dance can only truly be embodied by dancers who "match" the nationality of a given dance form. If one were to follow this logic, only a Chinese national could perform Chinese dance successfully, but the company stakes a proprietary claim to authentic Chinese culture while excluding cultural practices emerging from the contemporary dance scene in the People's Republic of China itself.

That is, Shen Yun's claim to aesthetic purity aims to differentiate the company from the West, where the company tours, and from the People's Republic of China (PRC). Though Shen Yun proposes that its version of classical Chinese dance is entirely free from non-Chinese influence, marketing materials for the company and recruitment material for the Fei Tian academies characterize their musical accompaniment as a perfect blend of Eastern and Western instrumentation. The academies are extolled as an ideal environment able to provide its (Asian American) students a bridge between East and the West. In the company's promotional videos, Shen Yun denounces the Chinese classical dance taught in the PRC as shallow, political, revolutionary, and otherwise contaminated by communist ideology, ballet, and modern dance movement. Dancer testimonials consist of stories in which former Chinese nationals can only discover the essence of Chinese culture by learning and performing classical Chinese dance choreography outside of the People's Republic of China. Shen Yun's assertion that real traditional Chinese culture "can no longer be seen in China today" is bolstered by the company's emphasis on their own role in preserving and sharing classical Chinese dance with the world (the West).

In her study of state-sponsored dance in Reform Era China, Emily Wilcox interviews professional dancers who, like the Shen Yun dancers, lament the state of dance in the PRC. However, these dancers blame the perceived decline of spiritually and artistically fulfilling dance jobs on the influx of Hong Kong and American-style popular culture. Dance jobs that were once considered socially and politically relevant have been replaced with commercial entertainments.[20] This description of a complicated relationship between dance, neoliberalism, and a resulting Maoist nostalgia for purposeful choreography runs counter to Shen Yun's characterization of communism as responsible for the ruin of Chinese dance. By making use of a simplistic binary between pure and contaminated cultures, Shen Yun masks the extent to which the company capitalizes on differentiating themselves from the West, while giving over to the West the authority to recognize and value their difference. More importantly, Shen Yun views its repertoire as a museum object that can only be preserved on Western stages.[21] Promotional videos feature diplomats, government officials, dignitaries, and corporate CEOs extolling the beauty, grace, and virtuosity of the performances, and of Chinese culture in general, while dancers in the company emphasize Shen Yun's goal of unearthing and upholding ancient Chinese practices and morals.[22]

Such recovery projects are not unfamiliar within dance studies. The recovery and reinvention of classical Indian and classical Cambodian dance in the aftermath of cultural imperialism in the former, and genocide in the latter, is well documented within dance studies; and the practice of "cultural forms" by diasporic communities is often hailed by practitioners and scholars as an essential element for performing identity.[23] To this end, it might be useful to think through Shen Yun's recovery project in relationship to Sau-ling C. Wong's history of the Chinese Folk Dance Association (CFDA) of San Francisco.[24] Founded in 1959, the CFDA held a near monopoly on teaching and performing Chinese dance in the San Francisco Bay Area until the 1980s. Wong tracks changes in the organization's membership from dispossessed, working-class, Cantonese-speaking immigrants in San Francisco's Chinatown in the 1950s to a more affluent,

Mandarin-speaking, white-collar, middle-class professional population in the suburbs of Silicon Valley in the 2000s. Originally founded as a means for the Chinese American community in San Francisco's Chinatown to support the People's Republic of China, the CDFA's repertoire in the 1960s as Wong reports was overtly political and decidedly Marxist. An emphasis on regional folkdance mirrored the types of choreography promoted within the communist regime in the PRC. Coupled with performances of pro-communist Chinese songs, the CDFA allowed Chinese Americans to support the New China. As the Cold War escalated and members of the CDFA came under surveillance for their pro-communist activities, the organization scaled down its political activities in favor of nonpartisan cultural activities. Once performed as embodied identifications with the politics of the People's Republic of China, Chinese folk dance became instead apolitical celebrations of cultural heritage. Although Wong does not outline what exactly these depoliticized performances of cultural heritage signify, one can infer that cultural heritage does not include one's political leanings.

Wong's study disrupts a common belief that Asian American subjects are by nature apolitical, valuing traditional culture over participation in progressive politics. (In the case of the CFDA, the organization was punished for its leftist politics.) By separating out political systems and ideologies from cultural heritage, heritage is cleaned up and made into a blank slate available for different uses. "Culture" is made into an object of the past that can then be brought forward into the present. This prevalent practice of disassociating cultural heritage from political ideology has allowed Shen Yun to operate under the radar of its anticommunist political agenda.

Shen Yun claims that its version of Chinese classical dance is derived from a pre-Communist Chinese tradition entirely free from modern aesthetic influences. The dance vocabulary and choreography supposedly hearken back to a Chinese imperial past, replete with romanticized narratives extolling Confucian values that include clearly gendered roles for men and women.[25] The company thus insists that its classical repertoire belongs to an ancient and unsullied tradition, but it is hard not to see the influence of the very elements Shen Yun claims are absent from its aesthetic—namely, Russian classical ballet and the Moiseyev-influenced, Soviet-era theatricalization of folk dance that is characteristic of state-sponsored dance companies in the PRC.[26]

On the surface, the contradictory claims made by Shen Yun about their inherent difference from the West may appear uncritically essentializing or auto-exoticizing. Perhaps to fully understand the context of its claims, then, one must delve into the company's role as the performing arts arm of Falun Dafa (Falun Gong) and the repression of Falun Gong by the People's Republic of China.[27] Historian David Ownby links the rise of Falun Gong and other Qigong-related practices in the early 1990s in the PRC to a longer history of redemptive societies, through which Chinese citizens sought in popular religious practices a means for identity, self-improvement, or social change.[28] To extend Ownby's arguments, Shen Yun's reference to a mythologized and generalized five-thousand-year-old Chinese past is not unique, but part of a longer history of religious revival movements in China throughout the Republican period (1912–1940s).

Whatever the specific political motivations of Shen Yun's claims to authenticity, and the ease with which one can easily tease apart the contradicting claims that the company makes, it is important to recognize the appeal that such claims yield. Authenticity plays an important function within marginal or immigrant communities as a mode of self-making in the face of invisibility, erasure, or misrepresentation. Equated with truth, authenticity often serves two temporal functions within immigrant communities. As a call for the return to a truer past or the truth of the past, authenticity is located in a return to roots in the form of national or ethnic origins. National or ethnic origins may be generalized or may not align with internationally recognized geographic borders. As a call to the truth of the present moment, authenticity can also be framed as the truth of the immigrant experience—what is happening now versus a return to the past. Very seldom is the racialized subject allowed to be authentic in the existentialist sense of "being true to oneself," as though an individual devoid of history.

Claims to authenticity by the Chinese Folk Dance Association and Shen Yun Performing Arts are complicated by the fact that they do not necessarily have to claim authenticity in order to be perceived as authentic. As Srinivasan argues, the assignation of authenticity is often naturalized as a duty imposed upon the bodies of Asian women.[29] Investments in and projections of authenticity are not exclusive to the Asian American dance community and are evident in other communities as well. Here I find it useful to reflect on uses of authenticity within the context of African dance to illustrate the malleability of authenticity as a path to access artistic, social, political, and economic claims and resources.

The 2013 Performing Diaspora Symposium hosted by CounterPULSE in San Francisco included a panel on "Representing Africa: The Changing Face of African Dance in the San Francisco Bay Area."[30] Questions about what constitutes African dance, the problematic conflation between a continent and specific regional practices, and debates over who could teach African dance were framed within and against an academic language that distances and objectifies authenticity as a performative category. I refer to authenticity as a performative category to describe the deliberate positioning of one's self or a form within a spectrum of authenticity as truthfulness, inheritance, or skill. To parse or question that authenticity can be anything other than what it is, is to objectify that which is perceived as rightful or already proven.

The resulting discussion revealed the mismatch between the theoretical notion that one can frame and speak of authenticity as something other than itself—that its own truth could be in question—and the idea that lived experiences of believing in and desiring one's own experiences to be authentic via proximity (marriage to someone from Africa, travel to the African continent, or study with someone from Africa), or the sincerity of self-discovery through the dance practice, could be subject to critique (not criticism). The topics broached in the discussion solicited a range of emotional responses from anger, anxiety, and exasperation over comments perceived as veiled criticisms—that African American dancers were more entitled than African nationals in the United States, that African nationals enjoyed the privileges of unproblematic relationships to genealogical Africanness, that African nationals had been excluded from the panel itself. The conversation came to a close after an appeal was made to the communal, color-blind, genderless, and inherently subjectless idea of dancing—that the practice of dancing itself (in this case African dance) would erase all external concerns tangential to the moving that is the dancing—such that questions of dancing would loop back and center in on itself.

Is this looping back a cop-out? The idea that one might return to the essence of dancing itself is an appeal to the idea that there is something real that one could aspire to in the practice. In spite of all the discussion about grappling with the politics of one's position within the economy of African dance, and the storied politics of Africa itself, the takeaway seemed to presume that African dance symbolized a site of authenticity regardless of what was happening in the countries and regions that make up Africa. Yes, it was possible to experience inauthentic Africanness, but the potential of authenticity through dance remained unchallenged.

Similar dynamics can be observed when it comes to the question of defining Asian American dance. Shen Yun defines itself as an authentic Chinese dance company unmoored from any geopolitical designations of Chineseness. The North American training of most company members does not register as a contradiction within the company's framing of Chineseness, and the metaphysical source of the company's actual aesthetic is never specified. Shen Yun makes vague references to Tang dynasty (618–907) court dance coupled with a hazy spiritual past as the source of their classical technique. In comparison to the ideological specificity of Shen Yun's anticommunist stance toward dance within the current PRC, Shen Yun invokes a flattened Chinese past with the Tang dynasty as a singular beacon marking the Golden Age of Chinese art and literature. In many ways, the overt theatricality and spectacular insistence on authenticity belies the real political forces at work, such that Chinese nationals in the company are living in a state of exile due to their affiliation with Falun Dafa.[31]

Shen Yun offers an example of a dance company inhabiting two extremes. Next to the Jabbawockeez stage shows in Las Vegas, Shen Yun is probably the most visible Asian American dance company in the world, although they do not identify as such—culturally, nationally, or aesthetically. While academic discourse has deconstructed authenticity such that there does not appear to be anything new to say about it as a performative modality, both the emotional responses from the audience at the Performing Diaspora Symposium and the emphatic claims made by the Shen Yun Performing Arts underscore the continued valence with which authenticity continues to operate in the context of performing, learning, and teaching what are obviously hybrid diasporic dance practices.

If authenticity retains its traction, how do we evaluate the actual dancing itself? Are there such things as "bad dancing" and "good dancing" under the rubric of authenticity? Perhaps the question with which critical dance studies has not yet contended is the place of authenticity in judgments of "bad dancing" and "good dancing." At the risk of being accused of harboring regressive desires for aesthetic judgment and wanting to engage with criticism rather than critique, I believe the distinction between "good" and "bad" dancing does ultimately come into play.

To designate something as bad dancing is shorthand for the failure to not just embody but also to become indistinguishable from the dance, suspending the social codes of the body in service of a dancerly anonymity. Since Shen Yun distances its own practices from all dance that is happening in China, Shen Yun's claims for authentic Chineseness are free-floating within an ambiguous precommunist past, such that the inclusion of non-Chinese citizen or multiracial dancers go unnoticed given the company's ability to execute "good dancing" on a large scale. Good dancing can justify and smooth over the contradictions between the dance and the body performing the dance, whereas bad dancing does not. Bad dancing highlights any mismatches between the dance and the dancing body. In order to privilege dancing over the subject of who is doing the dancing, dancing becomes distanced from the dancing body.

There is a desire to claim that Chinese dance or African dance can exist without nationally identifiable bodies, but that the dances themselves are intimately tied to particular national or cultural traditions. In order to fulfill these two contradictory desires, one must ultimately believe that the traditions can exist solely within movement, and that movement can be split by the body, such that the body is simply the vessel that makes visible the idea of the movement. This is a Cartesian formulation against which dance constantly struggles by appealing to an affinity for the oneness of mind and body and to the special status of having access to alternative modes of knowing or being an alternative way of knowing.

Asian American dance studies can mine these contradictions to understand why arguments over authenticity continue to hold sway, even when it seems like the political moment to "move on" has already passed. Authenticity as a vehicle for self-representation is useful for reclamation projects and to identify histories of unacknowledged appropriation, such as those found in representations of "Asia" in the history of Western concert dance. It is more difficult to address the metaphysical questions such as the concept of "being true to oneself" in the moment of performance. Within Asian American studies, artistic questions of "being true to oneself" have often taken on the mantle of representational accuracy as a response to stereotypes. For dancers, "being true to oneself" also carries with it a psychic dimension, through which following one's impulses and desires enhance one's creative life and artistic fulfillment. These two approaches are at odds, sometimes with each other, and at other times work together.

The essays in this collection represent a broad range of theoretical approaches that define the contours of what is considered Asian American dance. The dance practices represented in this volume are by no means exhaustive of what can be considered Asian American dance, and the essays should be read for their theoretical and methodological approaches to framing practices as Asian American. The contributors to this volume attend to the aesthetic and political forces that give form to choreographic works that can be understood under the rubric of Asian American dance, and to these practices that are enmeshed in tensions between national belonging/migration, narrative content/aesthetic form, local specificity/universality, and agency/orientalism.

The contributors further develop the themes broached by the earlier literature on Asian American dance with an eye toward filling in gaps in the field. Central to understanding the debates over what constitutes Asian American dance is the question of form as the material from which dance emerges as a choreographic entity. The essays in this volume analyze the work of artists engaged in a diverse range of genres that include popular genres (taiko and hip-hop), classical theatrical traditions, and modern/postmodern forms (U.S. modern dance, butoh, postmodern improvisation and German *Neue Tanz*[32]). The authors pick up threads hinted at by others, such that each essay can generate discussion via multiple points of entry, and collectively the essays are meant to be read as a conversation.

The essays in part I, Dancing Citizenship, address questions of Asian American choreography in relationship to performances of citizenship. Angela K. Ahlgren's (chapter 1) study of San Jose Taiko situates taiko as a Japanese American performance tradition. Ahlgren maps how Japanese American taiko is derived from Japanese taiko traditions and ideologically is shaped by the 1960s civil rights movements, cultural nationalism, and pan–Asian American identities. To counter the common misreading of Asian American taiko as simply a cultural expression of Japanese heritage, Ahlgren demonstrates how the performing of Asian American taiko is a corporeal dissemination of Asian American history. In contrast to Ahlgren's study of Japanese American taiko as a practice that is grounded within the assertion of Japanese American belonging in the United States, Roko Kawai (chapter 2) writes from the point of view of a binational Japanese and American dancer. Reflecting on her experience of returning to Japan after a twenty-year absence to collaborate on a contemporary dance project and study Japanese classical dance, Kawai uses the term *muzukashii* (translated as "untenable") to describe the precarious nature of cultural belonging. *Muzukashii* also describes the state of her body as it exists outside formations of nation, of race, and of culture, as she attends to the microsensations of dancing and being itself. Her account of dancing in Japan is haunted by a murder and suicide in her family, highlighting the disjuncture between her body's physical closeness to other bodies and her distance from the demands of psychic closeness that Western conceptions of postmodern improvisational dance assumes about the rhetoric of openness.

The inclusion of Asian Canadian dance in this volume allows for the resonance of cross-border histories of Asian immigration within North America. Eury Colin Chang's (chapter 3) analysis of Jay Hirabyashi's *Rage* situates Japanese American internment (a key historical period defining Japanese American identity) within a larger global context in which Japanese Canadians were also interned. Chang also addresses the ways in which Asian Canadian choreographers navigate Canada's official policies on multicultural nationalism and its manifestation in arts funding. The subject of citizenship and national belonging in Brian Su-Jen Chung's essay (chapter 4) takes a critical look at Asian American viewers' engagement with Asian American participation on MTV's *America's Best Dance Crew*. Chung examines the ensuing controversy over race and the perceived place of Asianness in the show's presentation of hip-hop as universal and inclusive of difference, while maintaining investments in hip-hop's blackness.

The essays in part II, Choreographing Aesthetics, focus on the works of Asian American choreographers active in the contemporary dance scene whose engagements with avant-garde aesthetics have not been previously read as Asian American. Using Asian American critique, Ellen V. P. Gerdes (chapter 5) positions Shen Wei and Kun-Yang Lin as contemporaries whose choreography is praised by critics because their work fulfills public expectations of what contemporary Asian (American) dance is supposed to look like. Conversely, Rosemary Candelario (chapter 6) revisits the careers of Eiko and Koma to propose a reconsideration of their choreography as an exercise in marking, evoking, and creating Asian American space. Likewise, Maura Nguyen Donohue (chapter 7) deploys ambivalence and ambiguity to analyze the works and careers of Yasuko Yokoshi and Sam Kim, who have actively resisted the label of Asian American.

Asian American dance is a framework for understanding the diverse movement practices and aesthetic concerns in which Asian Americans engage as choreographers and performers. The term is both specific and vague as it signals both niche programming and marketing, all the while signaling a geographically delimited understanding of race. In different contexts, Asian American modern dance is a descriptor of form, content, or authorship in various combinations. Read together, the essays illuminate the ways that Asian American dance shapes, troubles, and pushes against the contours of what counts as Asian American cultural production and how one consumes dance. In shifting notions of from where Asian ancestry is transmitted, and by illuminating how bodily proximity and closeness to forms can highlight distance between bodies, the attention to techniques of transmission can disrupt the assumed affinity between Asian bodies and their "matching" forms (Ahlgren and Kawai). Given the ubiquity of televised dance, a consideration of Asian American bodies allows us to think about accessibility as consumption and hope as labor (Chung). Asian American dance also asks us to think about the relationship between space and place in terms of bodily belonging (Candelario and Chang), as well as the legibility of representational power (Gerdes). Finally, Asian American dance also challenges ideas about dance as pleasure (Donohue).

The last chapter in this volume returns to the question posed at the beginning of the introduction. If Shen Yun Performing Arts can be theoretically framed as Asian American dance, can a self-proclaimed Asian American artist be unframed as Asian American? The afterword is a dialogue between Denise Uyehara and myself. Once the poster child for autobiographical, Asian American feminist performance, Uyehara relocated to Tucson, Arizona (a decidedly non–Asian American space), which has recast the artist's approach to her subject matter and working process. The chapter delves into the intellectually murky area of artistic inspiration to consider art making as a series of embodied free associations that make up a body of work.

The process of art making informs Asian American dance studies as an ongoing project shaped by scholars and artists such as those represented in this inaugural volume. Given the interdisciplinary nature of both Asian

American studies and dance studies, the essays in this volume represent a methodologically diverse approach to Asian American dance studies that includes ethnography (Ahlgren), autobiography (Kawai), media studies (Chung), history (Chang), and cultural studies (Gerdes, Candelario, Donohue). The inclusion of the dialogue placed at the end serves as a reminder that the multiple ways in which we can think about Asian American dance are oftentimes hashed out in informal conversations about the nature of art making. The themes running throughout the collection are part of a dialogue that exists beyond these pages and acknowledge that Asian American dance studies continues as a conversation between artists and scholars to consider the place of Asian America within dance and dance within Asian America.

NOTES

1. Yutian Wong, "Situating Asian American Dance Studies," in *Choreographing Asian America* (Middletown, CT: Wesleyan University Press, 2010), 27–56.

2. Ibid.

3. Amy Chua has followed up the success of *Battle Hymn of the Tiger Mother* with *The Triple Package*, which identifies culturally superior groups in the United States. Amy Chua, *Battle Hymn of the Tiger Mother* (New York: Penguin Books, 2007); Amy Chua and Jed Rubenfeld, *The Triple Package: How Three Traits Explain the Rise and Fall of Cultural Groups in America* (New York: Penguin Books, 2014). For a critique of Chua, see Ellen D. Wu, "Asian Americans and the Model Minority Myth," *Los Angeles Times*, January 23, 2014.

4. In 2011, Lee Siegel penned a scathing review of *Battle Hymn of the Tiger Mother* in which he cast Amy Chua as a narcissistic mother living through her children, a position from which he backpedals in his 2012 article for the *Wall Street Journal*. See Lee Siegel, "Declawing the Tiger: A Spanking for Amy Chua," *New York Observer*, January 19, 2011; and Lee Siegel, "Rise of the Tiger Nation," *Wall Street Journal*, October 27, 2012.

5. Mari Yoshihari, *Musicians from a Different Shore: Asians and Asian Americans in Classical Music* (Philadelphia: Temple University Press, 2008).

6. Anthony Tommasini, "Virtuosos Become a Dime a Dozen," *New York Times*, August 12, 2011.

7. David Palumbo-Liu, "Double Trouble: The Pathology of Ethnicity Meets White Schizophrenia," in *Asian/American: Historical Crossing of a Racial Frontier* (Stanford: Stanford University Press, 1999), 295–336.

8. *Forbidden City*, directed by Arthur Dong (1989; San Francisco: Deep Focus Productions, 2002), DVD.

9. Following Arthur Dong, SanSan Kwan takes up similar arguments. See SanSan Kwan, "Performing a Geography of Asian America: The Chop Suey Circuit," *TDR: The Drama Review* 55, no. 1 (Spring 2011): 120–136.

10. Shelley C. Berg, "Sada Yacco: The American Tour, 1899–1900," *Dance Chronicle* 16, no. 2 (1993): 147–196.

11. *Michio Ito: Pioneering Dancer-Choreographer*, directed by Bonnie Oda Homsey (Los Angeles: Los Angeles Dance Foundation, 2012), film; Helen Caldwell, *Michio Ito: The Dancer and His Dances* (Berkeley: University of California Press, 1977); Mary-Jean Cowell and Satoru Shimazaki, "East and West in the Work of Michio Ito," *Dance Research Journal* 26, no. 2 (Fall 1994): 11–23; Mary-Jean Cowell, "Michio Ito in Hollywood: Modes and Ironies of Ethnicity," *Dance Chronicle* 24, no. 3 (2001): 263–305; Naima Prevots, *Dancing in the Sun: Hollywood Choreographers, 1915–1937* (Ann Arbor, MI: UMI Research Press, 1987); Yutian Wong, "Artistic Utopias: Michio Ito and the Trope of the International," in *Worlding Dance*, ed. Susan L. Foster (New York: Palgrave Macmillan, 2009), 144–162.

12. Carolina San Juan, "Ballroom Dance as Indicator of Immigrant Identity in the Filipino Community," *Journal of American and Comparative Cultures* 24, no. 3–4 (Fall/Winter 2001): 177–181; and George Russel Uba, "International Ballroom Dance and the Choreographies of Transnationalism," *Journal of Asian American Studies* 10, no. 2 (2007): 141–167.

13. Lucy Mae San Pablo Burns, "Splendid Dancing: Filipino 'Exceptionalism' in Taxi Dance Halls," *Dance Research Journal* 40, no. 2 (2008): 23–40.

14. Theodore Gonzalves, *The Day the Dancers Stayed: Performing in the Filipino American Diaspora* (Philadelphia: Temple University Press, 2009); Jessica Falcone, "Garba with Attitude: Creative Nostalgia in Competitive Collegiate Gujarati American Folk Dancing," *Journal of Asian American Studies* 16, no. 1 (February 2013): 57–89.

15. Priya Srinivasan, "Negotiating Cultural Nationalism and Minority Citizenship," in *Sweating Saris: Indian Dance as Transnational Labor* (Philadelphia: Temple University Press, 2013), 117–140; SanSan Kwan, "America's Chinatown: Choreographing Illegible Collectivity," in *Kinesthetic City: Dance and Movement in Chinese Urban Spaces* (New York: Oxford University Press, 2013), 98–126.

16. Erika Lee and Naoko Shibusawa, "Guest Editor's Introduction: What Is Transnational Asian American History? Recent Trends and Challenges," *Journal of Asian American Studies* 8, no. 3 (October 2005): vii–xvii; Sau-Ling Wong, "Denationalism Reconsidered: Asian American Cultural Criticism at a Theoretical Crossroads," *Amerasia Journal* 21, no. 1 & 2 (1995): 1–27.

17. Schiller defines long-distance nationalism as a spectrum of practices in which immigrants engage to maintain ties with a home country. Practices can include actual involvement in the political affairs of a home country, such as voting

or political organizing on behalf of social or political causes in a home country, to less direct involvement, such as sending remittances to family members or participating in cultural events representing one's home country. See Nina Glick Schiller and Georges Eugene Fouron, "Long Distance Nationalism Defined," in *Georges Woke Up Laughing: Long Distance Nationalism and the Search for Home* (Durham, NC: Duke University Press, 2001), 17–35.

18. In *Choreographing Asian America*, I discuss Club O' Noodles, a Vietnamese American performance ensemble whose self-described mission was to create work that delved into social and political issues within the Vietnamese American community. Much of their work involved parody and satirized mainstreams representations of the Vietnam War in Hollywood films and on Broadway.

19. Shen Yun Performing Arts, "Reviving 5,000 Years of Civilization," http://www.shenyunperformingarts.org/about, accessed March 25, 2012. See Marta Savigliano, *Tango and the Political Economy of Passion* (Boulder: Westview Press, 1995), for a discussion of auto-exoticism.

20. Emily Wilcox, "'Selling Out' Post Mao: Dance Labor and the Ethics of Fulfillment in Reform Era China," in *Chinese Modernity and the Individual Psyche*, ed. Andrew Kipnis (New York: Palgrave Macmillan, 2012), 43–65.

21. See Diana Taylor, *Archive and the Repertoire* (Durham, NC: Duke University Press, 2003); Inge Baxman, "At the Boundaries of the Archive: Movement, Rhythm, and Muscle Memory; A Report on the Tanzarchiv Leipzig," *Dance Chronicle* 32, no. 1 (2009): 127–135; Jens Richard Giersdorf, *The Body of the People: East German Dance since 1945* (Madison: University of Wisconsin Press, 2013); special issue on "Preserving Dance as a Living Legacy," *Dance Chronicle* 34, no. 1 (2011); and Anthea Kraut, *Choreographing the Folk: The Dance Stagings of Zora Neale Hurston* (Minneapolis: University of Minnesota Press, 2008).

22. NTD (New Tang Dynasty) is the media outlet for Falung Dafa and Shen Yun Performing Arts. NTD produces post-tour videos promoting the success of the company's performances in different countries. Most follow a similar format in which government officials and business leaders make glowing remarks about the company interspersed with excerpts of performance. ShenYun Performing Arts: Zuschauer-Feedbacks Europa, http://www.youtube.com/watch?v=e80SyQQGv9s, accessed April 13 2014.

23. Gonzalvez, *The Day the Dancers Stayed*; Srinivasan, *Sweating Saris*.

24. Sau-ling C. Wong, "Dancing in the Diaspora: Cultural Long-Distance Nationalism and the Staging of Chineseness by San Francisco's Chinese Folk Dance Association," *Journal of Transnational American Studies* 2, no. 1 (2010), https://escholarship.org/uc/item/50k6k78p, accessed October 23, 2013.

25. Conversation with Linda Song, a representative of Feitian Academy, August 29, 2013.

26. See Kraut, *Choreographing the Folk*; Anthony Shay, *Choreographic Politics: State Folk Dance Companies, Representation, and Power* (Middletown, CT: Wesleyan University Press, 2002); Giersdorf, *The Body of the People*; and Dina Roginsky, "Folklore, Folklorism, and Synchronization: Preserved-Created Folklore in Israel," *Journal of Folklore Research* 44, no. 1 (2007): 41–66.

27. Terry Polnick, "Art, Truth, Politics Clash at Kennedy Center," *Washington Times*, February 7, 2013; Gina Salamone, "Shen Yun, the Show Beijing Doesn't Want You to See, Returns to New York's Lincoln Center," *New York Daily News*, March 25, 2012.

28. David Ownby, *Falun Gong and the Future of China* (Oxford: Oxford University Press, 2008), 23.

29. Srinivasan, *Sweating Saris*. Srinivasan deals specifically with the cultural labor imposed upon the bodies of second-generation Indian girls, but the model is applicable to other Asian cultural forms as well.

30. "Representing Africa: The Changing Face of African Dance in the San Francisco Bay Area," Performing Diaspora Symposium, August 10, 2013, podcast available at http://counterpulse.org/performing-diaspora/symposium/2013-sympo sium/, accessed August 10, 2014.

31. Shen Yun's publicity materials feature a series of dancer profiles posted on YouTube. A majority of the dancers are ethnically Chinese and either born in the United States or immigrated to the United States as young children. "Shen Yun Dancer Profile: Alison Chen," YouTube video, 5:36, posted by Shen Yun, December 12, 2011, https://www.youtube.com/watch?v=P18S4BLx-Vg, accessed March 25, 2012; "Shen Yun Dancer Profile: Tim Wu," YouTube video, 7:09, posted by Shen Yun, December 12, 2011, https://www.youtube.com/watch?v=H_JAAj2VJbk, accessed March 25, 2012; "Shen Yun Dancer Profile: Chelsea Chai," YouTube video, 6:01, posted by Shen Yun, December 12, 2011, https://www.youtube.com/watch ?v=bARWHUOcTYc, accessed March 25, 2012; "Shen Yun Dancer Profile: Miranda Zhou-Galati," YouTube video, 4:36, posted by Shen Yun, December 12, 2011, https://www.youtube.com/watch?v=NP12OZQDMlE, accessed March 25, 2012.

32. *Neue Tanz* is a little-known term used by Eiko and Koma to describe the work of Manja Chmiel, who was an assistant to Mary Wigman. Chmiel, who was Czech, established the Neue Tanz Dance Company in Germany in the 1960s. Eiko and Koma use the term *Neue Tanz* to describe the dance style that they studied with Manja Chmiel. Deborah Jowitt, "Dancing in Tune with the Earth," *Dance Magazine*, April 2006, http://www.dancemagazine.com/issues/April-2006/Dancing-in -Tune-With-the-Earth, accessed June 3, 2013. For more information on Manja Chmiel, see *Kultiversum*, http://www.kultiversum.de/Tanz-Ballet-Tanz/Celebrities -Manja-Chmiel.html, accessed June 3, 2013.

Part I

Dancing Citizenship

A New Taiko Folk Dance

San Jose Taiko and Asian American Movements

ANGELA K. AHLGREN

"Dig! And pick! And dig! And pick!" A woman's voice shouts over the din of makeshift taiko drums and excited voices as hundreds of taiko players spill out of the Aratani Japan America Theater in Japantown, Los Angeles. It is nine thirty at night, a rousing taiko concert has just ended inside the theater, and the audience—mostly participants in the 2009 North American Taiko Conference—have now gathered outside on the one-acre plaza and are ready to dance. Together, we bounce forward and backward in rhythm while rolling our forearms in front of us, we hop on one leg, and we wipe sweat from our brows. These movements are the stylized gestures of *Ei Ja Nai Ka?* (Isn't it good?), a participatory folk dance and one of San Jose Taiko's signature works. By digging, picking, and sweating together, we dancers honor the memory and labor of the Issei, who were the first generation of Japanese immigrants in the United States. A swingy rhythm from the *chappa*, small hand-held cymbals, cuts through the rumble of plastic garbage-bins-turned-drums keeping the base beat for a widening circle of dancers. Drummers shout, "Ei Ja Nai Ka!" and dancers respond, "A So-re, A So-re!" Then, "Ei Ja Nai Ka, hai!" "A So-re, So-re, Yoi-sho!" This call-and-response continues for a few rounds before the *shinobue* (a bamboo flute) joins, and voices singing in Japanese float over the din in a melodic song.

It is a hot summer night in Los Angeles, and after a few rounds of digging, picking, and jumping my way around the plaza, I step back to watch. The crowd is racially mixed, mostly Asian American, with many white, as well as a few black and Latino/a, men and women. There are people in their twenties, those who are middle-aged, and those with bodies small and

large. Some execute the gestures with confidence. Others shuffle through
the steps looking confused. There are people who, instead of dancing, loiter
at the center or outside of the circle to watch and socialize. For some participants, this is their first introduction to this folk dance, while others
anticipate dancing *Ei Ja Nai Ka?* in this participatory ritual that happens
after the Saturday night *Taiko Jam* concert performance at every North
American Taiko Conference. After years of trying to pick it up on the fly
at different conferences, I am glad to have finally learned the dance in a
workshop with San Jose Taiko members earlier that day. The dance continues for twenty more minutes before the circle begins to break up and the
summer sky continues to darken above the downtown lights.[1] Flushed with
the joy of dancing, the participants collect their belongings and disperse
to the hotels, sushi counters, and karaoke bars of Japantown. This small
business district tucked south of U.S. Highway 101 (referred to locally as
the 101) in downtown Los Angeles bursts to life during taiko conferences,
as hundreds of taiko players patronize businesses selling Japanese pastries,
noodles, newspapers, imported knick-knacks, and other goods and services.
For some LA-based taiko players, this is home base, a familiar site of many
years of civic, political, community, and cultural gatherings, but for many
taiko players from across the United States and Canada, these few blocks
are as close to Japan as they have ever been. Similarly, for some participants, the histories evoked in *Ei Ja Nai Ka?* are familiar, and for others, it
is an embodied introduction to early Japanese immigration history.

This essay focuses on how the politics of the Asian American movement
inspired and continue to resonate within the performances and practices of
San Jose Taiko. The "Asian American Movements" in the title refers to the
embodied and choreographed aspects of taiko performance itself and the
constellation of political activities undertaken by Asian American activists
beginning in the late 1960s. To explore the intertwined relationship between
these two meanings of "movement," this essay undertakes three readings of
taiko. First, I situate North American taiko within the emergence of Asian
American identity and politics to contextualize San Jose Taiko's effort to
develop an Asian American sensibility in their group in the face of external
demands for Japanese authenticity as a complex navigation of aesthetic
and sociopolitical terrain. Second, I analyze San Jose Taiko's taiko folk
dance *Ei Ja Nai Ka?* as a tribute to Issei labor and pre-internment history.
In performing and sharing this work, developed in the early 1980s, San

Jose Taiko reflects Asian American movement–era values of developing an Asian American consciousness and creating grass-roots, revisionist Japanese American histories. With its specific focus on the Issei, the first Japanese immigrants to the United States, *Ei Ja Nai Ka?* demonstrates San Jose Taiko's commitment to taiko as an Asian American art form and suggests ways for others (non–Asian Americans) to participate in and construct "Asian America" through participatory performance. Finally, I offer an analysis of the marketing materials for San Jose Taiko's national tours to highlight how the group attempts to remain grounded in Asian America when presenters and advertisers frame their performances as exotic and foreign. I have been attending San Jose Taiko performances and workshops as a taiko player for over fifteen years.

Taiko is the Japanese word for drum. While drums are integral to many Japanese musical traditions, taiko (also called *kumi-daiko* or *wadaiko*) in a U.S. context generally refers to the recent practice of ensemble drumming that developed in 1950s Japan and spread to the Americas, Europe, and other parts of Asia in subsequent decades. I refer to this contemporary practice as simply "taiko," since that is the most common way for players in the United States and Canada to refer to their art form.[2] Instrumentation for taiko is drawn from older performance traditions in Japan, but the practice of playing large barrel drums in group formation is a twentieth-century development. Martial arts–inspired movement and vocalizations also distinguish taiko from other, more static forms of drumming.[3]

San Jose Taiko's *Ei Ja Nai Ka?* is a taiko and dance piece that the group teaches widely in workshops and at festivals.[4] *Ei Ja Nai Ka?* is different from most taiko songs, in which drummers' movements stem from striking the drum, rather than dancing separately. San Jose Taiko describes the piece as a "taiko folk dance," situating the work within taiko musical repertory and other participatory group dances performed at *obon* festivals, Cherry Blossom festivals, and other Japanese American community celebrations.[5] In referring to *Ei Ja Nai Ka?* as a taiko folk dance, the use of "folk" signals both its demonstration of ethnic roots and its participatory nature. The Saturday night *Taiko Jam* concert is the pièce de résistance of the biannual North American Taiko Conference, an opportunity for attendees to see a carefully curated lineup of four taiko groups. It is a tradition for the audience— largely comprised of taiko players—to erupt into the now-expected, but seemingly spontaneous, performance of *Ei Ja Nai Ka?* immediately after the *Taiko Jam*. Many taiko players learn the song as I did during a workshop at the taiko conference.[6] Non-taiko players might learn the dance part as well, if they happen to see San Jose Taiko perform at an *obon* festival or in another community setting that encourages audience participation. *Ei Ja Nai Ka?* is intentionally participatory. The choreography is simple and the musical composition is catchy enough to encourage audiences to embody its rhythms and gestures by joining the circle of dancers. Much taiko repertoire, including other San Jose Taiko pieces, emphasizes technical prowess, group cohesion, and rhythmic complexity. But with its relative simplicity, *Ei Ja Nai Ka?* closes the gap between the audience and performer's experiences, blurring the boundaries between the two. Participants who are just learning can dance and chant alongside seasoned San Jose Taiko members. Even as a novice at the dance steps, I was at once performer and spectator.

The members of San Jose Taiko have long held leadership positions among North American taiko players and in particular at the North American Taiko Conference (NATC). San Jose Taiko's teaching of *Ei Ja Nai Ka?* and the planned spontaneity of its performance in the plaza have become traditions of the biennial gathering. Held every two years between the years 1997 and 2011 and again in 2015, NATC brings together taiko practitioners from the United States and Canada, guest teachers from Japan, and attendees (albeit in smaller numbers) from Europe and other areas of the world.[7] Other regional and collegiate taiko conferences and gatherings are sometimes held in the interim years between national conferences. Scholars and event organizers have only recently begun to formally track the demographic makeup of conference attendees, but in my observations at five conferences between 1999 and 2009, Asian Americans made up the majority of participants, and the number of white taiko players in attendance visibly grew during that time. As the taiko community expands and its practitioners come to taiko through avenues not linked to Japanese American or Asian American cultural contexts, the tradition of dancing *Ei Ja Nai Ka?* can be seen as a way to remind taiko players of the form's genealogy in the United States, which is inextricably linked to Asian American history and cultural politics.

San Jose Taiko formed in 1973, and the founding members describe their involvement in Asian American movement activities as connected to their taiko activities.[8] The Asian American movement (AAM), influenced by the civil rights movement, Black Power movement, and global Third World activism, coalesced Asians of different ethnic backgrounds to fight for broad-based social change. The AAM encompassed ethnic consciousness-raising efforts as well as antiwar demonstrations, education reform, and grassroots activities focused on service for underserved communities.[9] For the most part, Japanese Americans involved in the movement were Sansei, or third generation, although some younger Nisei (second generation) were also involved.[10] In his book *The Asian American Movement*, the historian William Wei contends that the AAM began to wind down in the early 1970s, but more recent scholarship by Michal Liu, Kim Geron, and Tracy Lai argues that AAM activities extended beyond the early 1970s and that movement participants continue to be community leaders who make significant change both within and beyond Asian American communities.[11] While the height of AAM activism took place in the late 1960s and early 1970s, the AAM had a lasting impact on the participants who continued to work in Asian American community contexts. The formation of San Jose Taiko was a result of Asian American movement activism, and situating taiko within the narrative of the AAM foregrounds the role of performance in enacting the movement's ideals and in political protest more generally. Many of the ideals that San Jose Taiko embraced were informed by the Asian American movement; these include negotiating identity-related issues as well as the instantiation of practices that reflect "peace, social justice, and equality."[12] These ideals are reflected in the choice to honor early immigrant labor through their performances.

When San Jose Taiko performs *Ei Ja Nai Ka?*—their self-described "North American taiko folk dance"—at concerts, festivals, and other community gatherings, they stage a history of Japanese American immigrant labor. San Jose Taiko dedicates the song to the Issei and "celebrates Japanese American history through movements that reflect the Issei's work in agriculture, mining, and railroad construction."[13] This re-membering of Issei labor through dance and music has historiographic implications.[14] Theater historian Charlotte Canning argues for performance as a viable means of conveying history: performance "can encourage considerations of the gestural, the emotional, the aural, the visual, and the physical in ways beyond print's ability to evoke or understand them."[15] *Ei Ja Nai Ka?* connects its performers and spectators—some of them the grandchildren or great-grandchildren of the Issei about whom the song is written, some of

them newcomers to Japanese American history—to "the past" through the
gestural life of manual labor. The piece "actively place[s] the past in the
community context of the present time" through a complex interplay of
dancing, drumming, singing, and chanting.[16] Given its specific link to Japanese immigration and labor, *Ei Ja Nai Ka?* articulates Issei history in ways
beyond those available in narrative histories. Within the layers of music
and dance, and within the various contexts in which the piece is offered,
the dance invokes pre-internment labor and immigration histories, aspects
of Japanese American history often overshadowed by the intense focus on
internment itself. It is important to acknowledge that internment is only
one, albeit traumatic, event in the longer narrative of Japanese American
history, which encompasses exploitative labor conditions, racist property
laws, and other injustices, many of which reflect ongoing issues within
U.S. immigration activities.

DOING AUTHENTICITY, NAVIGATING ASIAN AMERICA

Founded in 1973, San Jose Taiko is one of the most recognized and respected
North American taiko ensembles and was the third taiko group to form
in the United States. In 2011 the National Endowment for the Arts recognized founding members and directors PJ and Roy Hirabayashi with a
National Heritage Fellowship, a prestigious award that celebrates the recipients' artistry and acknowledges their craft as of national importance.[17] As
of this writing, the pair, a married couple, has handed over their official
roles as artistic director and executive director to longtime San Jose Taiko
members Franco Imperial and Wisa Uemura, but they continue to be involved with the group and to offer artistic and leadership-focused workshops and mentorship to taiko groups both nationally and internationally.
Begun by Roy Hirabayashi, Reverend Hiroshi Abiko, and Dean Miyakusu,
three Japanese American men interested in drawing youth to the San Jose
Buddhist Temple by hosting "cool" activities,[18] San Jose Taiko was inspired
and guided in its formative years by the two other U.S. taiko groups in
existence at the time, San Francisco Taiko Dojo and Kinnara Taiko, and
later by several Japanese taiko groups that had formed in the late 1960s.
Several of San Jose Taiko's early members were involved in aspects of the
Asian American movement, including antiwar activism, community service projects, and the formation of ethnic studies in California colleges.
The group's philosophy was shaped to a large extent by the AAM's critique

of oppressive structures. Today, in keeping with San Jose Taiko's activist roots, as new members join, regardless of their ethnic identity, they are expected to learn about Asian American history and the Yellow Power movement, another way of describing the Asian American movement that emphasizes its connections to the Black Power movement. The group operates on a collective and consensus-based structure. San Jose Taiko's membership is open to people of any gender, race, or ethnicity; and although their membership has consistently been comprised mainly of Asian Americans, the group has included a number of non-Asian members throughout its history.

On stage, the group exudes a cohesion that exceeds its technical precision, as the performers communicate through glances, smiles, yells, and the ever-present bouncy pulse that seems to rise up from their feet, through torsos and arms, and into the drums. As one reviewer notes, San Jose Taiko's drummers are "not only one with their instruments, but with each other."[19] With few solo and duet numbers, San Jose Taiko's concerts emphasize their ensemble work. They move together with a light yet grounded energy. The ethnomusicologist Deborah Wong notes the "exuberance and joy" she feels while watching San Jose Taiko: "They have this fantastic energy, and it's different from any other taiko group. Their technique and their level of skill is very high—enviably so—but you can also see the community base in their playing. Or maybe I just think I see it because I *know* it's there: I know several of their members and I've seen how they interact with other taiko players."[20] San Jose Taiko has strong ties not only to other taiko players but also to San Jose's Japantown, particularly its annual *obon* festival at which they regularly perform *Ei Ja Nai Ka?*

As the group formed its aesthetic and philosophical style during its early years, San Jose Taiko members grappled with competing and overlapping notions of Japaneseness, authenticity, and Asian American identity.[21] As they sought training from other groups, San Jose Taiko contended with how to maintain cultural authenticity vis-à-vis Japanese customs, while also remaining true to their political beliefs. For many of the Japanese Americans who began playing taiko in the 1970s, taiko was appealing because it was both associated with Japan—and therefore a way to connect with their cultural roots and the Issei—and a powerful and engaging art form that countered prevailing images of Japanese Americans as quiet and passive. Interviews with taiko players from this period reveal that for many of them, other traditional Japanese arts such as ikebana, or flower arranging, and traditional dance were not considered "powerful" but rather delicate and meditative—exactly how they did not want to be perceived in the 1970s. While taiko served these two distinct purposes, they did not always mesh. Some of the Japanese customs San Jose Taiko was encouraged to adopt went against the grain of their ethics, particularly regarding oppressive hierarchies and gender equality issues.

When the group formed in 1973, they were a small but dedicated group of Asian Americans—activists, students, and music aficionados—who had bought a thousand dollars' worth of drums from another fledgling taiko group in Los Angeles, who made up their own rhythms in the basement of the San Jose Buddhist Temple because they believed taiko gave expression to their experiences as Asian Americans. A black-and-white photograph of a 1979 informal gathering shows seven young shaggy-haired, bell-bottomed Asian American men and women standing behind their taiko drums on a paved courtyard. It appears to be a candid snapshot, taken during a jam session (see fig. 1.1). While in a more formal performance they might have

FIGURE 1.1. San Jose Taiko members play taiko at an informal gathering in 1979; Roy Hirabayashi is pictured third from the left, and PJ Hirabayashi is pictured third from the right (photo by San Jose Taiko Conservatory Archive)

worn *happi* coats, *tabi*, and *hachimaki*, here the puffy jackets, bell-bottom jeans, and feathered hair situate the group squarely in the 1970s, part of the counterculture.

Early San Jose Taiko members were largely improvising this newly adopted art form, but they nonetheless experienced taiko as a material connection to Japanese diasporic culture, a relationship they would continue to negotiate throughout the group's history. Christopher Small's term "musicking," which is meant to unburden musical criticism from its fetishization of the text, sheds light on my perspective here. Like Richard Schechner's definition of the performance process as extending from the conception and rehearsal stage to the "aftermath" of the performance event, "musicking" is a term that includes any aspect of taking part in making music, from composing to performing, or simply listening, even half-consciously, thereby shifting the focus from the art object to the acts of taking part in musical performance.[22] This shift from performance object and text to the acts of making music also opens up an important shift to the bodies that participate in performance as performers and audience members. My work thus focuses not only on the performers' choices but also on the corporeality of taiko performance and how taiko players move—what Matthew Rahaim calls the "musicking body."[23] Small writes, "For performance does not exist in order to present musical works, but rather, musical works exist in order to give performers something to perform."[24] For example, current executive director Wisa Uemura emphasizes that San Jose Taiko made a conscious choice to compose new music, rather than learn any existing Japanese repertoire, because "the charter members were not as familiar with Japanese music stylings (taiko or not) and they wanted music that represented them as Japanese-Americans."[25]

Like many performers working in neofolk or invented traditions, San Jose Taiko players grappled with notions of being authentically Japanese while also embracing taiko's relative newness. Looking at taiko as musicking—as a "doing and a thing done," to borrow Elin Diamond's definition of performance—positions taiko as a space for "doing" authenticity, rather than succumbing to a notion of authenticity as a stable or static state of being.[26] As the historian Gary Okihiro writes, "Like all identities, although but a script, Japanese gains form and currency through theory and practice."[27] That is, identities—Japanese, Asian American, and others—are called into being, in part, through repeated performances.

Rather than measure themselves against an elusive, yet seemingly fixed, quality of Japaneseness, San Jose Taiko sought to create an authentic, pan-ethnic Asian American practice. Looking back on the early years of San Jose Taiko, Roy Hirabayashi says, "Well, naturally, when we first started, there was no real *kata* [form] for us. There [were] no costumes. Our look was Kikkoman Shoyu happi coats with bellbottom pants and long hair."[28] Most likely referring to Seiichi Tanaka and San Francisco Taiko Dojo, Roy recalls, "We got in trouble early on because people, the traditionalists, were complaining that you can't use a tambourine with taiko or a cowbell. That's not taiko." While San Jose's early attempts to incorporate non-Japanese instruments into their practice met with criticism, their innovations are now standard practice for many taiko groups.

While many American taiko players see Japanese taiko as authentic, the Japanese tradition too is comprised of multiple influences, including American jazz.[29] Even if authenticity is an elusive goal, it nonetheless circulates as an important concept in taiko circles. PJ Hirabayashi highlights the conundrum of attempting to achieve authenticity in a diasporic form. She says, "We'll never be Japanese from Japan because we didn't grow up in the environment. And therefore, you could never play Japanese taiko like Japanese taiko. So we have to be very realistic that what we play is definitely from our experiences."[30] The performance theorist Joni L. Jones writes that although it is tempting to eschew authenticity as hopelessly essentialist, this viewpoint "disregard[s] the passionate longing that undergirds the hope of authenticity." Jones offers a definition of authenticity as something one does rather than something one finds. Performance allows one to embody aspects of culture, creating a "new authenticity, based on body knowledge, on what audiences and performers share together, on what they mutually construct."[31] Jones's formulation acknowledges performance as a site that is constituted both by performers' choices and audience members' responses.

Rather than imitate Japanese taiko, San Jose Taiko consciously constructed their group as Asian American. Distinguishing themselves from San Francisco Taiko Dojo, whose leader Seiichi Tanaka's way of "doing" authenticity relied on his direct connections to Japan, San Jose Taiko created new music and practices that reflected their members' Japanese American and Asian American identities. Realizing that they could not be "Japanese from Japan," San Jose Taiko reframed their endeavor as an authentically

Asian American taiko group, one that was inspired by their experiences as community activists and their eclectic musical tastes. While San Jose Taiko adopted some of Tanaka's practices, their choosing the term "Asian American taiko" was in part a way to forge their own practice, based on their own experiences as Asians in the United States. This was not a move away from Japanese taiko but rather a way to purposefully embrace a multiply influenced form that drew inspiration from their own musical tastes, including American vernacular music and Afro-Cuban rhythms.

San Jose Taiko members' desires for a connection to Japan were also mediated through AAM-related activities and ideology. In particular, the U.S. war in Vietnam gave rise to a burgeoning ethnic consciousness among young Asian Americans in the late 1960s and early 1970s.[32] PJ Hirabayashi describes how antiwar protests shaped her racial awareness and led her to see herself as an Asian American, rather than as a "progressive white, antiwar" college student. As she began to believe, as many Asian Americans did, that the United States was fighting a racist war in Asia, she also "really became aware of the social injustices within America."[33] Hirabayashi was one of many Asian American students at UC–Berkeley to become politicized during the late 1960s.

In addition to identity-related issues, San Jose Taiko's involvement in the Asian American movement also created an impetus toward structural change. The group, over the course of its many years, committed themselves to creating an organizational structure in which all of its members operate as equals. Issues of equality outweighed adhering to what many perceive as a Japanese tradition of organizational structure, in which members are ranked according to seniority. PJ Hirabayashi believes that hierarchies create oppressive structures in groups, and they made a conscious choice to adopt a collective, rather than hierarchical, structure. She began to recognize that "just because it's Japanese, you don't have to embrace it . . . if it's something that's oppressive, don't embrace it. That was very conscious."[34] Although San Jose Taiko learned technique and performance skills from Tanaka, they chose not to embrace his group's seniority-based hierarchy. Decisions are made by consensus, and all members share responsibilities in the group's operations, from costume making and maintaining the rehearsal space to teaching classes and mentoring new members. While several members do have administrative and artistic positions, San Jose Taiko purposefully encourages all members to serve as leaders in a variety of capacities.

From Los Angeles–based Kinnara Taiko, founded in 1969, and later from others, San Jose members learned how to make their own drums out of wine barrels, and today the entire group shares responsibility for creating and maintaining the drums and other instruments they play.[35] In performance, all members wear exactly the same costume, without any visual markers of seniority or skill. In some taiko groups, men and women wear slightly different costumes, while in others, a group's sensei, or leader, wears a special *happi* coat indicating his or her status. All San Jose Taiko members, including PJ and Roy, wear the same costumes. San Jose Taiko also requires an intensive training program that allows all members to play any part in the repertoire, giving all members opportunities to play the most desirable or challenging parts. This not only allows a uniform movement style on stage but also discourages any member from becoming the virtuoso or star.

In large part out of necessity, San Jose Taiko members began to compose their own songs early on, fitting the rhythms of their musical influences into the form and movement style they'd learned from their mentors. In the early 1980s, PJ Hirabayashi created a new taiko composition that was based on a Japanese style of drumming and dancing, but pulled its content from the experiences of the Issei, many of whom relied on hard manual and railroad labor for survival. This new composition, *Ei Ja Nai Ka?*, made the connections between politically motivated Sansei and their grandparents' generation explicit through performance.

LABORED GESTURES, PERFORMING RACIAL PROGRESS

When San Jose Taiko performs and teaches the taiko folk dance *Ei Ja Nai Ka?* at festivals, concerts, or taiko gatherings, they explicitly connect their artistic work to their Asian American movement and community roots. It also makes explicit how taiko bridged a generational gap between the Issei and Sansei generations. The piece highlights the Issei experience, as did historian Yuji Ichioka, as a "labor history."[36] The first three U.S. taiko groups—San Francisco Taiko Dojo, Kinnara Taiko, and San Jose Taiko—are often referred to in taiko circles as the "pioneer groups."[37] Pioneering not only evokes the American frontier but also rhetorically connects these Sansei-led groups with Issei historians, who cast the first generation as pioneers with a legitimate stake in American "frontier expansionism" in the early twentieth century.[38] Not only did San Jose Taiko's early members and other Sansei respect the "adventurous" spirit of the Issei, but Sansei in many cities started social service organizations dedicated to caring for the Issei—and later generations—as they aged.[39] Sansei, especially those who had become politicized during the Asian American movement, diverged from what they saw as the Nisei generation's "accommodationist and assimilationist" political strategies.[40] Many in the Nisei generation came of age during the World War II era and lived through the experience of internment. The fear of persecution before, during, and after internment partly explains the difference between the Nisei generation's more cautious political stances and the more radical activism undertaken by many Sansei.[41] The political climate in the midcentury United States reinforced the Nisei tendency toward assimilationist politics. Many avenues of political maneuvering were foreclosed for the Nisei, due to a number of national and international sociopolitical pressures during the early twentieth century. The Great Depression, the troubled U.S.-Japan relations leading to World War II, domestic racism, and wartime internment all compelled Nisei toward assimilationist politics and away from "affirm[ing] their ethnicity and practic[ing] ethnic politics."[42] Thus, some Sansei raised by Nisei parents not only practiced more radical politics than their Nisei parents but also sought cultural avenues for exploring their Japaneseness.[43]

The Sansei push to reclaim their Japanese heritage was informed by a complex dynamic of domestic racism, ethnic pride, and radical AAM politics. Sansei taiko players saw the Issei generation as their link to Japanese heritage. Many Sansei connected directly with Issei through community activism—for example, by providing badly needed social services to the older generation (a branch of AAM embraced not only by Japanese Americans but also by other Asian American communities). Others made this connection to the Issei through the arts, and taiko was one avenue through which to connect. PJ Hirabayashi recalls that after performing taiko at an Issei picnic in the late 1970s, many of the Issei audience members were very moved and told San Jose Taiko members, "'Oh, I'm so happy that you are being in touch with your Japanese culture. It makes me very proud.'" PJ continued, "And to hear that made it sound like it's coming from my grandmother."[44] Even though taiko was a recently developed folk art form, the Issei recognized and appreciated Sansei efforts to embrace Japanese culture through this new tradition. For Sansei, the sense of connection with Japan was deeply felt, and taiko as a Japanese art form (albeit hybrid in many ways) became a means of connecting with Issei, many of whom could not speak English. Thus, Sansei embraced taiko as a new Japanese American cultural practice produced by historical circumstances that created markedly different experiences for Issei, Nisei, and Sansei generations.

San Jose Taiko specifically honors the connection between the Issei and Sansei in *Ei Ja Nai Ka?* through gesture and lyrics. Creator PJ Hirabayashi notes that she was inspired by specific Japanese folk performance traditions and ensembles, tying the piece aesthetically to Japanese performance. The gestural movements in the piece mimic the very movements of labor performed by Issei—and, by extension, other immigrants and exploited populations—in their first years in the United States. Group members explain that the rough translation of the title, "Isn't it good?," implies an acknowledgment of the good things among the bad and a recognition of the sacrifices that have contributed to the good life people appreciate today. San Jose Taiko member Wisa Uemura says the song is "really about gratitude . . . for what has had to happen to make what we have good and blessed."[45] *Ei Ja Nai Ka?* is composed of parts for drumming, singing, *kakegoe* (chanting), and simple dance phrases that move in a circular pattern. PJ Hirabayashi created the dance, drum, and *kakegoe* parts in 1994 and later, in 2001, asked Yoko Fujimoto—a folk singer, member of Japanese performing arts troupe Hanayui, and former member of KODO—to write a melody and lyrics to accompany the dance.[46] *Ei Ja Nai Ka?* is performed widely throughout the taiko community, both by San Jose Taiko and by groups to whom they have taught the song. The piece is part of San Jose Taiko's touring repertoire and is also familiar to many taiko players through the North American Taiko Conference, as indicated in the introduction to this chapter. San Jose Taiko created *Ei Ja Nai Ka?* as a public domain performance and teach it to other taiko groups who want to learn and perform it for their own communities. The piece thus has wide influence as far as taiko compositions go.

Additionally, while the musical and gestural vocabulary are inspired by contemporary Japanese folk performance, it is also a staple in the San Jose Obon repertoire of *bon* dances, which are part of *obon*, the Buddhist festival honoring the dead, a tradition observed in the late summer.[47] While the content of the piece draws on an aspect of the Japanese American past, its form is inspired by music and dance conventions that are currently practiced both in Japan and in Japanese American communities. In *bon-odori*, or festival dances, a drummer and flutist accompany dancers who move in repeated patterns, usually in a circle or lines. Inspired by the Japanese folk arts group Warabi-Za,[48] and the traditions of Kyushu's Kokura Gion Matsuri and Awa Odori of Shikoku, Hirabayashi began to contemplate a folk dance piece that would be unique to San Jose Taiko and that would reflect a Japanese diasporic experience. While it is fairly common for taiko groups to participate in *obon* or other festival dances by either giving a concert or playing the drum parts for the large group dances, *Ei Ja Nai Ka?* is unique in that it was created both as a piece for San Jose Taiko to perform (in concert, at festivals, etc.) as well as to teach to its various audiences and communities, taiko players and nonplayers, Asian Americans and non-Asian Americans. It is highly participatory because, while the group members always perform the piece, festival-goers are encouraged to join in the dance circle.

Although Japanese laborers supported themselves in a number of ways, including through business and entrepreneurship, *Ei Ja Nai Ka?* focuses on manual labor, including gestures that mimic digging, picking (as if in a mine), fishing, steering, and wiping the sweat from one's brow. When the San Jose Taiko members perform these movements, they have a crisp yet buoyant energy. As they dig and pick, they sing the call and response: "Ei Ja Nai Ka!" "A So-re, A So-re!" "Ei Ja Nai Ka, hai!" "A So-re, So-re, Yoisho!"[49]

FIGURE 1.2. San Jose Taiko member Yurika Chiba (in costume) dances *Ei Ja Nai Ka?* with San Jose Obon participants (photo by Higashi Design)

As I stumble through the movements, I have to remind myself of the choreography, repeating, "Dig, dig / Pick, pick," in my head as I step sharply with my right foot on the first and second beats ("Dig, dig"), while at the same time jutting my fisted hands down and to the right, as if I'm thrusting a shovel into the earth. On beats three and four ("Pick, pick"), I step sharply to the left and raise my arms, jutting my imaginary pickax at the mine wall above my head. Song lyrics that accompany the drumming, chanting, and dancing refer to the physical effects—dyed fingers and "stretched" backs—of harvesting strawberries in the field. These gestures and lyrics point to the kinds of work the Issei performed. Japanese immigration to the United States began in earnest in the 1880s, when Japanese workers, both men and women, came to the United States to labor in farms, mills, mines, and railroads. It was largely halted in 1907 after Japan's emperor and U.S. president Theodore Roosevelt created the Gentlemen's Agreement that effectively barred Japanese immigration. After the passing of Alien Land Laws, Issei farmers barred from owning land were forced to move every two or three years. Still, although many continued the back-breaking "stoop" labor throughout their lives, others created their own businesses. Between 1900 and 1909, Japanese-owned businesses boomed. Despite these successes, the Issei faced racial discrimination, as had Chinese and Filipino laborers before them. Few spoke English or had access to education, and efforts to establish anti-racist labor unions failed. By 1913, legislation sought to halt the opening of more Japanese-owned businesses and farms.[50]

Throughout the lyrics, which are sung in Japanese, the singer/narrator is figured as someone in present time, speaking back to earlier generations. The song literally addresses "Grandpa" and "Grandma," though one might also take those monikers as figurative of ancestors rather than literal references to lineage: "Ei ja nai ka, ei ja nai ka, Grandpa, ei ja nai ka? / Ei ja nai ka, ei ja nai ka, Grandma, ei ja nai ka?"[51] Although "Grandpa" and "Grandma" are English words, they are sung in Japanese pronunciation. Rather than pronounce them as two-syllable words, they are sung in four syllables: "Gu-ra-n-ma" and "Gu-ra-n-pa." This line solidifies the piece's dedication to the Issei, using direct address and asking, essentially, wasn't the sacrifice—the "sweat dripping"—worthwhile? As the Asian American historian Ron Takaki points out, Issei came to be thought of as immigrants only in retrospect, since many came as temporary laborers, only to see their options for return to Japan dwindle once they arrived on U.S. shores.[52] The dreams they held may have been of return to their homeland rather than beginning a new life in the United States, but this lyric nonetheless recognizes the hardships of the Issei's early years in the country.

One of the most expansive movement phrases, the steering move, highlights the way *Ei Ja Nai Ka?* elevates manual labor to an honored—and honorable—symbol of progress. PJ Hirabayashi notes that one gesture in the song, in which the dancer spreads her arms wide and rotates them as if steering a giant wheel, was inspired by her grandfather's work as an engine wiper on the Southern Pacific Railroad. "Engine wiper sounds like a very menial and almost demeaning type of position, but . . . it's that kind of labor that has built this nation."[53] In a workshop, PJ demonstrates the effects this labor had on her grandfather by bending forward, explaining that her grandfather's back was permanently hunched. The shift from Hirabayashi's grandfather's position of "engine wiper" to steering is more than simply a wishful revision of history. On one level, steering is more legible a gesture than wiping, and also more easily connected to railroad work. But this steering motion requires more than the limited range of driving an imaginary car. To steer this train, I spread my arms full-length to each side, hands fisted, and tilt forty-five degrees with a bent right knee and straight left leg, the horizontal arms tilting along my body's line. I repeat it to the left, and once more on each side. The steering motion is the simplest and broadest of the dance, requiring me to extend my body to its limits. Each tilt is punctuated with a shouted phrase: "EI! JA! NAI! KA!" It is a full and celebratory movement, one that is pleasurable to execute. It transforms exploited physical laborers into powerful leaders performing rewarding work; and while it accomplishes this through a revision of history, the gesture (both the physical movement and the sentiment) highlights how crucial Issei labor was to the industrial and economic progress of the nation.

In the song lyrics, the railroad imagery is explicitly tied to notions of progress:

Smoke puffs out, making a roar
A sora ei ja nai ka—Railroad—ei ja nai ka
Ei ja nai ka—Steam engine—ei ja nai ka
The railroad expands from west to east,
Carrying today's load toward tomorrow.[54]

In accounts of Asian American history, the railroad is most commonly associated with Chinese American labor, specifically the vast numbers of Chinese laborers who built the Central Pacific Railroad, only to be erased from mainstream histories' commemorations of this marked achievement. But as many as ten thousand Japanese laborers worked on railroads in 1909, suffering under harsh labor conditions and extreme temperatures.[55] The railroad can be read as a symbol of achievement and national progress. Asian American histories generally mark railroad labor as a site of unfair labor practices, since Asian laborers were largely left out of official national histories. Notably, *Ei Ja Nai Ka?* honors the labor of Issei railroad workers and uses the railroad as a symbol of a different kind of progress. Here, perhaps, the railroad symbolizes progress toward equality and justice for Japanese immigrants rather than industrial achievement. On the other hand, perhaps viewing Japanese Americans' part in American industrial achievement is itself a vehicle for racial progress.

Ei Ja Nai Ka? frames Issei struggles as ones that were overcome and resulted in the success of future generations. Yet the historian Yuji Ichioka has argued that the Issei struggle for survival was "far from being a success story."[56] Japanese laborers, like other Asian and Mexican immigrant laborers, worked under harsh conditions, including extreme cold and hot temperatures, insufficient lodging, and long hours, among other injustices.[57] But the fervent racism that many Issei suffered goes unmentioned in this song. Further, the focus on agricultural and industrial labor belies the fact that many Issei became successful merchants who founded businesses both small and large during the first decade of the 1900s. In 1910 there was roughly one business per twenty-two people within the Japanese population in the western United States.[58] For women in both agriculture and merchant sectors, household duties fell to their shoulders in addition to their jobs, leaving them with a double workload.[59] While *Ei Ja Nai Ka?* highlights pre-internment manual labor, its celebration of racial and community progress eclipses other aspects of the Japanese American past.

Hirabayashi and San Jose Taiko are well aware of Japanese American history and are very likely also aware of the pitfalls of ascribing a teleological history. The internment of 110,000 Japanese and Japanese Americans during World War II is clear evidence that racial progress is not linear. Many taiko groups have songs about or dedicated to this dark chapter of Japanese American history or reference the event as a kind of originary moment from which American taiko has proceeded. That this piece notably omits internment indicates that the piece has more to do with the connections between the Issei and Sansei than it does with relating a complete and accurate timeline of Japanese American history. As member Wisa Uemura says, the song recognizes "the first Issei coming to this country, [and] that we can benefit from even playing taiko is from their hard work."[60] The song acknowledges the Issei for the economic and social foundations they provided for later generations' successes, achievements, and leisure.

In festival settings, where all of the elements repeat for an unspecified length, and the purpose is to join in the dancing and chanting, the kinesthetic aspects of participating in the dance take precedence. At the North American Taiko Conference, dancing, drumming, chanting, and singing this piece reminds taiko players—many of whom are not Japanese American or Asian American—that our ability to practice taiko at all is thanks to Asian American activism and the parents and grandparents whose labor made this elaborate leisure activity possible in the first place. In that context, *Ei Ja Nai Ka?* teaches Asian American history to taiko players with a range of backgrounds and investments in the form. When San Jose Taiko performs at the San Jose *obon* festival, perhaps some of the effects are similar. In the context of a San Jose Japantown event, *Ei Ja Nai Ka?* may speak more directly to Japanese Americans, Asian Americans, or those who have a specific connection to those communities. In both situations, the piece affords people the opportunity to move together in the present moment, and engage with the past through the shared labors of dancing, singing, and chanting.

The significance of *Ei Ja Nai Ka?* in San Jose Taiko's repertoire is evidenced not only by its being taught at taiko conferences, community festivals, and other performances but also through its inclusion in the group's thirty-fifth anniversary concert, recorded on DVD. In this abbreviated version of the piece, the progress narrative is made more obvious through cutting the middle verses of the lyrics dedicated to specific types of labor, while the audience participation elements are reduced because the piece is performed in a proscenium auditorium, rather than in a less formal festival setting. The anniversary arrangement begins with a slow and somber pace, emphasizing laborious movement, and proceeds to a fast, celebratory dance. These aspects seem appropriate to an anniversary concert celebrating the group's longevity, but I am interested in how this shortened version, as embodied history, emphasizes teleology and the notion of progress. Moving from slow to fast, mournful to celebratory, dark to light, this arrangement gestures to the memory of sacrifice and labor in order to celebrate the fruits of that labor in the present.

The piece begins with the stage bare, except for two *chu-daiko* (medium-sized barrel drums) standing upright stage left and right, in front of a red cyclorama. Slow single beats on the *atarigane*, a metal hand gong, precede one performer's entrance. The *atarigane* player begins to sing as the performer slowly enters from stage left and stands still on the platform that stretches across upstage. Almost as soon as she initiates the song, the company's voices join hers from off stage. Four men enter from stage right, four heavy left feet landing in time with the *atarigane's* slow beats. They continue to put one foot in front of the other. They grasp their *bachi* with both hands, as if holding the handle of an axe, and as they begin each step, their arms hoist the *bachi* above their heads, and then let the imaginary weight of the axe pull their arms down. They are working on a railroad, in a chain gang. One of the men pushes a drum onstage as though it is filled with lead. They continue across the stage, and once in place stage left, they root their feet in a wide stance and continue, in a round, to swing their axes. Meanwhile, three performers enter stage left, singing, facing the audience, stepping sideways as they plant rice with their hands. Holding *uchiwa* (hand-held fan drums) with their left hands, they use their right hands to dip into their *uchiwa* as if they are baskets. In time to the music, they pick seeds and throw them, pick and throw, then pick and bend down to plant them, and finally pick and scatter the seeds. Their eyes, like the railroad workers,' are downcast, concentrating on their labor.

After several beats, the long introduction ends, and the energy shifts subtly. All the dancers continue their gestures, but with a slight bounce in their feet, as if some new energy springs up through the ground into their bodies. Two or three people shout *kakegoe*: "Hai!" "Za!" Soon the somber formality dissolves, and the performers scatter into different positions: The railroad workers wipe the sweat from their brows, roll drums downstage, and begin to play. The rice planters beat their *uchiwa* as they leap and chant. PJ Hirabayashi and Wisa Uemura enter upstage right with a large *okedo* drum on wheels, which they begin to beat with buoyant energy. Franco Imperial sets a *shime-daiko* down upstage left and smiles as he lays down a peppy swing beat. The *chu-daiko* players play through one round of the drum melody, then the *uchiwa* players rush downstage, each taking brief solos down center. This section has the informal feel of an impromptu jam session. It is a typical taiko composition format: play the "song" and then allow for short virtuosic solos. But in the context of the song's focus on labor, it also is reminiscent of laborers' impromptu entertainments, showing off for each other with their individual moves as an appreciative crowd looks on.

The company chants a long phrase of "Sore, sore, sore, sore, sore, sore, sore, sore!" in crescendo and scatters once again into another formation. Imperial, Hirabayashi, and Uemura continue to drum on the upstage platform and are now joined by three *uchiwa* players. All the other performers form a circle on the main stage and begin the folk dance as they sing the melody again: Dig and pick, roll and sweat, steer, steer. This setup mirrors as closely as it can the festival version of the song: the musicians accompany the dancers, and they all sing together. They run through the dance twice and then re-form into two lines, facing the audience. They dance, some sing, and some chant. Here, all parts of *Ei Ja Nai Ka?* come together in its layered complexity. By this point in the performance, although the labor is still present in the dance gestures, it is layered with so many songs, chants, and beats that it is woven into a celebratory cacophony. The lighting is brighter, the pace is faster, and the dancers move with buoyant energy, the signature San Jose Taiko bounce, with glittering smiles on their faces. The piece ends abruptly, as the melody, dance, and chant end. As the last line of the lyrics, "Tatako yo, Odoro yo!" (Let's beat the taiko! Let's dance!) is sung, the dancers hoist their nets toward the audience, pointing their *bachi* right at them, and shout a final "Yoi Sho!"

This shortened version of the piece omits the lyrics that focus on types of Issei labor and skips to an ending verse that celebrates dancing and drumming. But even if spectators could not recognize the Japanese lyrics, the brevity of the piece, along with its dramatic shifts from dark to light, slow to fast, somber to upbeat, suggests a celebratory teleology. *Ei Ja Nai Ka?* as staged in this DVD performance conveys a triumphant success for Japanese Americans and for the United States. The piece draws on Japanese performance traditions, world music influences, and the diasporic tradition of *obon* festival to re-member and revise our understanding of Japanese immigration and intergenerational dynamics. While Japanese American history and traditions may be familiar to San Jose Taiko's Asian American and Japanese American audiences, this story of racial progress may be new to mainstream audiences in the United States and abroad. As the piece continues to be performed, it is significant that it celebrates and honors immigrant labor against a backdrop of hostility, fear, and violence that too often accompanies immigration discourse in the United States.

The creation of Japanese American histories, whether through writing or performance, not only connects Issei to Sansei, present to past, but also connects San Jose Taiko to the Asian American movement itself. The writing of Asian American histories has been instrumental in Asian American movement politics, given the movement's involvement in the creation of ethnic studies programs in California colleges. Josephine Lee connects these impulses to those that have shaped plays that evoke Asian American histories as well: "The eagerness to write history points to the desire for an authenticating past that will support a communal future; within the enactment of the meticulous details of history are purposes that shape theatrical presentation."[61] San Jose Taiko's *Ei Ja Nai Ka?* enacts a revision of the past through gesture and sound in ways that not only complement and extend written histories of Asian America but also encourage, in Lee's words, "a communal future" in which all willingly participate in and remember those histories as a route to structural equality and social justice.

MARKETING ASIAN AMERICAN TAIKO:
BETWEEN WORLD DANCE AND ACTIVISM

When San Jose Taiko performed at the Long Center for the Performing Arts in Austin, Texas, on September 27, 2009, their last number did not end in the usual way concerts and other performances end, with bows and quick exits. Rather, the last number only ended after the entire ensemble danced down the aisles through the applauding audience, still playing instruments—small hand-held gongs, cymbals, and large drums strapped to their bodies—smiling and shouting spirited cries along with the rhythms. Once they arrived in the large, glass-fronted lobby that overlooks the river and the colorfully lit buildings of downtown Austin, the San Jose Taiko members positioned themselves strategically throughout the space so that they could greet as many departing audience members as possible. Rather than disappearing backstage and exiting in street clothes much later, San Jose Taiko talks with audiences while the labor of their performance is still evident: they appear with rumpled costumes and sweaty skin, their breathing still heavy from performing. They are approachable and warm as they shake many hands, accept congratulations, and answer questions for almost an hour after the performance has ended.[62] Bringing the performance out into the house and greeting their audiences in the lobby, even in the formal setting of a large performing venue, is part of how San Jose Taiko reaches out to communities when they tour nationally and internationally.

Gathered around PJ Hirabayashi in a cluster by the large windows is a group of local taiko players. They are identifiable as such because they sport sweatshirts and T-shirts with the names of their groups, Austin Taiko and Kaminari Taiko, and because they are chatting with Hirabayashi about upcoming workshops that have been scheduled in Austin later that week. In another spot near the theater doors, the performer Franco Imperial speaks animatedly with interested audience members, some of whom I later learn are his relatives who live in the Austin area. Around the lobby, several other group members field questions and compliments from a range of people: tall white Texan men in dress jeans and cowboy boots, young women in high heels, and couples leading their children by the hand. Other San Jose Taiko members obligingly sign the programs of the many Asian and Latino/a children standing in line for their autographs. The crowd San Jose Taiko has drawn is decidedly more racially diverse than audiences at other Long Center performances, such as the ballet, symphony, and other national touring shows, and the presenter's brochures have been designed to attract crowds interested in performances that lie outside the European/American canon.

Despite San Jose Taiko's complex understanding of its grounding in Asian American politics and history, presenters often rely on Orientalist rhetoric to promote the group's shows. In some cases, their performances are imagined as Japanese rather than Asian American. Much of San Jose Taiko's work over its four decades has been to make Asian Americans legible—visually and sonically—in a variety of contexts. Taiko players in the 1960s and 1970s often saw taiko as a way to replace negative images of stereotyped Orientals with a more active and positive picture of themselves. Part of San Jose Taiko's adopting an Asian American stance for themselves was a way to distinguish the group from Japanese taiko groups, as well as to acknowledge the different histories and experiences of Japanese and Asian American people. Current members are clearly still invested in these aims. In some performance contexts, San Jose Taiko can articulate their history, influences, and philosophical aims. On their tour to large performance venues, some of these opportunities to articulate their history and philosophy fall under the control of presenters' marketing departments and PR materials.

The brochure announcing the 2009–2010 season of the Long Center for the Performing Arts in Austin, Texas, sports a montage of its varied offerings: classical music, dance, and musical theater, among others.[63] The Long Center, which opened in 2008, is home to Austin's ballet, symphony, and opera and presents a variety of national touring performances. In 2009 San Jose Taiko was among them, and a slice of the cover montage was accordingly filled with a San Jose Taiko image. Member Wisa Uemura is dressed in a *happi* coat and *hachimaki*, her face and left arm reaching skyward against a deep red background. Uemura's smiling face is lit brightly, and the rim of a *chu-daiko* almost fades into the adjacent photograph. To the left of Uemura is a black-and-white photo of the classical pianist Lang Lang gazing philosophically skyward, and to the right, the actors playing Danny and Sandy in the musical *Grease* grin happily from the cover. Inside the brochure, San Jose Taiko's upcoming performances are listed under the "International" series.

San Jose Taiko's positioning in these marketing materials exemplifies what the dance studies scholar Susan Foster calls the "worlding" of dance. Foster argues that although the term "world" as applied to music, dance, and other arts purports to view all performance as equal under one category, the "colonial history that produced [the imbalance] continues to operate" in practice. Reading a brochure for the 2007–2008 Cal Performances at UC–Berkeley, Foster notes that only ballet and modern companies, danced mostly by white people, qualify as "Dance," whereas performance by artists of color are "World Dance."[64] In a similar fashion, the Long Center's season brochure relegates its performances by artists of color to the two categories "Dance with a Difference" and "International." The other categories—Broadway, Off-Broadway, Classical Variations, Musical Legends, and Specials—present work created and performed by white performers, with the exception of Lang Lang, the Chinese pianist whose repertoire of European classical music qualifies him as simply an artist. The "Dance with a Difference" category includes the presumably Latin-influenced, "sizzling" *Ballroom with a Twist* and hip-hop show *Groovaloo*, while the "International" category includes San Jose Taiko among its two other offerings, the *Ballet Folklorico de Mexico* and *Spirit of Uganda*. While San Jose Taiko is clearly not an international group when presented in the United States, its inclusion among performances from Mexico and Uganda that blend dance and music is not surprising. CDs of taiko music are often shelved as world music, and San Jose Taiko does, indeed, draw on musical traditions from around the world, including Latin and African music.

Nonetheless, the placement of San Jose Taiko in the International series disregards the long history of taiko as an American performance tradition and reinforces the designation of Asian Americans as perpetual foreigners. When San Jose Taiko tours nationally, presenters and agents capitalize on the ongoing commercial appeal of Asia as a cultural product by selling San Jose Taiko as "authentically" Japanese from "over there," rather than Asian American from San Jose, California. The image and copy that accompany San Jose's advertisement within the season brochure create what Emily Roxworthy calls a "theatricalizing discourse" around San Jose Taiko. Theatricalizing discourse presumes the maskedness and aesthetic distantness of Japanese people.[65] The brochure copy reads:

> These empowering and overwhelming sounds weave traditional Japanese music with the beat of world rhythms. It's extreme physical endurance, amazing theatrics and an [sic] transformative spirit that inspired an Empire. This is Taiko, a culture unseen for centuries and filled with the rituals of 5000 years. Percussionists will battle.[66]

Even if we dispense with the many factual and grammatical errors in this blurb (modern taiko does not date back five thousand years, nor is it a competitive or "battle" performance style), the text characterizes taiko as something ancient ("unseen for centuries") and ritualized. The notions that taiko "inspired an Empire" or that "Percussionists will battle" are pure fantasy. That this particular group, who clearly and consistently emphasize their connection to Japanese American communities and Asian American movement politics rooted in peace and equality, should be cast in such a mystical and militant light is indicative of the theatricalizing impulse of American culture.

The image against which the blurb is set reinforces the text's positioning of taiko as an ancient and exotic performance. Three drummers are shown in shadow against a luminous blue cyclorama—black, faceless figures with their arms held at 45-degree angles, about to strike the drums. The figures loom large against the backdrop, their shoulders broadened by the cut of the *happi* coats, any personal expression or detail obscured by the lighting technology. The performers' slender arms and silhouettes make them discernible as female, and the overall image, in concert with the text, makes the performers appear ominous, almost warrior-like. Although the Long Center appears to have edited the image only slightly, a browse through San Jose Taiko's publicity website reveals that the Long Center likely chose the only image out of thirty-three that obscures, rather than highlights, performers' facial expressions and colorful costumes.

When I asked San Jose Taiko members about marketing materials in our interview, they laughed knowingly. About this particular brochure, Wisa Uemura said that where the copy emphasized the ancient and traditional, "we tend to not think of ourselves as traditional. We are definitely a contemporary taiko company. . . . [The blurb is] not from any of our wording." Franco Imperial acknowledged that the Long Center had graciously changed the offending copy online but were unable to change the printed brochure because of deadlines.[67] The group does provide presenters' PR and marketing departments with web access to extensive group histories, descriptions, program lineups, images, and video, but whether this information gets passed along to other members of staff is often out of San Jose Taiko's control.[68] Perhaps part of the conundrum is that the Long Center's impulse to frame taiko as part of an unbroken lineage dating back thousands of years taps into their audience's wish for authenticity. That many taiko players, both Asian American and non–Asian American, see taiko in Japan as authoritative and seek training and inspiration from their Japanese counterparts complicates this issue.

The Orientalist leanings of advertising and marketing are not new to San Jose Taiko. PJ and Roy Hirabayashi both noted that in the past, agents and presenters have urged them to change the group's name, either to something "sexier" or "something Japanese." Roy also notes that, particularly in areas with fewer Asian Americans, "they're trying to represent us as a group from Japan. . . . And then the audience kind of thinks that's what we are when we really feel that we're trying to present a more American or Asian American perspective to what taiko's all about."[69] As San Jose Taiko no doubt tries to differentiate themselves from taiko groups from Japan who are, essentially, their competition, the very avenues through which to do so (agents and marketing departments) urge them to become *more like* other taiko groups, once again collapsing the difference between Asian and Asian American.

San Jose Taiko does not compromise its aesthetic or ideals by bending to Orientalist demands; it attempts to distinguish itself from other touring taiko groups by connecting directly with audiences. Franco Imperial says that in contrast to KODO, one of the well-known Japanese touring groups, who maintain a kind of "mystique" within and around their performances, San Jose Taiko mingles with the audience in an effort to connect with them. As I described in the introduction to this section, San Jose members carry their performance off stage, through the audience, and into the lobby, breaking the theatrical "fourth wall" and dissolving the distance between audience and performer. Once in the lobby, they talk at length with audience members. Imperial says this is all part of San Jose Taiko's "emotional accessibility."

Outside the touring venue, the group tries "as much as possible to connect with the local [taiko] groups."[70] While San Jose Taiko's full-scale concerts usually play in cities with large presenting venues, they also perform school shows in more rural or remote areas, many of whose populations include very few Asian Americans or other racial minorities. Wisa Uemura says that in schools, particularly where there may be very little exposure to Asian people or cultures, San Jose Taiko members may seem "different," but as she says, they "make 'different' cool . . . accessible, and acceptable."[71] Meg Suzuki adds that when audiences include very few Asian Americans, she feels particularly motivated to reach out to them. She says,

> I wish I could say, you know, like, "I actually grew up in rural Pennsylvania. . . . I'm like you!" I didn't know what other Asians, gosh, looked like even. It was just me. I mean, I lived in a place where the Klan came through town every once in a while, you know? Like, I wish there was some point where I could be like, "I know what you're feeling. I feel your pain. It's going to be okay."[72]

Both Uemura and Suzuki, like other members of San Jose Taiko, are invested in using taiko to connect with the communities in which they perform. In some instances, this means teaching their audiences to respect racial difference, while in others, it means reaching out to Asians and Asian Americans who might feel isolated in rural or largely white areas.

While outreach performances and encounters with audience members may in some instances disrupt Orientalist rhetoric that pervades marketing materials and too often audiences' perspectives, they continue to be a site of negotiation and even struggle for San Jose Taiko and other groups. These ongoing and sometimes seemingly futile attempts to redirect spectators' Orientalist impulses through direct audience engagement are part of the complex constellation of identities and influences San Jose Taiko navigates as an Asian American, Japanese American, and multiethnic performance ensemble in the United States.

San Jose Taiko members continue to shape and be shaped by Asian American movement politics through their enactment of embodied Asian American histories, organizational structure, and continued struggles with Orientalist representation. Through their negotiations among Japanese authenticity, Asian American activism, and their multiple artistic influences, San Jose Taiko has also deeply influenced the trajectory of North American taiko. The organizational structure of the group reflects the founders' involvement with Asian American movement activities. Moreover, through the group's leadership within the taiko community and PJ and Roy's extensive leadership outside the group, it is clear that these AAM participants' influence has extended well beyond the heyday of political activism in the 1970s. Because it has been so widely taught and performed, *Ei Ja Nai Ka?* and its impulse to connect audiences and participants with Asian American history has also carried out AAM ideals through performance. Finally, the group's continued negotiation of exoticizing and Orientalist assumptions by presenters and marketing departments highlights the continuing necessity of carrying out messages that early Asian American movement activists and pioneer taiko players brought to light. Not all taiko players and groups give as much explicit attention to the structural, political, and representational aspects of taiko, but we all must move through this complex negotiation of performance, politics, and everyday life.

NOTES

1. A YouTube clip of this performance is available: "Ei Ja Na Kai—Post Taiko Jam Jam 2009," YouTube video, 2:51, from North American Taiko Conference 2009, posted by kaukadj, August 20, 2009, https://www.youtube.com/watch?v=c8 Z7a4e5sBg, accessed August 21, 2009.

2. In order to emphasize its status as a twentieth-century U.S. form (that is, as not only Japanese, but also Japanese American and Asian American), I consciously do not italicize the word "taiko" in this essay.

3. Some instrumentation used in taiko performance comes from Shinto and Buddhist rituals or from Japanese performance traditions, such as *gagaku* (court

music) and Noh and Kabuki *bayashi* (musical accompaniment for Noh and Kabuki theater), but modern taiko distinguishes itself from these earlier types of music by making the drumming the focus of performance, rather than an accompaniment to dance, theater, ritual, or festival activities. Although taiko instruments from the festival traditions initially came to the United States with the first wave of Japanese immigrants in the 1900s, the later tradition did not take the same diasporic route from Japan to the United States but rather was taken up by *Sansei*, or third-generation Japanese Americans, in the 1960s as a way to connect to their ethnic roots. For a thorough explanation of the instrumentation, costuming, and other material and practical aspects of taiko in the United States, see Shawn Bender, *Taiko Boom: Japanese Drumming in Place and Motion* (Berkeley: University of California Press, 2012); Mark Tusler, "Sounds and Sights of Power: Ensemble Taiko Drumming (*Kumi Daiko*) Pedagogy in California and the Conceptualization of Power" (PhD diss., University of California, Santa Barbara, 2003); and Deborah Wong, *Speak It Louder: Asian Americans Making Music* (New York: Routledge, 2004).

4. PJ Hirabayashi, who created the piece, teaches *Ei Ja Nai Ka?* in workshops. With her permission, groups are allowed to perform the piece and teach it to their own groups.

5. *Obon* refers to a late-summer festival that honors the dead. These are common throughout Japan and the Japanese diaspora. Cherry Blossom festivals are celebrated in the spring.

6. In such a workshop, we learn the basic drum rhythms, the call-and-response chants, and the dance moves. There are other elements to the song—such as a melody with lyrics and other auxiliary percussion parts—that could be learned in further workshops.

7. The 2013 conference was postponed as conference organizers strategized about how to support future gatherings, and a 2015 conference was held in Las Vegas, Nevada, in June of that year. The 2015 conference's primary sponsor was the newly formed Taiko Community Alliance, a nonprofit organization founded and run by taiko players, after the long-time sponsor Japanese American Community and Cultural Center of Los Angeles refocused on other efforts. Further attention to this organizational shift is beyond the scope of this essay, but more information about Taiko Community Alliance and North American Taiko Conference can be found at www.taikocommunityalliance.org.

8. See, for example, Roy Hirabayashi, "Life History Interview," with Art Hansen and Sojin Kim, (transcript, *Big Drum: Taiko in the United States* exhibition, Hirasaki National Resource Center, Japanese American National Museum, 369 East First Street, Los Angeles]hereafter HNRC/JANM], January 26, 2005).

9. For more on the Asian American Movement, see Yen Le Espiritu, *Asian American Panethnicity: Bridging Institutions and Identities* (Philadelphia: Temple University Press, 1992), 25, 31–32; Michael Liu et al., *The Snake Dance of Asian American Activism: Community, Vision, and Power* (Lanham, MD: Lexington Books, 2008); William Wei, *The Asian American Movement* (Philadelphia: Temple University Press, 1993).

10. See, for example, George Abe, "Life History Interview," with Art Hansen and Sojin Kim (transcript, *Big Drum: Taiko in the United States* exhibition, HNRC/JANM archive, December 10, 2004).

11. Liu et al., *The Snake Dance*, xv.

12. Liu et al., *The Snake Dance*, xv.

13. PJ Hirabayashi and San Jose Taiko, "Ei Ja Nai Ka?" handout, unpublished score (1994) distributed in the "Ei Ja Nai Ka?" workshop at the 2009 North American Taiko Conference.

14. I use "re-membering" here following Ngugi wa Thiong'o's formulation. Re-membering, for Thiong'o, is a set of practices deployed by African writers in a "quest for wholeness" after the dis-memberment of Africa under colonialism. He writes, "Creative imagination is one of the greatest of re-membering practices. The relationship of writers to their social memory is central to their quest and mission. Memory is the link between the past and the present, between space and time, and it is the base of our dreams." *Ei Ja Nai Ka* re-members Japanese American history both in that it enacts social memory and re-embodies that history in the present. See Ngugi wa Thiong'o, *Something Torn and New: An African Renaissance* (New York: Basic Civitas Books, 2009), 39.

15. Charlotte Canning, "Feminist Performance as Feminist Historiography," *Theatre Survey* 45, no. 2 (November 2004): 230.

16. Ibid.

17. See NEA National Heritage Fellowship page, http://arts.gov/honors/heritage.

18. Roy Hirabayashi, "Life History Interview."

19. Jennie Knapp, "Ensemble's Mix of Drumming, Dance Thrilling," *Richmond Times Dispatch*, March 2, 1999, D6.

20. Deborah Wong, "Moving: From Performance to Performative Ethnography and Back Again," in *Shadows in the Field: New Perspectives for Fieldwork in Ethnomusicology*, 2nd ed., ed. Gregory Barz and Timothy Cooley (New York: Oxford University Press, 2008), 76.

21. Roy Hirabayashi and PJ Hirabayashi are the only two members currently in San Jose Taiko who were also part of the group's formative years. Other founding members were not interviewed either by me or the JANM staff during the *Big*

Drum exhibit. My analysis, therefore, is based largely on the memories of these two individuals.

22. Richard Schechner, *Performance Studies: An Introduction* (London: Routledge, 2002), 191; Christopher Small, *Musicking: The Meanings of Performing and Listening* (Middletown, CT: Wesleyan University Press, 1998), 9.

23. Matthew Rahaim, *Musicking Bodies: Gesture and Voice in Hindustani Music* (Middletown, CT: Wesleyan University Press, 2012), 1.

24. Small, *Musicking*, 8.

25. Wisa Uemura, e-mail to author, March 29, 2012.

26. Elin Diamond, "Introduction," in *Performance and Cultural Politics*, ed. Elin Diamond (New York: Routledge, 1996), 1.

27. Gary Okihiro, "Acting Japanese," in *Japanese Diasporas: Unsung Pasts, Conflicting Presents and Uncertain Futures*, ed. Nobuko Adachi (New York: Routledge, 2006), 195.

28. Roy Hirabayashi, "Life History Interview."

29. For a further discussion of Japanese taiko's multiple influences, see Shawn Morgan Bender, "Drumming between Tradition and Modernity: Taiko and Neo-folk Performance in Contemporary Japan" (PhD diss., University of California, San Diego, 2003), 71–74; and Angela K. Ahlgren, "Drumming Asian America: Performing Race, Gender and Sexuality in North American Taiko" (PhD diss., University of Texas at Austin, 2011).

30. PJ Hirabayashi, "Life History Interview."

31. Joni L. Jones, "Performance Ethnography: The Role of Embodiment in Cultural Authenticity," *Theatre Topics* 12, no. 1 (2002): 14.

32. Wei, *The Asian American Movement*, 11.

33. PJ Hirabayashi, "Life History Interview."

34. San Jose Taiko members (Yurika Chiba, PJ Hirabayashi, Roy Hirabayashi, Franco Imperial, Meg Suzuki, and Wisa Uemura), personal interview, September 29, 2009 (hereafter, San Jose Taiko members, personal interview).

35. Ibid.

36. Yuji Ichioka, quoted in Eiichiro Azuma, "Editor's Introduction: Yuji Ichioka and New Paradigms in Japanese American History," in Yuji Ichioka, *Before Internment: Essays in Prewar Japanese American History*, ed. Gordon H. Chang and Eiichiro Azuma (Stanford: Stanford University Press, 2006), xvii.

37. Taikoprojects's theater-taiko piece "Pioneers," for example, weaves monologues with performances of these three groups' most popular songs.

38. Eiichiro Azuma, *Between Two Empires: Race, History, and Transnationalism in Japanese America* (Oxford: Oxford University Press, 2005), 91.

39. See Masumi Izumi, "Reconsidering Ethnic Culture and Community: A Case Study on Japanese Canadian Taiko Drumming," *Journal of Asian American Studies* 4 (2001): 35–56.

40. Jere Takahashi, *Nisei/Sansei: Shifting Japanese Identities and Politics* (Philadelphia: Temple University Press, 1997), 2. This sentiment was also echoed in the interviews I conducted and the oral history transcripts I read.

41. Takahashi, *Nisei/Sansei*, 85.

42. Ibid., 197–200.

43. The search for Japanese cultural activities by Sansei is a prevalent theme in the interviews I conducted as well as the oral history transcripts I read. For a detailed thorough exploration of generational dynamics between Nisei and Sansei, see Takahashi, *Nisei/Sansei*.

44. PJ Hirabayashi, "Life History Interview."

45. San Jose Taiko members, personal interview.

46. PJ Hirabayashi, e-mail to author, June 17, 2010.

47. *Big Drum: Taiko in the United States*, dir. Akira Boch, Sojin Kim, and Masaki Miyagawa, DVD, Frank H. Watase Media Arts Center, Japanese American National Museum, 2005.

48. Warabi-za's website indicates that the group "prides itself in depicting contemporary society through the arts." In addition to seven performing troupes, Warabi-za also runs a Folk Arts Research Center, which houses thousands of folk songs and dances; see http://www.warabi.jp/english/aboutus.html.

49. The general meaning of the chant is "Isn't it good?" "Ready, ready!" "Isn't it good?" "Ready, ready, here we go!" In taiko, "Sore!" is often shouted just before beginning a number, something like "Five, six, seven, eight!" or "Ready, and!" in dance. Similarly, "Yoisho!" has no particular meaning, but keeps time.

50. Ronald Takaki, *Strangers from a Different Shore: A History of Asian Americans*, rev. ed. (Boston: Little, Brown, 1998), 221–223.

51. Yoko Fujimoto, "'Ei Ja Nai Ka?' Lyrics to Accompany Dance," unpublished manuscript, 2001. Just as the dance is gestural, using simple, stylized movements to convey its meanings, the song lyrics too use a spare, poetic style to create a progress narrative moving from migration to labor to progress to celebration. The lyrics (different from the call-and-response chanting) were added later in the song's development. The lyrics are written and sung in Japanese, with only a few English phrases throughout, so only audiences with an understanding of the Japanese language would have total access to the piece's layers of meaning as they watched a performance. San Jose Taiko has provided me with two translations, one that is (in PJ Hirabayashi's words) more "literal" and another that is "poetic." Since my analysis depends on the general meaning of the song, rather than a close textual analysis, I refer to the poetic translation here. The song is composed of four verses, with the refrain "Ei Ja Nai Ka?" (Isn't it good?) repeated in the second and third lines of each verse.

52. Takaki, *Strangers from a Different Shore*, 44. As Takaki writes, many Issei "saw themselves as *dekaseginin*—laborers working temporarily in a foreign country."

53. San Jose Taiko members, personal interview.

54. Like "Grandma" and "Grandpa" in the first verse, "Railroad" and "Steam Engine" are pronounced "Suti-ime En-gine" and "Ra-il ro do."

55. Takaki, *Strangers from a Different Shore*, 182–185.

56. Ichioka, quoted in Azuma, "Editor's Introduction," xvii.

57. Takaki, *Strangers from a Different Shore*, 180–197.

58. Ibid., 186.

59. Ibid., 191.

60. San Jose Taiko members, personal interview.

61. Josephine Lee, *Performing Asian America: Race and Ethnicity on the Contemporary Stage* (Philadelphia: Temple University Press, 1997), 137.

62. Members who performed in this concert, part of the 2009 Rhythm Journey Tour: Yurika Chiba, PJ Hirabayashi, Alex Hudson, Franco Imperial, Dylan Solomon, Meg Suzuki, Wisa Uemura, and Adam Weiner.

63. Long Center for the Performing Arts, Austin, Texas, season brochure, author's personal archive, 2009.

64. Susan L. Foster, "Worlding Dance—An Introduction," in *Worlding Dance*, ed. Susan L. Foster (New York: Palgrave Macmillan, 2009), 2.

65. Emily Roxworthy, *The Spectacle of Japanese American Trauma: Racial Performativity and World War II* (Honolulu: University of Hawai'i Press, 2008), 21.

66. Long Center for the Performing Arts season brochure.

67. San Jose Taiko members, personal interview.

68. Ibid.

69. Ibid.

70. Ibid.

71. Ibid.

72. Ibid.

2

We Should Bring Our Muzukashii

ROKO KAWAI

Introduce yourself as ロコ.カワイ, "ro-ko ka-wa-i," using the katakana alphabet.

Your name, written in katakana, will signify immediately that you are a special visitor.[1] This will protect you from "appearing too Japanese." Trust us, this will help you while you're here. Your position is 微妙 bi-myoh: weird, delicate, uncomfortable, nuanced, odd though possibly exquisite— or, just untenable.

—Advice from the Japan United States Friendship Commission upon my arrival in Tokyo for a seven-month fellowship, March 2005

Themes of identification and sourcing, belonging and soloing, comfort and battle, and who-sees-who-interpreting-whom had always been the current that drove me, plagued me, carried me in my dance/culture work.

PART 1: MUZUKASHII

What is untenable? It's my own translation of the Japanese word *muzukashii*. While more frequently translated as "difficult" like a math problem, or "complicated" like a divorce, neither English word captures the fullness of the coded non-answer, the ellipses to the enduring questions that come up when I am in Japan. Such as: Why do funny consequences occur when I use official Japanese characters on my business card? Why is it important to feign foreignness (i.e., pretend to only speak English) in conversations with my landlady or during my interview with a leading contemporary choreographer in Tokyo? When a Japanese colleague introduces me to important individuals, why does my Japanese parentage, my coming of age in both countries, and my extended interest in Japanese classical dance frequently get replaced by a more "exotic" American modern dancer narrative?

I suspect I'm being protected from an unspoken danger, caused by over-complicating a Japanese identity.

In 2002 I toured with a Pennsylvania group of cultural practitioners for two whirlwind weeks in and around Tokyo. We interfaced with the most prominent choreographers, presenters, and critics who were working on the edges of the contemporary dance scene. I recall the exhilarating connection between the city's high-tech intensity and the defiant, absurdist freneticism of the contemporary work we saw. During the tour, an uncomfortable tension emerged. While I was intellectually thrilled by the urbanized edgework, I felt a deeper physical affinity to classical Japanese form, which is often reviled by contemporary artists there. Introducing what I stood for, again, became further complicated.

In Japan, I often hear the complaint that the classical dance world is elitist, scorned as a hobby for privileged children and retirees who are loaded with savings. In order to perform in a fully produced recital (with professional costumers, stagehands, makeup and wig masters, and live musicians), apprentices might put out the equivalent of a down payment on a house. On top of that, apprentices must prepare gratuity monies for the teacher, the teacher's mentor, that mentor's headmaster, the headmaster's association, the backstage staff, and even one's own invited guests. Japanese classical dance also places emphasis on extreme etiquette. Apprentices are required, for example, to bow at precise times in precise ways according to one's relative place in the hierarchy of those around you. To many, teaching such complicated customs is seen as a distraction from nurturing artistic excellence. Abiding by such a system may be too anachronistic for contemporary artists. Moreover, for postmodern dancers especially, I imagine that Japanese classical dance repertory is utterly problematic. The choreography thrives on predictable and cathartic narrative, emotive and outdated gender roles, the warrior's code of honor, glorified technique, and entertainment.

But from where I was standing in the diaspora, I could not help but also note the exciting commonalities between the classical and contemporary performances we saw during that tour. Examples include hypercrystallized visual moments, the juxtaposition of the monumental to the miniscule, the use of *ma*,[2] and the compositional buildup from restraint-to-accumulation-to-climax. However, when I initiated dialogue about this correlation with our Tokyo hosts, I was surprised by how cold their reactions were: a drop in energy, a grunt, and a single word, "hmmmm . . . *muzukashii*"—difficult to explain, untenable.

Okay, I get it: having been thrust into westernization in the late nineteenth century, Japan needed to put out a bold signature national art form. Kabuki and classical dance seemed to fill the bill. But then with the war, industrial collapse, and the rise of new sociopolitical movements, some felt that these traditional genres overexoticized Japan's growing international profile. Furthermore, what began as street theater for common people in the sixteenth century has since been repositioned as an expensive pastime for the wealthy and nostalgic. Or that is one theory. But what makes it so hard to discuss and deconstruct this openly? We did not have much time to explore this issue fully. I wanted to return one day to revisit this tension.

So, it was a godsend when, in 2005, I received a Japan-U.S. Friendship Commission Fellowship, which provided me the opportunity to live in Japan for half a year to carry out artistic research. For seven months I absorbed the visceral, physical energy of Japan today, which is so different than the Japan of my childhood. I was born in Tokyo, but my family immigrated to Pennsylvania when I was three. In many ways, my life has been a continuing dance between these two countries, subliminally shifting how I carry my torso, how I project my voice, how I weight my touch, how I use my eyes, how I see myself, how I interpret others interpreting me. I returned to Japan at the blinding age of twelve but left again at a tumultuous seventeen. It had always been a dream of mine to go back as an adult, as a professional dance artist. I wanted to discover where my own views were still naive. Before this trip, it had been twenty-three years since I last lived there.

My focus was on studying with Japanese classical dance master Hanayagi Kazu: teacher, dancer, fire.[3] Charismatic, eloquent, and unconventional, she emphasizes that all movement must be researched—deconstructed and understood—in the body, by the body. Kazu-sensei,[4] as fierce a preservationist as she is a passionate performer, pushes dancers to transcend assumptions about perfect form and to let go into the rough and the gruff, the humor, the surprise, and the breath. I was delighted by an anecdote she once shared. By coincidence, she was at a wedding that Kazuo Ohno also happened to be attending. "Out of nowhere," she recalled, "he stood up and started to dance. It didn't matter at all [that there was no recognizable form], it was so real."

17.40

2005. Before beginning my training with Kazu-sensei, I had written:

each repetition in japanese classical dance practice offers me a vehicle through which i can find new depth in stillness, new sophistication in transition, and new clarity in phrasing. the discoveries have been rich and infinite. like a yoga practice, re-visiting over and over the exacting, "non-negotiable" forms and sequences of classical dance has allowed me to find greater nuance in each moment, expanding my range from intense focus to ease in carriage, refining and refining awareness of my front and back, my inside and outside, the dance moment just past and the gesture about to come. it remains a mystery somewhat. why should such a traditional form, so sentimental, narratively driven, and entertainment-focused (not to mention utterly politicized!) open me to this new depth of technique and presence? i continue to muse on that question.

So calm and philosophical then; however, one month into the fellowship I am writing:

4/3/05—can i stop acting like a fugitive? a nervous wreck? important realization today: i need to stop feeling so ashamed. the last time i really lived here was when i was 17. now I'm 40. i can't believe i'm still terrified enough that i would rather get on the wrong train (to god knows where) than to let on to the station staff that i can't read the signs and schedules.

17.40. these ages mean totally different things in japanese society. it's no longer everybody's business to put me in my place, as a japanese child-in-training-to-become-a-perfect-japanese-citizen. i am returning as an adult and an artist/researcher with some U.S. credentials to boot. but i'm still operating like i'm 17, an embarrassment. in the past, i always started each visit with a robust sense of self, a "multicultural right to exist." but the longer i stayed, i would lose it and inevitably get sucked into the vortex of i-suck-ness, never-enough-ness. but now (gasp), i'm 40 (exhale), and an invited scholar/artist! (sweating bullets). i'm still just getting used to every little thing.

but i recently discovered a new strategy that's working better—i re-vamped the important self introduction—even with strangers at a train station or department store. after a friendly, light-hearted and confident bow and smile, i say upfront in Japanese—"i'm so sorry to bother you. i'm visiting from america and my japanese isn't as good as it should be, but i have a question and wondered if you might help me . . . please forgive me."

i've always eschewed this tact because it felt like such a cheat—like i failed at being a regular-japanese. a japanese-japanese would think it cheap to call attention to oneself. politically, i never wanted to lean on "america" as a power-symbol. but by frontloading, this prelude has helped the other person comfortably place me, instantly. they feel less tense (they don't have to worry that i'm mentally disabled). and, by "setting up the scene," people even feel invited to chat me up—to compliment my japanese (which i deny) and inquire about my fellowship and research. paradoxically, this "conceit" has given me a more workable re-entry. "working the fiction" and "facilitating the truth" may not be as evil as i'd originally thought. perhaps this is the way to establish a ground that is more—tenable—in order to engender longterm trust and dialogue.

Uso-mo hohben: A Lie Is Also Useful

yokohama: at nibroll's[5] open rehearsal at the gallery space yesterday, we had a comical little stint around "uso-mo hohben," "a lie is also useful" or "lying is a temporary expedient." a proverb. a social tact. when the dancers went on break, the receptionist suggested we use the time to go check out another gallery where they were having a photo exhibit. normally, i would be non-committal upfront: thanks, maybe we will. But my friend says, 'yes, we definitely will!' I gave him a look. the receptionist maps out detailed walking directions. he even asks clarifying questions. we took the walk, but blew off the photo show. as we head back to the rehearsal, my friend is also rehearsing—sample lies, like: 'we didn't make it to the gallery because we ended up having tea and lost track' or . . . 'we saw the show and particularly liked the one photo in which there was a . . .'(!!) it was all very funny as our "creative lies" got more preposterous.

at the same time, in my recent quest to live "more accurately" (y'know, face your fears, discover what you truly enjoy), i had to think. the so-called truth is slippery. to me, this was such a no-brainer: we weren't interested so we won't lead her on. no love lost on the receptionist. what I got, though, was that it behooved us to engage, to effort. the japanese would argue that this is truth. that what is really being danced here is that we are helping her maintain a comfortable equilibrium. she plays her role as the friendly receptionist and we accept her intention whole-heartedly. anyway, after all that, we got back and the receptionist was gone for the day!

That was 2005.

PART 2: A GROUND

2008. Returning, revisiting, researching, belonging, striving, driving, musing, battling, conflicting, colliding. WAIT. Stop. Be still now . . .

It is impossible to look back on—or forward to—my dance and autobiographical explorations without disclosing the thing that now defines me most. On June 18, 2007, my forty-year-old sister and her daughters (eight and six years old) were murdered point blank by her husband, who then shot and killed himself. Needless to say, the understanding of "body" has now forever changed.

My continuing dance between two countries suddenly feels like a past project, important but dimmed. Belonging—and the will to tease it out as a concept—is dependent upon a center from which to orient and reach. Aground: A ground inextricably created with *her*, who had robustly co-lived my crisscrossed history. Through this new viscerality, this absence, this shattering, I reflect on dancing. I feel a longing to be still and to have things come to me now.

Izu House

Chihan-an, named after Nobuko Awaya's maternal grandfather Chihan, is the two-hundred-year-old traditional house of the Suganuma family, located in the tiny town of Ohito on the Izu peninsula two hours south of Tokyo.[6] The house is historic enough to be an architectural museum, and Nobuko decided to keep it in the family and to revive her grandfather's tradition of using it as both a home and a place where artists could gather and workshop.

I met Nobuko toward the end of my 2005 fellowship, and she invited me to create a dance piece at Chihan-an.[7] We scheduled it for October 2007. No one could know it that it would be eclipsed by the murders, just three and a half months earlier. After much deliberation, I decided to go ahead as planned with longtime collaborator Leah Stein, a Philadelphia-based choreographer known for her site-specific work.[8] From Tokyo, we invited the dancer/performance artist Hideo Arai[9] and the vocalist Mika Kimula[10] for a multiyear workshop that would eventually culminate in a

2008 premiere. During the first workshop, we explored the architecture of Chihan-an, Nobuko's oral histories, and each of our own separate relationships to this place. To hold it together, I packaged away my nightmare. I call this work *Izu House*.

All four artists, Nobuko, and the two video-artist photographers slept, cooked, bathed, and played together at Chihan-an. By modern Japanese residential standards, the house is vast—a single-story structure with a thatched roof and a foyer with its original earthen floor. The expanse can be subdivided by a grid of sliding door-walls, both wooden and *fusuma* (paper screen door-walls), from the Edo (1600–1867) to Taisho (1912–1926) periods.[11] Most of the house is a stretch of unfurnished *tatami* (straw-based) floor space. A good chunk of it, like the kitchen and bath areas, is modernized for everyday needs.

In Ohito, we greeted elderly farmers who were squatting low, tending tidy fields. We joined neighbors in an autumn festival, dancing late at night to disco-infused *obon* music on loudspeakers.[12] In daylight, we discovered that local residents still observed Shinto customs at their homes (vs. at shrines only). During rice harvest time, for instance, people hung ceremonial rope across the front of their houses. Just one train line connects this cozy valley to the larger cities. Down below the tracks, golden rice fields lay like brilliant mats between generic box buildings. There were other small reminders of modern Japan: ubiquitous vending machines, punky teenagers, and diesel-spitting mini-trucks. APITA, the Crayola-neon red and yellow home grocery complex, the Ikea of Izu, stood like a sibling next to the town's other landmark—the rugged and beauteous Mt. Joh.

My work often asks: "Who are we in this place? Who are we with one another?" Leah worried if she, a strawberry blonde, fair-skinned American, looked weird or out-of-place in this cast, in this setting. But did any of us look like we fit in this historical but not totally traditional space? Even Nobuko herself, a descendent of 450 years of the Suganuma line, whom neighbors still call Non-chan, is a feminist scholar and journalist of intercultural studies who lives in Jiyugaoka, one of Tokyo's most cosmopolitan districts.[13] Hideo and Mika are longtime residents of Tokyo's congested working-class neighborhoods, far from the relaxed greenery of Izu. And me? I have lived and worked most of my adult life in the United States, absorbing parts of contemporary and classical Japan through visits. How do I belong here? How can any of us speak to this place?

We're just beginning to tackle these questions—not by tackling them but by playing with them. We accept our naïveté and our fascinations, our interpersonal attractions and anxieties, our hidden agendas, our trial and error—all without too much historical, identity-based postmodern judgment. We use free association: with food and late-night stories in translation; by teaching each other Noguchi Taiso,[14] authentic movement, contact improvisation, and vocal scales. It's full-on work, but lighthearted.

The sliding door-walls are movable *and* removable. In the vastness, a tiny room can be sectioned off, enclosed to become "the birthing room," for example, where Nobuko and her ancestors were born. Inside this cubicle, women participated in the bloody red, chaotic messiness of birth while, on the other side of the *fusuma*, the men-folk concentrated on a game of Go: gridded, calculated, black and white.[15] To create an expansive public space, these same doors could be removed entirely for ceremonial events such as weddings or funerals. The outermost doors can also be thrown open, offering those inside a cross breeze or a "borrowed," framed view of the mountain or the moon. Tokyo relatives fled to Chihan-an during World War II's incendiary bombing of the capital. It was also a place of return for Chihan's divorced sister and her son. One night we discovered turn-of-the-century tax records hidden in a drawer. Evidently, as the local landowner, Chihan had collected rice duties from tenant farmers.

The road that passes in front of Chihan-an is named Shimoda Kaido. Today it is fume-filled and noisy with traffic. Our soundscape is syncopated by the cries of doves and Mika's vocal scales. The road is named after historic Shimoda port, located at the southern tip of Izu. It was there that the U.S. Black Ships first landed in 1853 and forced Japan to open for trade, catapulting the society into rapid westernization. To negotiate the terms with the Shogunate in Edo (now Tokyo), the American emissaries traveled up Shimoda Kaido. To imagine American emissaries walking right by this house! I cannot ignore the magnitude of working in a site so close to such history. Had the U.S. ships not come and Japan not westernized, albeit with great internal conflict, would my family have immigrated to Philadelphia?

A Language of Us

If I hadn't left Japan and found myself at this diasporic distance, would I have been drawn to, would my body have found a home in, Japanese

classical dance? Would I have this lifelong socioanthropological-artistic
interest in Japan?

Leah, Hideo, Mika, and I moved and removed doors, we staged views
near and far, we came home, and we set out. Multiple bodies shifted from
one space to another. We created vignettes: a family spat, a shadow play
behind translucent screens, a figure seeking refuge behind a grated doorway,
a head birthing out from behind a *fusuma*.

Dancers looped through the house with folk dance–like agricultural
movements, a time lapse of generations. A scene emerged around the *irori*
(fire pit) of late night conversations: ancestors listening in.

We developed movements sourced from our own visceral response to
this place. Hideo took on character-like personae (the mythological *kappa*-
creature or Chihan, the grandpa).[16] Leah was more ethereal, a disembodied
ghostly hand "riding" the sliding door-walls. I was the most grounded, like
the physical house itself, enduring with gravitas and pathos, accumulating
memories. A language of us began to coalesce. We started to belong.

While working in a context already laden with so much familial, local,
and national history, it was important to constantly evaluate what felt or
did not feel authentic. We would dig further, we agreed, the next time we
came together in October 2008. In a lighthearted e-mail just prior to our
return, Mika wrote: "For the second part of our exploration we should
bring our different selves, having changed within the year."

We Should Bring Our Muzukashii

This next time I wondered if I should disclose my actual postmurder body
state. Will it be *untenable*? Our collaborative explorations were so playful,
daring, open, and rigorous. Was this contingent upon keeping my emotional implosion and physical vulnerability out of view? In this next workshop, would I overburden my Japanese collaborators if I called attention to
my tragedy? Should I "work a fiction" to maintain a safe, uncomplicated
relationship? "Murder and guns," my in-laws sternly warned, "are too shock-
ing here in Japan. It will be untenable and, most importantly, it will irre-
versibly impact how people see you and interact with you. If you have to
mention it at all, call it a car accident."

In such a state, how do I dance a fiction, a negotiated, facilitated self?
How odd to be excavating this house—with its hidden objects and sense

memories, its birthing room and altar for the deceased—while being cautioned against bringing into the process my most vivid body-self. Which things are best left tucked away, or re-presented as something more palatable? At what cost? Who is the authority? I sense an unknown invisible line that may be risky to cross. Risky to not cross? But where is this line?

How do I dance this fiction?
—Roko Kawai, 2008

∽

It is now 2013.
It is now 2013.

PART 3: AGROUND

Gladly, decidedly, necessarily, I have truly stopped. I am still. Aground. The thing that defines me most is the murder and growing absence of my sister Moink (her nickname) and her daughters, Nikki and Lena. He shot them in the head, one by one, at point blank range. My understanding of body remains, today, smashed. Movement, unless absolutely necessary, is an anomaly: thinking, a monster. "Research" has been hacked to "-search" and has come to mean desperately locating handholds, finding any respite from the nightmare.

Studies show that survivors of traumatic loss often present radical changes in physique. At the Parents of Murdered Children support groups, I met survivors who had become very ill, losing hair and teeth and suffering from chronic pain. I heard about other survivors who did not, ultimately, survive. They died shortly after the murder of a loved one, of cancer or by suicide. In Moink's community, one of Nikki's friends (a little girl who was six at that time) dropped seven pounds from her already tiny frame. Seized by fear and confusion, she never let her parents out of sight even to go to the bathroom at home. It was only after intensive, specialized therapy that she was able to regain a sense of safety and functionality.

"Why eat? . . . why stop eating?" wrote Elisabeth Kübler-Ross, the renowned early pioneer of grief research, and writer David Kessler.[17] I know individuals who clearly embodied the first of these two questions. They are ashen, thin, and their clothes hang on them. I went for the second rhetorical question, "why stop eating?" Now, after six years, I no longer recognize myself, physically.

In the first months after the murders, I remember a bottomless despair, a gasping and a drowning, a never-ending undertow. There isn't a word for this type of "crying." "Weeping," "sobbing," and "wailing" seem but pale descriptors to the physical action of what happens to the human body after complete and traumatic loss. Ugly, ugly face; magnified grimacing. Silent screaming for hours. To "sob" was too debilitating, best avoided; it was hard enough to draw breath. Unable to endure light, I stayed in bed with the shades drawn. If I was lucky enough to fall asleep, I dream-traveled to a moment when it hadn't happened yet; I could still save them. I would rush to their aid. Violently, I tried to protect them, thrashing and clawing until my clenched muscles strangled me awake. In time, my teeth and gums began to lock, and my sternum pressed sharply back into my lungs. Maybe this full-body grip was helping me to survive. Opening was risky; it made me too vulnerable. If I softened, Loss would stampede over me. I think the body knows not to release too soon.

I could do so little. I hid in bed, suicidal. I did the barest minimum required of me—clean the cat box, eat something, seek help. Answering e-mails was no longer a necessity. Imagining a future was no longer a necessity.

I could barely drive or even remember my telephone number. I felt perpetually exhausted and cloudy. I'd forget where I'd parked my car only to discover that it had been towed. I joked that this was the price of "brain damage." The upside of "brain damage" was that I simply didn't care anymore. I'd pay the fine, get the car, go to bed, and call it a day.

I used to thrive on cavalier to-do lists. Every day I prided myself on doing it all—run five miles, do the day job, teach at the university, studio rehearsal, write a grant, fix the printer, catch up with a neglected friend, fifty sit-ups before bed. Now, if I managed to take a shower, I'd call it an achievement, and I'd call it a day. Eventually, when I had to go back to full-time work, I would rally for just those hours, and then come home, and call it a day.

Every once in a while, I had to gear up for something more monumental: facilitate the cremation and burial, order and submit death certificates, clean out their house, return to Japan to create *Izu House* (2008), weep. And then "call it a day."

I remember a session with my grief counselor K. I was worried about how much pleasure I was getting at the local café, savoring a chocolate croissant, spending the whole day researching bipolar disorder, which is what we suspect my brother-in-law had. I'd always struggled with my weight, so admitting to *enjoying* these moments felt criminal; surely, the beginning of the end. K told me I should be grateful for anything that gives me a modicum of relief. I needed to "shore up," she said, for the many more "drownings" I would still have to endure.

Visiting my surviving sister and her family in California was also, literally, a lifeline. Days with her toddler and baby were luminous; at the time of the murders, her sons were ages eighteen months and seven weeks, respectively. Because my surviving sister, their mom, was in her own shattered state, it felt good to help out. I loved the motions and simplicity of this new dance, of being "nothing more" than a housemaid and a babysitter.

In an e-mail just after the first *Izu House* (2007), I had written:

> been re-sifting "my truth" since getting back. i'm still in pain & will be for a long while yet. japan was "wonderful" but, as K put it, it was by sheer magnitude of my ability to compartmentalize on cue. and now i can get back to the wobbly process of grieving. if i move to calif, there will at least be people there who share the loss, the sudden and bitter disappearance of this entire family.
>
> K pointed out that the "old strategies" of coping no longer apply during trauma. y'know—the bottom line get-exercise, put-yourself-out-there, set-new-life-improvement-goals, see-the-glass-as-half-full stuff. I GOT IT yesterday during my solo walk in Fairmount Park woods. yes, the trees are beautiful AND I don't feel better. that's my momentary truth. K says, it's enough just to deal with the present. that's all i can and need to engage in for now. this a relief. and clarifying.

Dancing a Fiction Seemed Like a Stupid Exercise.
Dancing at All Seemed Irrelevant.

After the second *Izu House* in 2008, I built a thick cocoon around myself and hid away from the world entirely. To stay alive, I sought out only simple joys, avoiding all unnecessary "should's" because "shoulding" would send

me down a hell-vortex. I couldn't risk becoming too fragile. If I was unable
to recapture my bearings, who would take care of my surviving family?

Ironically, at about the same time, the world of Facebook exploded.
All around me, people were broadcasting themselves publicly and widely,
"friending" everyone. I went in the opposite direction. I let go of most of
my (actual) friends and secretly stowed away to California.

I now live within walking distance of where Moink, Nikki, and Lena are
buried, in Oakland. I am also within walking distance from "5511," the
former house they lived in during a happier era. I know this neighborhood
well from my frequent summer visits back then. The flora and crisp California light, the streets and the shops still reverberate with them. I pass
Buffalo Exchange, the trendy used clothing store where many years earlier
I was hanging out with a five-year-old Nikki. I flashback to a scene: as I try
on a cute tight sweater, Nikki stares up at me. As though she were the mom
and I the child, she says, "You will grow out of that very soon." But I have
to avoid the "5511" block now. It is too painful. Thankfully, my surviving
sister and her sons are within driving distance. Suddenly, family is Local.
I feel "belonged" here—with a clarity I had never experienced in my life
before.

Moink's community is my community now. This includes the network
of her "fabulous female physician friends." Like Moink, they were extra-
ordinary family practitioners and, well, downright gorgeous. They now do
local public health work with STDs, advance AIDS policy in Africa, admin-
ister urgent care for the homeless in San Francisco, and provide long-term
treatment to victims of the 1984 Union Carbide Gas Disaster in Bhopal,
India. Moink's community also includes the thousands of her Japanese
patients as well as the Japanese Sycamore Church congregation where she
had volunteered. With her sunny disposition and her "kindergarten-level"
of spoken Japanese, she gave end-of-life care to their elderly parents, provided flu shots when there was a shortage, and did free house calls when a
child was injured. She was widely beloved.

Embraced by everyone, I am normalizing the details of the tragedy.
With her doctor friends, we flip-flop easily between serious talks about the
murders and cracking morbid jokes about it. As a Japanese American in
California, I am also normalizing my cultural sense of self. I now socialize
regularly with other Japanese here, some who still prefer to speak only in
Japanese. I celebrate traditional holidays with them, locally and collectively,

such as the winter *mochitsuki* (pounding rice cake), or joining the summer festival *obon* dances. It's good to already feel a part of something without having to "perform into the belonging."

A new practice was emerging. Visiting the cemetery was critical for me. I needed to tend to and beautify their stone, to take care of them, to feel viscerally close to them. Jobless when I first arrived in California, I went nearly every day. I found it soothing to picture myself as dead in life, lying in the grass next to them. I created installations for them with cut flowers and foraged plants. It was nourishing to work with living things. And some of those early installations were quite stunning. I took joy in photographing the installations, often with me in the frame "sleeping dead" by their side.

I began seeking information about other people's traumatic losses. I devoured books written about the grief process and looked for other horrific tragedies throughout history. I cut out photos from newspapers that depicted acute loss. Two Iraqi brothers, faces distorted in grief, clutching each other after learning of their father's death. A row of eleven children's bodies laid side-by-side on the ground after the 2004 Tsunami in Thailand.

(re)Search

Am I still speaking to the field of Japanese/American dance or even to "dance-proper?" My explorations are intensely individual, internal, and invisible. Right after the murders, I told a dancer/choreographer friend that the last thing I wanted was to be onstage. She compassionately replied: "That's the last thing I would want for you too, all those eyeballs on you like that." With no eyeballs on me now, and very little outward movement, wherein lies the dance? Where did the dancer/researcher go?

What is clear to me is that even in the midst of despair and disorientation, and even as I considered suicide, I was still observing and following dynamic movement shifts in my body and consciousness. The movement now was simply stripped of performance conventions. If, for example, I had cried too long and too hard, I "directed" my gums to relax, knowing that this would stave off debilitating neck strain later. While I knew intellectually that my daily capacity was limited, I could also *feel* how much "sand" I had left in the "hour glass." Over time, I became more masterful at calibrating my to-do lists and at building in—or "scoring"—recovery strategies. During memorials and their birthdays, for instance, since these times were always so devastating, I learned to move through my days in slow motion, honoring that it was best to "dumb down" and operate in a suspended state until the blinding, crushing fog dissipated.

This brings to mind the experience of Dr. Jill Bolte Taylor, the brain scientist most popularly known through her TED talk and her book *My Stroke of Insight*.[18] At age thirty-seven, Bolte Taylor suffered a massive stroke in the left hemisphere of her brain. In the four hours before help arrived, she was able to observe what was happening to her brain as she rapidly lost the ability to talk and control movements. With her left hemisphere disabled, her right brain began to envelope her in a directionless euphoria. Occasionally, however, she noticed that the left brain function—pragmatic and action-driving—would resurface. During those moments, she recognized that this was in fact a stroke and that she should get help. Identifying which mental capacities were still available to her, she problem-solved a way to dial a telephone and save her own life. During her right brain overrides, which she affectionately calls "la la land," the quality of light, color, and expansiveness was so profound that she still uses that memory-sensation as a tool, a "reset button," to relocate that state of peace and interconnectedness.[19] She calls this noticing, and the action that follows the noticing, "tracking."

In my own tumbling and drowning, in my unacceptable loss, I wonder if I too might have been "body-tracking" toward new strategies for "authentic action." Was I using skills that I had cultivated as a dancer and cultural researcher to track, improvise, and ultimately integrate what was unacceptable into a new dynamic identity?

2009. Cambodia

Cambodia is a part of a continuum that leads to the end, not a beginning unto itself. I went because I was at a standstill, consumed by a white-hot hatred toward my brother-in-law. I needed to be somewhere where they had also "killed one's own." I wanted to understand the mind of the killers, the world where such violence could be justified, where cruelty was a vehicle for "creativity." I wanted to see how the victim-survivors were doing, thirty years after this Khmer Rouge reign of terror.[20]

I wanted to be close to my friend Toni Shapiro-Phim, who was the first person I called when I got the news of the murders. As one of the world's leading scholars on Cambodian dance and human rights, Toni was on a three-year work assignment with the Khmer Arts Ensemble, the classical and neoclassical dance troupe based in Takhmau, Cambodia, headed by the choreographer and National Heritage award-winner Sophiline Cheam Shapiro. After decades of field research on the role of dance during and after genocide, Toni was in Cambodia creating a research archive and educational curriculum for the current generation of Cambodian dancers.[21]

Earlier that year, I had received a Leeway Transformation Award for women and transgender artists working in social justice.[22] With this support, I traveled to Cambodia for three weeks, observing hours of rehearsal with and teaching workshops for the Khmer Arts Ensemble. I also wanted to speak to dancers who had suffered losses (far worse than my own!) so Toni introduced me to a few of the elder masters of Cambodian court dance whom she had interviewed over the years. Two were willing to be interviewed by me, with Toni present and translating. From an e-mail dated March 2009 to friends in the United States, I wrote:

as far as the interviews, it was more about what wasn't expressed in the end. i am, after all, a complete stranger to both interviewees. i'm sure i wouldn't necessarily open up either out of the blue. Toni explained to both women that I had experienced a recent loss and was interested in how unspeakable violence affects the dancers' body and psyche. i couldn't stop crying during these meetings.

The first interviewee—Em Theay, an elder master dancer and singer (seventy-something? she doesn't know herself the year of her birth)—had had eighteen children.[23] Only five (or four?) survived the Khmer Rouge. Her answers to my questions were quick and "friendly." Right after the fall of the Khmer Rouge, she taught dance wherever she could, even at places where she stopped on the road back home from the prison camp. she is very happy now that the royalty is restored. she said she would pray for me.

As honored as I was to be able to meet and speak with Em Theay, toni had originally set us up to interview her daughter (also a dancer/survivor). we're not sure what happened. toni said that it would have been very different with Em Theay's daughter who is more vocal about her anger and her grief.

I met with one other elder singer and former dancer, Hun Sarath, but that too felt odd. Perhaps, I was asking too much of her to meet with me; I also wondered if my questions were too "American":

—did you dream about dancing/singing during the Pol Pot regime? what songs did you sing to yourself for comfort?

—what was the first moment like when you were able to dance/sing again without the threat of being killed? how did your muscles, body, vocal chords respond?

—is there a difference between the way you danced/sang before the genocide and after?

And . . .

—if you could have a conversation now with those you lost, what would you want to say to them?

the answers again were curt and plain: "we couldn't think of anything else but surviving, not being killed." or, "no difference from before and after." my last question did seem to cause pause, however. Sarath was silent for a while, and then said: "it's too hard a question. i have no words."

This morning, we visited the infamous Tuol Sleng Genocide Museum.[24] toni & i talked about the madness—how could it have gotten to that level, that scale? of course there's no answer.

Although, many complicated factors did contribute . . . child soldiers who were "re-educated," disenfranchised people who were suddenly given absolute power and deadly weapons, everyone terrified of consequences should they oppose the killers.

being with toni was an amazing opportunity. can't believe she first came to Southeast Asia in the '80s. It was a few years after the genocide but a civil war was still raging between the Khmer Rouge & invading Vietnamese forces. Toni was conducting unprecedented research at refugee camps for the Cambodians who had fled to Thailand; her relationships with dancers young and old started then. In those camps, the act of dancing represented hope. amidst random artillery shelling, abuse by guards, malnourishment, disease, rampant crime, and a very uncertain future, the refugees chose to use their scarce resources to build makeshift dance stages so they could teach, perform and watch one another. As toni points out, they also spent time singing, storytelling, reciting poetry and making art with their hands. But dance was by far the most important, as though it was a necessity for survival. What's wrong with me, then? Why did I choose to stop dancing?

In 2009 I saw evidence everywhere that Cambodian society still suffers from the by-products of genocide and civil war—corruption and land grabbing, rape and domestic violence, inadequate medicine and education. I happened to be there just one month before the long-overdue Tribunal.[25] There was a pervasive sense of national cynicism. In my post-travel research, however, I was heartened to come across the work of the human rights activist and author Theary Seng. In partnership with the German psychotherapist and intercultural trauma and reconciliation specialist Dr. Mattias Witzel, she edited and published a research handbook titled *Understanding Trauma in Cambodia*, which is used throughout Cambodia for trauma recovery programs.[26] In her autobiography *Daughter of the Killing Fields: Asrei's Story*, she writes:

> I believe healing requires a very conscious, deliberate and honest processing of one's circumstance; it involves utilizing tools that are not readily available to a people who attribute everything to karma reflexively and who are generally unaccustomed to self-reflection and introspection. It seems a fatiguing discipline deemed too individualistic and emotionally exhausting . . . But I am making a gross generalization that may need a qualifier. For me personally, ever since I can remember, I possessed a heightened need to comprehend the unintelligible elements of my experience. I believe all survivors . . . have this desire for interpretation of their experiences . . .
>
> I was deeply and chronically depressed and gained a lot of weight. . . . I lived in a state of grogginess, almost a hallucination.[27]

How thankful I was for Theary Seng's candor and specificity. In no way did I want to compare my own loss to the suffering that she and the Cambodian people endured, but her desire to look analytically at the changes in the post-trauma body/psyche closely mirrored my own efforts toward reorientation. Moreover, her documentation of what was happening in her own body/psyche was actually contributing to the field of culturally attuned trauma treatment. I admit that my research in Cambodia sometimes did feel selfish, as though I had gone there to be validated by tragedies that clearly outscale my own. Yet my hope is that it also opened up a new area of study, not only for my purposes but in service of others one day.

To Be as Vivid as Possible

The Leeway award required that each recipient complete the grant year with a public presentation of some kind. I knew I did not want to perform "onstage with all those eyeballs on me." So I pondered, "What might I really *want* to do? What am I most interested in?" I knew I wanted to help others. I also knew that the thing that got me up in the morning was the research on traumatic grief. I had spent two and a half years body-tracking and observing the reintegration of my own loss into this new life. I had clear thoughts about why some of the early care I received from well-intentioned but reckless professionals nearly did me in. I also knew how easily some of their methods could be remedied.[28] Perhaps I could present a forum for direct service providers, from the perspective of a family survivor of murder who is still "in it." I could articulate what worked and what didn't, and offer firsthand recommendations.

In partnership with the Institute for Safe Families, a Philadelphia-based organization for anti–domestic violence advocacy, I co-organized a panel of three speakers, which included myself; Kathleen O'Hara, author of *A Grief Like No Other: Surviving the Violent Death of Someone You Love*; and Julie Campbell, coordinator of trauma-focused projects for the Children's Crisis Treatment Center. In attendance were a group of about twenty-five psychotherapists, social workers, academics, and a counselor from the medical examiner's office. Our venue was the Painted Bride Art Center, on whose stage I had premiered many dance works. This time, however, there was no bodily warm-up for me. I just needed to be present and welcoming to my audience, and to know where to start. I would simply begin with who I had been the day before I got "the phone call," followed by the changes I noticed in myself immediately afterward. It was excruciating to tell it. I had written an outline, but I abandoned it. I improvised. After finding a point of entry, my main task was to keep the "inner story" connected to "the room" and to be as vivid as possible.

"The devil is in the details" was the resounding response I received. The direct service providers said it was rare to get such a clear picture of the effects of trauma from someone who is still experiencing it. Most survivors, the attendees said, are too wrecked in the early stages to be able to articulate what is or is not working for them. Once they are stronger, they quickly want to disassociate and move on with their lives. I began to see a potential new role for myself—something about the telling and the ongoing discovery during the telling.

Tether

Theary Seng, the Cambodian human rights activist and writer, spoke of the feeling she had as a six-year-old, in a Khmer Rouge prison the day her mother was taken away from her and her brother. When her mother failed to return the next morning, Theary Seng knew she was dead. "[From that moment on,] I felt a new sensation . . . where I was just an empty frame, I felt like my whole inside was gutted."[29] Below is an excerpt from an article I wrote in 2010 for the Parents of Murdered Children newsletter about the day that Moink, Nikki, and Lena were cremated:

> Three body-sized cardboard boxes, one large, the other two smaller, were raised in formation. Their names were written with a black sharpie at the head of each box. They had misspelled Nikki's name as "Nicky." We were required to sign a waiver before entering the crematorium, promising that we wouldn't tear through the cardboard to touch them or . . . ? It had been two weeks; they had been kept at the coroner's for autopsy. For my surviving sister, it may have been four weeks since she last saw them. For my mother and me, living so far away, it would have been much longer. And yet, here they were. We stroked the cardboard for a long time. I sang them a lullaby.
>
> I must have aged 10 years in that room. When I exited, I felt like a mass of clay that had been cleaved and hollowed by giant talons, a triple amputee, a shard, just a remnant of who I was before.[30]

Eating for me, aside from the pleasure of sweets, gave me a much needed tether, an anchor in my belly. It grounded me from spinning off into a wild panic. In the first nine months after their murders, I fantasized that I was pregnant with them, "gaining them back," readying myself to nurture and care for them again.

With every passing memorial, however, I did secretly fantasize that "this" would be the year that my body would turn. Like a young girl in love, the adrenalin would flood my cells and the pounds would miraculously melt away. After all, that's what several women reported at the Parents of Murdered Children national conference. One woman in her fifties said that in the ninth year after her husband's murder, sans diet or new routine, the pounds just dropped off. K talked about waiting at least five years to turn a major corner; 2013 technically is my sixth.

My body mass index is now verging on medical obesity. I've bought new fat clothes, then another set of fatter clothes, and will expand soon into another. I am still determined not to get on a treadmill until I truly want it, vividly desire it. As I experiment with this body-tracking, though, I fear I am also aging. I was forty-two at the start. Now I am forty-eight. Did I blow my prime? I flash back to when I was nearly anorexic in the early 1990s, and the panic that I felt then when I didn't recognize myself in the dance studio mirror. I have similar shock moments now when I see my current reflection.

2011. Tsunami: I Must Find a New Feeling for My Activity

"I'll just be a rock in the rock garden." As usual, I set the bar low for my role as a performer. After our two workshops in Izu, Leah, our Tokyo collaborators, and I had created an adaptation in 2010 for Philadelphia's Shofuso Japanese House and Garden.[31] In 2011 Leah and I were preparing for our next iteration at Shofuso when the catastrophic earthquake and tsunami hit northern Japan. Our collaborators in Tokyo were reeling, and rightly canceled coming. Hideo Arai in particular was deeply affected. He joined a group of artists who volunteer regularly in Fukushima, offering movement workshops for children and hand massage for the elderly. He said via Skype in spring 2001:

> Many things furniture broken. Town suddenly changes no buildings, oh my god. This side survived this side not. But so many small lives still survive. 1 minute walking from seaside the flowers blooming. Seaside unbelievably clear and beautiful. Starting and stopping at the same time. I must find a new feeling for my activity.

Leah and I decided to dedicate this next work to those affected by the earthquake, tsunami, and subsequent nuclear disaster. We explored the destruction, loss, and eerie grace that followed. Leah asked me to do a solo. Then, during our performance weekend, Hurricane Irene hit Philadelphia and ripped apart our site. This solo felt inevitable.

I don't know what happened except that I felt carried, as though I was riding a furious energy, ecstatic and tragic, stomping and hunkering, gesturing, crying, singing, suspending, spinning into the shamanistic. The structure of the piece was looped, so I did this over and over. My feet opened. The water in my skull tipped a little further behind my spine. My throat and heart hollowed and enjoyed the hollowing. My lower back playfully joined the balloon of my belly, and I allowed my expanded heaviness to tire me and then feed me. To my great surprise, others took note as well.

2012. Teaching Again

"I know you're on hiatus from performing, but are you still on hiatus from teaching?" I was asked to teach dance improvisation at San Francisco State University. I'd danced that solo at Shofuso and had some other one-offs, but I wasn't sure I could teach dance anymore. Could I even touch my toes still? How will I demonstrate the simplest of motions? I wasn't sure, but I said yes.

As my students walked in that first day, I heard a new "voice" come out of my body. It was smiling and had a slow, deep, and welcoming sound: "Go ahead and put your bags over there, and come sit over here in a circle." And that voice continued—almost without me—talking, guiding, listening, and discovering for the rest of the semester:

Do only what's already easy, what's already interesting. Don't skip steps . . . pause until you're sure. Follow your curiosity down "a road" . . . what's just around that corner? where have you arrived? Simply fold and unfold. Find phenomena!

2013. Body Destroyed / Body Remembered

At this point, I am starting to feel shame: I close my eyes when changing in front of a mirror. My "one size fits all" *yukata*, the cotton kimono I so loved donning for a classical Japanese dance lesson, no longer wraps properly around me. Maybe all this "seeking authentic joy" is nothing but magical thinking. But if I don't stay with this, this commitment to moving only when I absolutely want to, my physical body and mind, let alone my spirit, may never find lasting balance, health, and transformation. Can I own this as my present reality and feel comfortable, if not strong and unequivocally liberated, in this my ever-changing survivor body?

NOTES

An earlier version of this essay was originally published in 2010 in *Roko Kawai: An Artist's Workbook*, published by the Pew Center for Arts and Heritage, Philadelphia, Pennsylvania, as part of the danceworkbook series, which documents the creative practice of living and working with dance.

1. *Katakana, hiragana,* and *kanji* are the three alphabets used in modern Japanese—in combination and with clear rules about when to use which in a given sentence. As a preschooler, we first learn hiragana—all forty-eight phonetic

symbols. By the end of kindergarten, we also learn the corresponding katakana to each hiragana. I was taught that hiragana was used for most words, and katakana was used for words that were foreign in origin—like *kissu* (kiss) or *pan* (bread). To me, this made katakana the "second-class citizen" of alphabets. Visually, too, katakana wasn't as graceful as hiragana. It was very square and block-like, boring and not very "Japanese-looking." As an adult, then, it came to me as a surprise when I read that katakana had actually preceded hiragana, migrating from China via Buddhist and scholarly texts around the fourth century AD.

Starting in the first grade, I began to take on the more complicated kanji. Because the early Japanese had no written language of their own, they had adopted China's alphabet, this kanji, which is also sometimes referred to, consequently, as "Chinese characters." Chinese and Japanese pronounce the characters differently, but because kanji are hieroglyphic in origin, Chinese and Japanese people can sometimes communicate with one another by writing these pictographic characters.

Kanji is known for its multistroked complexity. A Japanese young person is not considered fully literate until sixth grade, by which time it is expected that we know two thousand kanji, about the number you need to read a newspaper. For me, a young Japanese-outside-of-the-homeland, kanji was the prize in the sky and the test of being truly Japanese. If you could read a novel in kanji, if you could beautifully pen those complicated strokes, then you had arrived. At my best, I knew 250–350 kanji. I was equivalent to a third-grade reader, but I had always dreamed that one day I would go live and study in Japan to become fully literate.

Thus it was a shock when, at the start of this fellowship, I was advised not to use the kanji characters of my name on my business card. Every formal Japanese relationship begins with the presentation of one's card. It is considered an embodiment of your personhood. On the receiving end, when someone offers you theirs, you must take it respectfully with both hands and gaze at it for a few seconds. But in this introduction, my personhood was being deleted. Without kanji on my business card, my lifelong desire to "arrive" was sidelined. More importantly, the kanji meaning of my name was being erased. "Child of Universal Knowledge" had been chosen by my parents as an expression of who they hoped I might become. Gone. I felt defiant. Was this an American response, this yearning to hold on to exotic name origins? A new game was in play now.

2. I think of *ma* as the empty space or moment in between. It is the silent scream between two majestic trees or the suspenseful breath between the cries of a bird. It is alive—both for the person creating it (a rock gardener, for instance, or a percussionist) and the person experiencing it (someone listening to a brilliantly told story). *Ma* is not calculated or measured; it is felt.

3. Japanese classical dance, as in all the traditional Japanese arts (including music, flower arrangement, tea ceremony, etc.), is organized into *ryuha*, or schools.

A *ryuha* is not a brick-and-mortar institution but a lineage that keeps its choreographic repertoire and teaching methodologies very well guarded. The Hanayagi school (founded in 1848) is one of the five main classical dance schools in Japan and currently boasts the largest membership at more than twenty thousand students.

Like ballet, the canon in Japanese classical dance remains universal. For example, *Swan Lake* retains its title, music, story, and characters regardless of choreographic attribution. While general audiences may not see differences between multiple versions of *Swan Lake*, aficionados will recognize that Balanchine's *Swan Lake* is aesthetically distinct from one choreographed by another artist. Similarly, a Hanayagi *Wisteria Maiden* will differ from one taught by the Fujima school (founded in 1704). In Japan the separation between schools is fiercely protected. It is taboo to mix choreographies between schools or for an apprentice from one school to take class at another school.

During lessons, beginner apprentices go by their own first and last names. Once they pass the advanced *natori* (name-taking) exam, within the context of the classical dance world, they adopt a new first and last name. The new last name is the name of their *ryuha*, in this case Hanayagi. The new first name starts with the first kanji character of the teacher's stage name, to which additional kanji are added to celebrate a special quality in the apprentice. For example, Hanayagi Kazu's leading apprentices are named Kazu-maika and Kazu-renka. In this way, lineage is very easily and sonically affirmed.

Once in a while, a rift occurs between the teacher and an apprentice. Hanayagi Kazu's teacher was Hanayagi Chiyo, known for authoring the first published manual on classical dance, *Fundamentals of Japanese Dance* (originally published in 1981 by Kodansha Shuppan Service Center, Tokyo). Technically Kazu's name should have started with the syllable "Chi." However, Kazu broke from the "Chiyo" line and boldly started her own, using her birth name "Kazu."

4. "Kazu-sensei" is what her apprentices affectionately call her. "Sensei" is the term used for master, teacher, doctor, scientist, or lawyer.

5. Nibroll is a multimedia dance/art collective, based in Tokyo, that was formed in 1997 by Mikuni Yanaihara. See the website, http://precog-jp.net/en/artists /nibroll, accessed April 6, 2014.

6. Since the Edo Period (1603–1867), Chihan-an has been home to the Suganuma family. The Suganumas were wealthy landowners and Nobuko Awaya's maternal ancestors. The year 2008 marked the two-hundredth anniversary of their residence at this home. It takes its namesake after "Chihan," the pen name of Nobuko's grandfather, who was a patron of the arts with a special love of poetry. The "an" of Chihan-an means "retreat" or "sanctuary."

The area is also well known for the short story "Izu Dancer" by Yasunari Kawabata, whose story takes place just a few hours south of Chihan-an.

Chihan-an still retains its original footprint but now includes beautifully designed modern additions. When entering the large foyer, one's attention is drawn
high up toward the thatched roof interior. From a spacious, contemporary kitchen,
the eye can follow dark, gigantic ceiling beams undulating through the house, and
extending into an inner room with a traditional hearth and ancestral altar.

Privately, the Suganuma family gave birth, celebrated weddings, and held funerals here. Publicly, as community patrons, they provided a center for town meetings and important gatherings. As a philanthropist, Chihan invited artists to come
for creative retreats, haiku contests, and cultural exchanges among one another.
Today, we can see some of the work they left behind as a "thank you." For example, Yuinen, a ninety-one-year-old monk, left his calligraphic painting of a snake.
Among his guests were such luminaries as the playwright Mantaro Kubota, the
novelist Fumiko Hayashi, and the filmmaker Heinosuke Gosho.

In 2000 Chihan-an was passed on to Nobuko Awaya. While there was some
discussion about whether to bequeath the property to the state as a historic site,
Nobuko decided to carry on her grandfather's vision: to use it both as a home and
a place of creative inspiration. In 2007 Nobuko launched the "Chihan Art Project,"
an ongoing artist series that includes live-in workshops, on-site performances and
installations, and a space for good food, drink, and company. In 2012 Chihan-an
was designated a National Treasure by the Japanese government but still remains
under the stewardship of Nobuko Awaya.

7. Nobuko Awaya is a descendant of 450 years of the Suganuma family in Izu,
Japan. She is also a freelance journalist/author and a professor of intercultural
communications with a special interest in gender issues and media at Shoin University, Japan. Since 2000, she has served as cochair of the Research Organization
for Asian American Experience and played an important part in inviting me in
2005 to lecture to this group. It was that meeting that spurred her to commission
me to create a site-specific dance at Chihan-an.

8. Leah Stein grew up in the Hudson Valley in New York State. She is a dancer,
choreographer, and teacher who has been making site-inspired dances for over
twenty years. In 2001 she formed the Leah Stein Dance Company, whose site-
specific dances have been performed internationally and throughout the United
States in train garages, open fields, corner parking lots, vacant city lots, historic
sites, gardens, and burial grounds. Her choreography refers to particular landscapes
and addresses the relationship between people and their physical surroundings.
Building on a background of Western dance, she has trained in Aikido, Javanese
dance, improvisation, and contemporary dance techniques. She has collaborated
with numerous artists including long-standing artistic partnerships with Toshi
Makihara, Josey Foo, Roko Kawai, Alan Harler of the Mendelssohn Club Chorus,
and Germaine Ingram. She received a 2010 Independence Foundation Fellowship

and three Pennsylvania of the Arts Fellowships for Choreography. In 2001 she won a Herald Angel Award for her dance "In Situ" in Edinburgh, Scotland. *A Lily Lilies: Poems*, by Josey Foo, with notes on dance by Leah Stein was published by Nightboat Books. Leah Stein website, http://www.leahsteindanceco.org/, accessed April 6, 2014.

9. Hideo Arai, interested in dance and bodywork from a young age, began studying under the famous Japanese movement and body expert Michizo Noguchi in 1989. Noguchi taught Hideo how to artistically express his own unique dance impulses through the most efficient physical movements possible. Hideo also learned how to link his personal artistic yearnings with the greater surrounding forces of nature. He once mentioned that he has no human dance teachers; that the inspiration for all his movement comes from the natural world. Taking place in temples, shrines, fields, and streets, Hideo's dances may be accompanied by live musicians and variously concocted sets, or it may occur in complete silence, punctuated only by ambient noise and wild grasses. His dance is intensely shamanistic yet playfully light, and as Hideo cavorts across his various stages, one is held in amazement at his mastery of juxtaposition: stillness and motion, light and dark, life and death.

In 1997 Hideo created the dance project-office KARADAKARA, joining two Japanese words—"body" (*karada*) and "therefore" (*dakara*), or "Therefore the Body"—creating a moniker to express his ideas of natural body movement. Hideo has performed throughout Japan, North America, Hungary, and Malaysia.

10. Mika Kimula has a keen interest in the use of voice and Japanese language in contemporary theater and music, with a specialty in the history and technique of early twentieth-century Japanese song. Like Hideo, she received intensive training in Noguchi Taiso. A constant researcher, she also worked with Shigeo Miki, MD, to investigate "life morphology" (how live beings respond to the voice). Presently, Mika performs, records, teaches, writes, and gives workshops throughout Japan and internationally. Most recently, she is featured in the book/DVD *Japanese Voice: A Video Archive of Singing and Techniques in the Japanese Language* (compiled by I. Nakayama, Osaka University of Arts, AD POPOLO, 2008), for which she has also translated an English supplement with explanatory notes on seventy-nine singers from thirty-two genres.

11. Edo (1600–1868) to Taisho (1912–1926) periods: an extremely rich swath of Japanese history. The Edo Period, ruled by the Shogunate, transitioned Japan from a medieval to a premodern society. Tightly ruled by Shogunate generals and fiercely resistant to foreign influences, the Edo Period gave birth to much of what is today considered culturally Japanese—Kabuki, Ukiyo-e prints, and the geisha quarters. After two and a half centuries, American warships did forcibly penetrate Japan's seacoasts (in 1853) and demanded an opening of trade negotiations. The

weakened Shogunate collapsed, unseated by a new government headed by Emperor Meiji, ushering in the Meiji Era (1868–1912). Meiji felt that in order for Japan to survive and "outsmart" European imperialism, it needed to "catch up" to Western ways first. Samurai swords were outlawed. The new elite learned how to wear Victorian dress, play violin, bake bread, and, eventually, to wage its own imperialistic war outside its borders. By the time of Meiji's death, Japan was well on its way to building an empire across Asia. In the following Taisho Era, Japan entered World War I.

12. *Obon*, next to New Year's, is one of Japan's most important celebrations of the year. Occurring in mid-August, it is a festival in which most Japanese return to their hometowns to honor their ancestors through massive gatherings in public spaces, folk dances, food, drink, and ultimately a respectful prayer. Each region prizes its own *obon* traditions, including its particular set of folk dances and songs. In modern times, the song "Soran Bushi," originally from the northern island of Hokkaido, has become a favorite for young people to set their own moves to the addition of a faster beat. We saw one of these disco-ized versions in Ohito and later created our own "Soran Bushi" for *Izu House*.

13. Non-chan was Nobuko's nickname; "-chan" is what you put at the end of a child's name to show endearment (vs. "-san" to show respect). When used for adults it's often an expression of continued affection, as though you were still the beloved child in someone's care.

14. Noguchi Taiso (literally "Noguchi Physical Exercise [method]") was developed by Michizo Noguchi (1914–1998) in the 1970s. It is a system of physical improvement and revitalization through specific physical exercises, and the use of metaphoric prompts including double-meanings found in Japanese kanji characters, as well as physical props such as cloth, eggs, water, nature, and God—all aiming to find the already innate balance and fluidity that we are born with. Both Hideo and Mika are certified in Noguchi Taiso. Hideo's work draws daily from this practice.

15. Go is a traditional Japanese board game for two players. It has the reputation, like chess, of requiring a high level of mental acuity.

16. Kappa (literally "River Imp") is a mythological creature, an anthropomorphized green being that looks like a long-legged frog or turtle, one of the "water deities" in indigenous lore.

17. Elisabeth Kübler-Ross and David Kessler, *On Grief and Grieving* (New York: Scribner, 2005), 21.

18. Jill Bolte Taylor, *My Stroke of Insight: A Brain Scientist's Personal Journey* (New York: Viking Penguin, 2008).

19. Jill Bolte Taylor, "My Stroke of Insight," TED Talk, video, 18:19, filmed February 2008 at TED2008, http://www.ted.com/talks/jill_bolte_taylor_s_power ful_stroke_of_insight, accessed April 6, 2014.

20. The reign of terror was the period in modern Cambodian history from 1975 to 1979, during which a communist faction called the Khmer Rouge militarily seized power with the goal of creating an agrarian communist utopia. Shutting down former medical, education, and economic infrastructures, the Khmer Rouge forcibly reorganized the population into mass agricultural labor and persecuted those perceived as part of the former elite, including aristocracy, intellectuals, teachers, scientists, and artists. In this genocide, close to two million people (between one-quarter and one-third of the population) are believed to have died from starvation, overwork, disease, torture, and execution. Inside of those statistics, an estimated 80–90 percent of the country's professional artists perished, leaving the future of Cambodian cultural and artistic traditions in a precarious state (most traditions are handed down orally from living teacher to student). For more information, see Toni Shapiro-Phim, "Mediating Cambodian History, the Sacred, and the Earth," in *Dance, Human Rights and Social Justice: Dignity in Motion*, ed. Naomi Jackson and Toni Shapiro-Phim (Lanham, MD: Scarecrow Press, 2008), 304–322.

21. From 2008 to 2010, Toni Shapiro-Phim worked with the Cambodia-based branch of the Khmer Arts Academy, founded and led by her sister-in-law Sophiline Cheam Shapiro. During her tenure there, Toni launched a new archive of classical Cambodian dance while also teaching dance ethnology to the younger generation of classical dancers and training other young Cambodians in research and archiving practice.

22. The Leeway Foundation supports women and trans artists and cultural producers working in communities at the intersection of art, culture, and social change. The Leeway Transformation Award provides awards to women and trans artists who create art for social change and demonstrate a long-term commitment to social change work.

23. Em Theay is a renowned Cambodian classical dancer, singer, teacher, and elder survivor of the Khmer Rouge reign of terror. She is featured in the film *The Tenth Dancer* (written and directed by Sally Ingleton, distributed by 360 Degree Films, 1993), named because only an estimated one in ten classical dancers of Cambodia's Royal Court had survived. Em Theay was separated from her star pupil Pen Sok Chea during the genocide. Both survived by taking on false identities and following the masses to work in the fields. Em Theay, like so many, lost numerous family members and colleagues during this time. After the fall of the Khmer Rouge, she and Sok Chea heard an announcement over a loudspeaker begging all dancers, musicians, and performers to return to Phnom Penh to help rebuild the classical and cultural traditions. As part of a small handful of survivors, Em Theay and Pen Sok Chea have made it their mission to keep the ancient stories and traditions of their ancestors alive.

24. The Tuol Sleng Museum of Genocide is located in Phnom Penh. Formerly called S-21, it had been a detention, torture, and execution center during the

Cambodian Genocide. Led by prison chief Kaing Guek Eav, it was notorious for its cruel and horrific atrocities inflicted on imprisoned men, women, and children. Today, while the grounds and building remain largely unaltered, the museum also features powerful historic and educational displays, including a haunting exhibition of photographs of each prisoner's "portrait" upon entry.

25. From 1997 to 2001, the Cambodian government lobbied the United Nations (UN) to assist in establishing a tribunal court to prosecute the Khmer Rouge senior leaders for serious crimes against humanity. Pol Pot, the leader of the Khmer Rouge, died in 1998, thus evading trial. Commonly referred to as the Tribunal, the hearings are still in session at the time of this writing. To date, the only convicted member of the regime is former prison chief Kaing Guek Eav for his role in killing more than fourteen thousand while running the Tuol Sleng torture and execution center. In July 2010 he received a shockingly lenient prison sentence of nineteen years. In 2013, after much outrage and protest, his sentence was changed to life in prison.

26. Matthias Witzel, *Understanding Trauma in Cambodia Handbook*, trans. Yim Sotheary and Om Chariya, ed. Theary Seng, Center for Social Development and German Development Service, 2007, http://www.matthias-witzel.com/index.php ?id=21&lang=en, accessed April 7, 2014. This manual is used widely as part of outreach efforts across Cambodia on the Khmer Rouge Tribunal, justice, and peace and reconciliation issues.

27. Theary Seng, *Daughter of the Killing Fields: Asrei's Story* (London: Fusion Press, 2005), 236–237.

28. In the first few weeks after the murders, when I was the most vulnerable but not shy about articulating how fragile, disoriented, and suicidal I was feeling, several "specialists" counseled me in reckless ways. Trying to talk me out of suicide, one counselor offered, "You have to stay in this world because your nieces need you." Of course, my nieces Nikki and Lena were murdered along with their mother, Mamiko! He just forgot to reread my file. It was like they were being killed all over again. This is the same counselor who told me just a week after the murders to stop focusing so much on myself and sign up to volunteer at a homeless shelter. At that point, I could barely get out of the house, let alone go into a challenging environment with strangers. Another specialist told me that the pain in my body was probably because I had stopped dancing and that I should start dancing as soon as possible. To the direct service providers at the forum, I was able to describe what it was like both emotionally and physically to hear such abominable advice, and to give alternative recommendations. For example, if service providers do nothing else, they should read the survivor's file and know the names and circumstances of the victims. The names and the intimate details of lost loved ones are the most precious thing to a survivor of murder.

29. *Judging Genocide*, Journeyman Pictures, video, 18:56, July 2007, http://www.journeyman.tv/57479/short-films/judging-genocide.html, accessed April 6, 2014.

30. Roko Kawai, "Untitled," Parents of Murdered Children (POMC), Contra Costa/East Bay Chapter newsletter, February/March 2010.

31. Shofuso Japanese House and Garden is a seventeenth-century-style traditional Japanese house that was never lived in. Designed by the Japanese midcentury modernist architect Junzo Yoshimura in 1953, the house was built in Japan, using traditional materials and techniques. The house was conceived as part of "The House in the Museum Garden" series exhibition at the Museum of Modern Art in New York City. At the conclusion of the exhibition in 1958, it was moved to its current site in Philadelphia, where there has been a continuous Japanese presence since the 1876 Centennial Exposition. Currently, Shofuso is a public museum.

3

Asian Canadian Dance

*Cross-Cultural Currents in Vancouver's Kokoro Dance
and Co.ERASGA Dance*

EURY COLIN CHANG

Asian Canadian studies, broadly defined, has embraced a transdisciplinary approach to studying issues related to a complex, heterogeneous demographic. In the last five years alone, the number of new published titles has increased exponentially.[1] At this time, it seems pertinent to take stock and point out that most of the work in Asian Canadian studies addresses sociopolitical history and literary arts. Less attention is paid to the performing arts, let alone dance. This is not to suggest that efforts have not been made to connect the work of cultural workers with social activism—and, in fact, this has been done to some degree—but rather to recognize Asian Canadian dance as a growing site of scholarly interest. Within Asian Canadian studies, Asian Canadian dance is relatively unexamined and undertheorized from a scholarly perspective, but dance as an embodied practice offers the opportunity to expand the field of Asian Canadian studies.

How does choreography represent notions of home and belonging? More specifically, what would a comparative analysis of the repertoire between Asian Canadian dance artists reveal about the impact of multicultural policies on artistic production? This essay argues that the choreographers Jay Hirabayashi of Kokoro Dance and Alvin Tolentino of Co.ERASGA Dance have benefited from state-level funding and multicultural discourses. In particular, the latter has encouraged, albeit in subtle and overt ways, a body of work that gestures toward cultural heritage and its relationship to the land. Seen together, the choreography of Hirabayashi of Kokoro Dance and Tolentino of Co.ERASGA Dance speaks to a decidedly contemporary, Asian Canadian theatrical dance practice that is growing in urban centers such as Vancouver and Toronto.[2] In order to build my argument, I examine the work of both choreographies as they intersect with key policy developments—namely the Canadian Multiculturalism Act and the Equity Policies at the Canada Council for the Arts—that have impacted arts funding in Canada.[3] As such, this chapter reflects upon the state-level instruments that support "diverse arts" practices and enable artists of Asian descent to emerge as a driving force in the Canadian and international dance scene. Positioning the works within theoretical concepts such as *abjection* and *subjection* has proven useful in teasing out the meaning behind Asian Canadian dance and its relationship to the nation-state, geography, and belonging.[4] Perhaps it is no surprise that Hirabayashi and Tolentino base their companies in Vancouver, which is British Columbia's largest urban center and a city whose global demographic is heavily influenced by successive waves of Asian immigration. It seems quite pertinent to recognize the work of Jay Hirabayashi and Alvin Tolentino as migrants; Hirabayashi is a Seattle-born American who migrated to Canada, and Tolentino is a Manila-born Filipino who migrated to Canada with his family. Both men have made significant inroads into the contemporary dance milieu, which historically honors the legacy of European and American founders while ignoring the work of "diverse" or "minority" artists (i.e., those of Asian descent) and those working out in the hinterlands (anywhere outside of the United States and Europe).[5]

Rage: Displaced Bodies Stripped of Land

Butoh is said to have evolved in post–World War II Japan, partly in response to the American bombing of Hiroshima and the growing disinterest in emulating Western or traditional Japanese forms such as Noh. Kazuo Ohno and Tatsumi Hijikata are credited as the founders of butoh. In 1980 Hirabayashi witnessed a butoh performance in Vancouver that would prove to be an inspirational turning point in his artistic development. Hirabayashi recalls seeing Koichi Tamano's Ankoku Butoh Dance Theatre performing at Robson Square Theatre in Vancouver. The show left an indelible mark on Hirabayashi and Barbara Bourget, and the two artists began researching deeply into the Japanese form.[6] In 1993 Hirabayashi and Bourget saw Kazuo Ohno and his son Yoshito perform *Water Lilies* (1987) at the Moore Theatre in Seattle. Two years later, Hirabayashi traveled to Tokyo to study with the father-and-son team.

The presence and enduring legacy of butoh in Canada can be attributed to the work and influence of Jay Hirabayashi and Barbara Bourget, who are the husband-and-wife team behind Kokoro Dance.[7] The Vancouver-based company creates dances rooted in Asian philosophy and aesthetics and is considered by critics to be on the vanguard of dance on the West Coast. Through their work as teachers, choreographers, and mentors, Hirabayashi and Bourget are considered senior artists within the contemporary dance scene who have forged the way for the next generation of dance artists. In addition to choreographing original works and performing, Jay Hirabayashi and Barbara Bourget are responsible for producing one of Vancouver's largest and longest-running dance festivals in Vancouver.[8] Jay Hirabayashi was born in the United States and raised in Seattle, Washington. He moved to and settled in Vancouver, British Columbia, where he completed his master's degree in Buddhist studies at the University of British Columbia. In 1982 Hirabayashi joined forces with other pioneers of Vancouver's dance community and formed Experimental Dance and Music (EDAM).[9] By 1986 Hirabayashi and Bourget left EDAM and cofounded Kokoro Dance Theatre, which is Canada's first contemporary butoh company.

The 1980s would prove to be a dynamic time for Hirabayashi and Bourget as they embarked on raising their son while building the foundation to develop what would become Kokoro's signature dance repertoire: *Rage* (1986/87) and, later, *Sunyata* (1997). Jay Hirabayashi was already privy to the nuanced history of the race-based politics of the United States and Canada. The birth of their son and company also coincided with the same year that Jay Hirabayashi's father, Gordon Hirabayashi, was to appear before the United States Supreme Court, petitioning to have misdemeanor convictions set aside. In 1942, after the United States entered World War II in response to the Japanese bombing of Pearl Harbor, Gordon Hirabayashi, a student at the University of Washington in Seattle, refused the curfew—the hourly restrictions and containment to specific neighborhoods during specific hours—that was imposed only on people of Japanese descent.

The senior Hirabayashi was convinced that the curfew was unconstitutional, and he failed to "register for evacuation from the military area." In addition, he "was away from his place of residence after 8:00 p.m. on May 9, 1942."[10] Gordon Hirabayashi was one of three Japanese American men imprisoned for resisting Executive Order 9066. Signed by U.S. President Franklin D. Roosevelt on February 19, 1942, Executive Order 9066 authorized the U.S. Secretary of War to relocate and intern over 120,000 Japanese Americans who were living on the West Coast of the United States. Refusing to be treated differently and wanting to exercise his civil rights as an American-born citizen, Hirabayashi was convicted of a misdemeanor and imprisoned for six months. In 1983 Hirabayashi wanted to have the misdemeanors cleared from his record and sought to obtain "writ of error coram nobis to vacate his convictions and thus make the judgments of the courts conform to the judgments of history."[11]

On September 24, 1987, these misdemeanors were successfully over-turned at the Court of Appeals for the Ninth Circuit because it was known that the U.S. government knowingly suppressed evidence that would have been favorable to him and other persons of Japanese ancestry. The evidence proved that the Japanese living in America posed no threat to the security of the nation. Almost five months after Gordon Hirabayashi passed away, Barack Obama, the president of the United States, awarded Hirabayashi with a Presidential Medal of Freedom on April 27, 2012. Jay Hirabayashi and other family members traveled to Washington, DC, to receive the award on behalf of their father. In early 2014 the family donated the medal to the University of Washington, Seattle, where it is held by the university's Library Special Collections alongside the Hirabayashi papers.

North of the border, a similar wartime hysteria would unfold, as Mac-Kenzie King, the prime minister of Canada, ordered the removal of twenty-three men, women, and children from British Columbia. Like their counterparts in the United States, Japanese Canadians were incarcerated as "enemy aliens," even though 75 percent of the people of Japanese ances-try in Canada were either Canadian-born citizens or naturalized Cana-dian citizens. Unlike in the United States, where Japanese immigrants were barred from becoming naturalized citizens, Japanese in Canada were allowed to become naturalized citizens. The British Columbia Security Commission set up a "protected zone" that extended along the West Coast and one hun-dred miles inland. Canadians of Japanese descent living in the zone were stripped of their citizenship rights, property, and personal belongings. Much of the latter were then sold without consent or proper reimbursement.[12]

Perhaps in homage to his father's wartime resistance and, more gener-ally, to the hundreds of thousands of Japanese North Americans who were interned throughout the United States and Canada, Jay Hirabayashi cho-reographed and performed *Rage* for Kokoro Dance Theatre's first show.

Rage would become a signature piece that would manifest in different in-carnations over the years (later renamed *The Believer*) and would evolve into one of the company's most lauded and widely seen productions. As a creative intervention and reflection of the issues surrounding the history of Japanese Canadian internment, *Rage* premiered at the height of the Japa-nese Canadian redress efforts that sought formal apologies and reparations for the Japanese Canadians and Americans who were forcibly removed from their homes during World War II. The National Association for Japanese Canadians (NAJC), headed by President Art Miki, mobilized throughout the 1980s to represent the Japanese Canadian community who were finally granted redress on September 22, 1988. At that time, Prime Minister Brian Mulroney provided an official apology to Canadians of Japanese ancestry in the House of Commons.

In his book, Roy Miki described how the newly established Japanese Canadian Redress Secretariat was established in order to implement the financial redress that included $21,000 provided to surviving internees, $12 million to undertake "educational, social and cultural activities or pro-grams that contribute to the well-being of the community or that promote human rights," and a further $12 million "for the creation of a Canadian Race Relations Foundation that will foster racial harmony and cross-cultural understanding and help eliminate racism."[13] Jay Hirabayashi's father, Gor-don, was part of the Reparations Committee of the National Japanese Canadian Citizens' Association. He was a vocal proponent of individual redress, exclaiming: "Individuals were uprooted, deprived of home, treated with indignity, delayed in income and education, confined like criminals. It is therefore the right of individuals to be given reparations/restitution."[14] Essentially, this meant that Hirabayashi was in favor of a model that fol-lowed the American example, where individual survivors were given redress payments, a strategy that for some was more favorable than receiving a lump sum payment that would go toward one representative group; in the end, monies went to individuals and were also collected by the National Asso-ciation of Japanese Canadians on behalf of the demographic and were to be distributed for community projects and outreach.

In many ways, the fight for Japanese Canadian redress was part of a larger discussion about identity and minority culture in Canada, a discussion that began as early as the 1970s and 1980s. These decades saw the expression of strained relationships between the various provinces, between English- and

French-speaking populations, and within Canada's growing multicultural demographic. It should also be noted that Japanese Canadian redress was settled the same year that saw the enactment of the Canadian Multiculturalism Act (1988), another policy document that sought to increase awareness of identity politics and dynamics between artists and citizens of various cultural backgrounds. Section 3, titled "Multiculturalism Policy of Canada," declares that all federal institutions shall "promote policies, program and practices and enhance the ability of individuals and communities of all origins to contribute to the continuing evolution of Canada," and that "enhance[s] the understanding of and respect for the diversity of the members of Canadian society."[15]

As a concept and value, discourses of multiculturalism would enter into the policy priorities of the arts and cultural milieu, especially the national funding bodies. Even as early as 1978, an Advisory Arts Panel was considering how to advise the Canada Council for the Arts on such matters of "diversity." Their report, *The Future of the Canada Council*, highlighted pertinent concepts of "diversity in Canadian culture" and "the challenges of Canada's demography and its distribution," citing the country's dispersed population base and American culture as potential threats to the dissemination of cultural products.[16] One of the programs that attempted to embrace artists working outside mainstream, Eurocentric, institutional arts groups in Canada was the Explorations Program. According to Andrea Monike Fatona, the existence and articulation of the program revolved around "the concern with fostering regional representation and culture" and, further, recognizing Canada as a "pluralist entity that is constituted of multiple cultural centres that produce a range of cultural expressions."

It is within this political climate and the Explorations Program that Jay Hirabayashi received money to develop Kokoro Dance Theatre's first work, *Rage*—a dance work that clearly uses choreographed movement, costume, and music to explore issues of social injustice, the politics of identity, and place. Xiaoping Li, a Canadian sociologist, coined the term "Asian Canadian Cultural Activism" to describe a movement of individuals who "affect the world through their cultural practices." More specifically, Li sees their role similar to what Gramsci ascribed to "organic intellectuals," describing them as "makers of this politically charged and socially committed cultural discourse" who connect "intellectual, artistic activities and community/ societal betterment."[17] Ethnographic in tone and rooted in the artists' need for "societal betterment," Kokoro Dance's signature work, *Rage*, clearly engages in a particular kind of "Asian Canadian Cultural Activism" espoused by Xiaoping Li.

Rage was not wholly autobiographical in tone; rather, the show gestured broadly and figuratively to the social injustices experienced by Japanese immigrants before, during, and after World War II. I saw the premiere of *Rage* in 1986 at the Firehall Arts Centre, which happened to be located a block away from the neighboring streets that used to comprise old Japantown in Vancouver.[18] In the show, Jay Hirabayashi honored his Japanese roots by wearing only a *fundoshi* (Japanese loin-cloth), referencing the bygone era when Japanese men wore such undergarments before the widespread introduction of Western-style briefs and boxers. He stood atop a large platform constructed specifically for the show with his arms bound with latex tubing that wrapped around his wrists and ran up to the platform on which he was standing. At the premiere, Jay Hirabayashi's body was full of tension: his biceps curled, and his hands balled into tight fists. His deep agony was palpable, exuding a heavy energy that was felt throughout the theater. As Hirabayashi pulled his arms upward, testing the strength and resistance of the latex tubes, his sinewy musculature glistened under the stage lights. Simultaneously, another male performer raised his arm to hit a thunderous *taiko* drum placed downstage but never seemed to have completed the task. The drummer's movement was also contained as if he were held back by internal and external forces. Both men stood naked, their bodies covered in the recognizable chalk-white rice powder often used by butoh dancers. The most memorable moment of the evening remains burned on my mind's eye: near the end, Jay Hirabayashi was blindfolded, and his mouth remained agape in a silent scream. His physical and facial gestures captured the pain and patience of Japanese internees, offering his audiences a reminder and mirror of this dark moment in Canadian history.

Rage is a highly self-conscious and politically astute work. Since 1985, there have been at least nine versions of *Rage*. While it is beyond the scope of this essay to compare each version, it should be noted that the original duet that inspired *Rage* was known as *Half-and-Half*, performed by Jay Hirabayashi and John Endo Greenaway. After the 1986 premiere at the Firehall, subsequent versions were performed at larger venues, such as the Vancouver Playhouse, and featured larger casts, which allowed for increasingly complex choreographic patterns and relationship dynamics. Other versions became interdisciplinary and foregrounded the story of redress with martial arts, contemporary set design, and mise-en-scène. Eventually, Hirabayashi states: "We changed the show name from Rage to The Believer, and it's become more personal. It's about my father who was sent to prison during the war. My father was a Japanese American, and was involved in a famous United States Supreme Court case, helping to bring attention to the redress movement in North America."[19] Clearly, the work began as a general reflection on Japanese internment and transformed into a more deeply familial story grounded in the story of the choreographer's own father, a born and raised American citizen. As such, the borders between various binary categories—tradition/modernity, Canada/United States, Japanese/European—become blurred in *Rage*.

While Hirabayashi pays homage to his Japanese roots by using the *fundoshi* and *taiko*, signifiers from a past "Japaneseness," the use of rice powder (common in butoh) and latex tubing can be seen as more recent artistic practices and innovations. Aesthetically speaking, the show utilizes the signifiers from both traditional and modern costumes, devices, and props. In an interview, Hirabayashi described how watching Koichi Tamano of Ankoku Butoh Dance pull wisps of red silk between his fingers inspired him to consider how fabric can embody both fragility and strength. Hirabayashi emulated Tamano's simple act, transforming and changing the whole scale: the use of long latex tubing in *Rage* acted as a physical metaphor for the perceived tension and confusion that Japanese internees must have experienced during their forced relocation. Similarly, *Rage* gestures broadly toward Japanese internment in North America and the notions of belonging. As forced relocation marked Japanese bodies as "foreign aliens," they became racialized, and yet Asian Canadians and Asian Americans "cannot be differentiated from the 'legitimate' U.S. American subject with an exclusion carrying the force of law and therefore cannot be openly, completely, or permanently expelled."[20] Karen Shimakawa explains this double bind, suggesting that in order "to maintain the legitimacy of the dominant racial/national complex, the process of abjection must continually be reiterated or re-presented."[21] In addition to having lived in the United States, Canada, and Cairo, Jay Hirabayashi is biracial, and this fact has colored the nature and quality of Kokoro Dance's repertoire: a border-crossing aesthetic that alludes to cultural heritage and relationship to the land. As representative of a displaced demographic that has literally been moved out of

their homes and interned into the hinterlands, the Japanese Canadian/
American body onstage marks the presence of a sociopolitical critique and
exploration.

To document *Rage* as part of the canon of dance history seems necessary
and vital, especially as it connects the impacts of multicultural policies
on contemporary dance expression in Canada. The funding of the Explorations Program offered by the Canada Council for the Arts has provided
Jay Hirabayashi with the means to explore his contemporary Japanese-
influenced dance within a society whose government has historically dis-
criminated against citizens of Japanese descent, especially during wartime.
Broadly speaking, *Rage* gestures toward the history of Japanese American internees. More specifically, *The Believer*, with its focus on Gordon
Hirbayashi's refusal to relinquish his rights as an American by abiding by
state-sanctioned curfews, signals dance creation as a particular brand of
Asian American political activism, which tends to be downplayed since the
"model-minority stereotype perpetuates the notion that Asian Americans
have nothing to complain about."[22] Yutian Wong further explains how
interned Japanese are not portrayed or seen as "prone to protest," which
decontextualizes the protest of the draft as well as the redress movement
of the 1980s. Karen Shimakawa makes the assertion that assimilated Asian
Americans are praised for their ability to "surpass even 'normal' Americans (that is, whites) at being ideal manifestations of American success."
Of course, as the image of America as land of opportunity erases its own
prejudices, the model minority myth still persists as a colonial discourse,
functioning "through racial stereotype, to establish a self in opposition to
an other by making the other abnormal, monstrous, and thereby fixed and
characterizable."[23]

As a form that manifests itself through the flesh, dance is particularly
adept at commenting on forms of punishment that involve the soul and
body—such as dislocation, war, and confinement. As a dance with activist roots, butoh—and by extension Kokoro Dance's production of *Rage*—
uses an internal and creative process to cope with the residual legacy of the
American occupation of Japan after World War II and the internment of
Japanese North Americans.[24] In her book *Bodies That Matter*, Judith Butler wrestles with notions of power and control by specifically citing Michel
Foucault: "The man described for us, whom we are invited to free, is already
in himself the effect of a subjection [*assujettissement*] much more profound

than himself. A 'soul' inhabits him and brings him to existence, which is itself a factor in the mastery that power exercises over the body."[25] Despite a seeming indebtedness and preoccupation with Foucault, Butler also seems uneasy with such a conclusion, questioning whether his efforts "fail to account for not only what is *excluded* from the economies of discursive intelligibility that he describes, but what *has to be excluded* for those economies to function as self-sustaining systems?"[26] By figuratively performing acts related to the internment, Kokoro Dance is able to temporarily challenge the "economies of discursive intelligibility," such as the preference for Eurocentric bodies and practices, or the exclusive and violent qualities of Western imperialism, while opening up possibilities for a new kind of subject formation. Perhaps butoh could be seen and understood as a particular embodiment that actively resists the soul's own subjection, even while revealing parts of itself and drawing attention to the exclusion of the enemy alien body.

Ironically, the Japanese translation and equivalent for *kokoro* is "heart," "soul," and "spirit," which makes sense given Jay Hirabayashi's reflection on his first experience training with Kazuo Ohno himself. The choreographer recalls being in the room with the teacher and twenty other students from Brazil, Spain, Portugal, France, the United States, and Canada. For an hour, Kazuo read poems and talked to his students. Hirabayashi recalls the moment just before the students got up to dance. "In the space between good and evil, Kazuo Ohno said, is the source of *love*. Then he asked us to get up and dance the source of *love*."[27] In many ways, drawing attention to his father's plight was *an act of love*, one that allowed Japanese redress to have a representative voice on theatrical stages. In doing so, Jay Hirabayashi provides literal and figurative space to reconfigure the subjective identity of "enemy aliens." Perhaps his open silent scream and tormented facial features in *Rage* are meant to express the anguish and *love* in the Japanese Canadian *soul*. This resistance to the external, racializing subjection imposed by the U.S. government manifested as Gordon Hirabayashi's resistance to the exclusion and the containment imposed upon his very own body and soul. After all, butoh evolved, at least partly, as a reaction to the American bombing of Hiroshima, a very traumatic event. By extension, Jay Hirabayashi's butoh dance expresses the lingering trauma from such large-scale atrocities while reclaiming the soul and resisting further subjection.

Butoh as practiced by Kokoro Dance works against the grain of commercial dance culture, which often values highly kinetic and overly adrenal-
ized bodies over old, frail-looking or "grotesque" bodies. The dance scholar
Samantha Mehra describes Kokoro's work as countercultural: a place where
youth and beauty are not valued. Instead, she argues, "the butoh-inspired
focus on emotional integrity and internal imagery override a demand for
thin, young, pleasant bodies."[28] In many ways, Kokoro Dance's butoh-
driven works may be seen as somewhat "grotesque," yet ironically this outsider status and distance also provide the company's choreographer with
enough distance from which to critique the values of mainstream culture,
which have sought to *racialize* and *otherize* Japanese Canadians.

Sunyata: HOMAGE TO THE HOLY LAND

Arguably, one of the most enduring works from Kokoro Dance's repertoire
is *Sunyata* (1997)—a trilogy composed of *Zero to the Power* (1989), *Aeon*
(1990), and *Elysian Fields* (1997). Together, *Sunyata* represents the depth
of Hirabayashi's interest in Buddhist philosophy, butoh aesthetics, and the
world literary canon. In an interview with the founders, Hirabayashi takes
inspiration from the world's literary canon and describes *Sunyata* as "a
Christian story based on Dante's *Inferno*, which of course references heaven
and hell within a Christian cosmology. But we call it *Sunyata* because it's a
philosophical principle of emptiness. In our own minds, it was about taking
Christian concepts and placing them alongside a Buddhist framework."[29]

In *Zero to the Power*, dancers pay homage to the fallen angels in *Inferno*
from the first section of Dante's *Divine Comedy*. The first scene opens with
dancers moving in unison. Together, they face the back of the stage, but
soon, they turn to face the audience by lunging deeply into second position. Here, their collective journey into hell and purgatory begins as each
dancer portrayed a character featured within Dante's stark and gruesome
world. The flat-footed, endless jumping sections are rhythmic, controlled,
and spirited but also mechanical in tone. Hirabayashi and Bourget use this
rigorous repetition of movements almost as a trademark of Kokoro Dance.
At times, the repetition gives the dance an inimitable trance-like quality. As
the scene progresses, the performers find themselves in a "mud-pit," a deep
square sandbox located upstage that actually contains a cold and sloppy
mixture of watery mud. They slither in-and-out of the pit, as if coming out

of the fiery, molten lava that symbolizes the depths of hell. In this scene, the dancers wear only undergarments: men bare their chests, and women bare their breasts. While this kind of minimalism and sensuality is quite familiar to Kokoro audiences, the aura of naked dancing bodies is heightened further by the presence of dripping mud that transforms moving bodies into primal beings. Together, the performers become an ensemble of anthropomorphized demons or animal-like humans who attempt to find their way from damnation and purgatory to salvation.

In the second segment, *Aeon*, Jay Hirabayashi and Barbara Bourget, dancing by themselves, manage to transform back into the more recognizable butoh-esque body covered in chalk-white rice powder. At first, they stand apart from each other, arms raised above their heads, open as if wanting to transmit a vital human message. Each dancer stands on opposite ends of the stage from the other and then moves toward the other by taking painfully slow and almost imperceptible micro-steps. The scene tests one's patience and takes seemingly forever for the two dancers to meet. As they become intimately close, the tension heightens as audiences anticipate their impending embrace. Just as their bodies are about to touch, both dancers pivot unexpectedly and literally pass each other like ships in the night, leaving viewers on an anticlimactic note.

The ending scene features the two dancers atop raised platforms comprised of loose, wooden planks. They fall backward from standing position: each body smacks the wood with a sharp sound that echoes throughout the theater. Shaking uncontrollably, they mimic each other's convulsions. The white rice powder covering their bodies drifts into the air, leaving a trace of ghostly dust. In this fantastic duet, art imitates life. The husband-and-wife team leaves this world as they entered it, but now as otherworldly figures present for all to see. The sharp sound of smacking bodies continues as the lights dim and blackness engulfs the room.

In the third segment of *Sunyata*, the dancers exude a more whimsical and graceful movement style, reminiscent of Bourget's training in classical ballet.[30] The finale, *Elysian Fields*, conjures ideas of Elysium in Greek mythology—the place where heroes and redeemed souls are rested. Anchored by universal characters seen throughout *Inferno*, and followed by the ironic, counterromantic butoh imagery in *Aeon*, the third segment closes *Sunyata* on a more hopeful and inspiring note. Dancers descend, literally and

FIGURE 3.1. Jay Hirabayashi and Barbara Bourget in *Rage* and *The Believer* (photo by Peter Eastwood)

figuratively, from the sky. One by one, they walk down a set of stairs wearing long, translucent, ivory-colored *chiton* (Greek tunics). Almost androgynous in appearance, the dancers begin running around the stage in a circular fashion: their celebratory dance is mildly reminiscent of Isadora Duncan's bare-footed salon performances at the fin de siècle.

For the closing scene of *Elysian Fields* Jay Hirabayashi returns onstage, once again covered in mud. His character is set apart from the others, who appear to be more emancipated dancing characters. Eventually, Hirabayashi seems to be released from eternal damnation as a jazz-inspired sound score full of horns and electro-acoustic drumbeats fill the air. Hirabayashi stands alone center stage. Powerful, muscular, and independent, he shakes his head back and forth, punching to the music in a manner that is controlled yet speaks to wild abandon. He shakes his body as if convulsing, and the white rice powder drifting into the air looks like dust particles under the house lights. The music continues loudly as the lights dim slowly over the bold, near-naked figure. Seen together, these three dance pieces represent the aesthetic range of Kokoro Dance's repertoire, which draws upon a distinct fusion of Japanese butoh, modern dance, and contemporary ballet.

As an embodied practice with the potential to engage in cultural activism, butoh has provided Jay Hirabayashi with the means to critique the cultural hegemony foregrounding the establishment of multicultural policies by creating choreographies that speak to the relationship of citizens to their homes and geography. Upon reflection, *Rage* provided a platform from which to speak about Japanese internment and the displaced body stripped of land; *Sunyata*, with its tripartite structure, provided a platform from which to speak about forbidden or holy land—whether that manifests as a kinetic exploration into purgatory, heaven, or imagined utopia. For Kokoro Dance the exploration of self in relation to land and the reclamation of soul, body, and spirit remains paramount to a progressive yet complex "Asian Canadian cultural activism" that seeks to disable, however temporary, the forceful acts of subjection and abjection. As one of Vancouver's most established contemporary dance companies, Kokoro Dance has offered a training ground for the next generation of dance artists. The company has hired, mentored, and provided performance opportunities for up-and-coming dance choreographers, such as Alvin Tolentino, who performed regularly with Kokoro Dance before founding his own company,

Co.ERASGA Dance. Since then, Tolentino has created a body of dance works that reflect his own immigrant experience and desire to be recognized as a gay, Asian male in the contemporary dance world.

Field: Land is the belly of man: NOSTALGIA FOR THE HOMELAND

Born in Manila, Philippines, Alvin Tolentino was introduced to the folkloric dances of his homeland. His family immigrated to Canada in 1983, and soon after he graduated from high school, Tolentino began formal dance training at the Royal Winnipeg Ballet's Training School (Winnipeg), York University (Toronto), SUNY Purchase (New York), and the Limon Institute (New York). Following this period of extensive training, Tolentino worked as a dance interpreter for many of the leading dance companies in Vancouver, including Kokoro Dance.

In 2000 Tolentino founded Co.ERASGA with a self-stated investment in creating work that addresses Filipino Canadian identity within a global context.[31] As someone whose choreographies are influenced by his cultural heritage and status as an immigrant living in Canada, Tolentino has carved a unique place for himself within the larger Eurocentric contemporary dance culture. Even as a relatively new dance company, Co.ERASGA has made considerable strides in terms of maintaining a visibility and presence within the local, national, and global dance networks.[32] Tolentino has reflected on his sense of identity and how his cultural heritage has informed his dance creations. At the age of twelve, he migrated from the Philippines to Canada and acknowledges experiencing a shock due to the new culture and new environment. He admits to "the longing for that physical statement to express the body and to celebrate the daily life. In the Philippines we dance on social occasions to interact with our friends and family."[33]

In many ways, the emergence of Co.ERASGA was also made possible through the values that evolved from the establishment of the Canadian Multiculturalism Act (1988). The values of this policy document were eventually turned into tangible resources and financial allocations for "diverse arts" groups and practices at the Canada Council for the Arts. Similar to those of Hirabayashi, the dance creations of Alvin Tolentino have benefited, in part, by the principles and policies recognized in Section 3 of the Multiculturalism Policy of Canada, which clearly acknowledged "the freedom of all members of Canadian society to preserve, enhance and share their cultural heritage" and the promotion of "understanding and creativity that arise from the interaction between individuals and communities of different origins."[34]

The language of the act is specific and attempts to create an inclusive realm where cultural heritage can be *preserved* (not assimilated, as were many Aboriginal Canadians), *enhanced* (rather than thwarted or excluded, as were many Chinese Canadians), and *shared* (rather than displaced and erased, as were many Japanese Canadians). The act is also specific to provoke "understanding," which in the Canadian context often means connection, empathy, and tolerance. The focus on "creativity" suggests that new ways of thinking and being are often evoked as individuals and communities of "different origins," birthplaces, or nationalities are encouraged to interact among themselves. Surely, theatrical dance, with its ability to bring people of "different origins" together in the same space, would qualify as a multicultural endeavor capable of creating a space to "preserve, enhance and share" one's cultural heritage, or at least representations of one's cultural heritage.

These values described above became part of the discourse and rhetoric surrounding multicultural arts practices and resulted from the realization that emerging and diverse companies have been historically underrepresented and underfunded at the national level. As argued by Andrea Monike Fatona in her dissertation, "the bulk of Council funding was allocated to large organizations and detrimental to small, emerging and emergent organizations. Barriers also existed that hindered the ability of individual applicants such as emerging and racialized artists to gain access."[35] Despite some resistance from those wishing to uphold the status quo, there was a growing need to acknowledge and embrace new cultural practices and communities in Canada's funding structure. This recognition lead to the establishment of the Equity Office of the Canada Council for the Arts in 1991, which had a deliberate mandate of "maintaining a strategic focus on supporting Canadian artists of African, Asian, Middle Eastern, Latin American or mixed racial heritage, and their artistic practices."[36] In 2002, shortly after its incorporation as a nonprofit society, Co.ERASGA Dance successfully applied for funding administered for Capacity-Building Grants available through the Equity Office of the Canada Council. With these additional funds, artistic director Alvin Tolentino began building an administrative structure for his vision by renting office space, hiring a general manager, and seeking other sources of financial support from local, regional, and federal funding bodies.[37]

A year before the company received its first major Capacity Grant, Tolentino was commissioned to create a new work for Ballet Philippines, resulting in *Field 1*, a work for five male dancers. *Field 1* coincided with the plight of Filipino rice farmers in his native homeland to preserve and share the natural landscapes within the province of Ifugao, which contains a mountainous region of rice terraces. In 2001 the terraces were inscribed on the list of World Heritage in Danger; on UNESCO's website, the site at Ifugao is described as two-thousand-year-old rice fields located in the high mountains. As a sacred tradition and knowledge handed down for generations, the harvesting of rice terraces dates back to the precolonial period, expresses the harmony between humans and the environment, and continues to evolve as a living landscape in the Philippine Cordilleras.[38]

Years later, the group show *Field 1* was reconfigured as a longer interdisciplinary solo performance, choreographed and performed by Alvin Tolentino, and retitled *Field: Land is the belly of man*, becoming a personal homage to the agrarian lifestyles, his home country, and the relationship between humans, food, and nature. It is a dance that speaks to the changing environmental circumstances and, more broadly, the struggle to maintain traditional farming practices in the midst of globalizing and industrializing forces. Similar to Jay Hirabayashi's *Rage*, which alluded to the history of Japanese internment in North America, Alvin Tolentino's *Field: Land is the belly of man* is another dance work that connects cultural heritage to notions of geography and place. The show began as *Field 1*, a group work for male dancers at Ballet Philippines in Manila. When Tolentino returned to Canada after this experience, he subsequently began work on a reinterpreted solo dance of the same thematic material, tackling themes of homeland, agriculture, and the plight of the rice farmer. The production premiered on May 12 and 13, 2005, at the Scotiabank Dance Centre in Vancouver.[39]

Field: Land is the belly of man brought together contemporary choreography alongside film, sound design, props, and costume into a complete mise-en-scène.[40] The performance begins with Tolentino walking onstage, wearing ivory-colored clothing. He moves toward an actual pot of boiling water, heated by a portable Bunsen burner placed atop a trolley cart. With an outstretched arm he lifts the pot's lid, and the scent of fresh rice emanates throughout the theater. Soon he begins stirring the water with a wooden

FIGURE 3.2. Alvin Tolentino in *Field: Land is the belly of man* (photo by Steven Lemay, courtesy of Alvin Erasga Tolentino and Co.ERASGA Dance)

spoon and then brings some rice up to his mouth to taste. For the first and only time in the show, Tolentino spoke a few words in Tagalog, gesturing toward an undeniable interconnectedness between language, culture, and territory. Suddenly Tolentino moves upstage right in a lithe and supple manner as if brought to life by the presence of the audience.

Ted Hamilton's music set the mood for the kinesthetic journey, and impending feelings of turmoil, celebration, and hardship are brought to the fore. A square light emerges downstage left, and the lone dancer moves into this space. The words of Paul Claudel, a diplomat who spent years as consul in China, are projected over the loudspeaker, paying homage to the life of the farmer. In the fourth scene a video created by Tad Armitanio and D-Anne Kuby-Trepanier and projected on the large screen presents the image of a falling cascade of rice grains. The soundscape mimics this image as crackling and dropping sounds of little hard nuggets of a golden harvest fill the theater.

Tolentino turns to face the back wall and video screen and crouches in order to pick up a triangular straw hat. Eventually Tolentino turns to face the audience, now rising so that his shadow can be seen against the backdrop video of cascading rice. The image was arresting and confirmed the show's twinned themes of man/land, man/rice, culture/place. Perhaps the most climactic moment in the show occurs when real rice grains fall from the sky. A steady stream of pearly white kernels descends upon the stage, creating a golden mound that almost touches the audience's feet. Near the end, the tone lightens as the music becomes more upbeat. Tolentino takes his straw hat and begins a sensuous dance, perhaps not what one might expect from a rice farmer, and yet the transformation of the farmer into a spiritual being capable of dancing and celebrating life onstage is acceptable. By now, an image of four enlarged rice kernels begins to twirl on the same screen where the cascades of rice once fell. Tolentino takes his hat and begins to fill it from the mound of rice. He flips the kernels in the air like popcorn flying in the wind and shakes the kernels with great ease and purpose. The last image offered in *Field: Land is the belly of man*, faces of farmers projected on the screen, is accompanied by the sound of birds chirping and provides all the reminders of life on land. They are the real farmers who lived and worked among the rice fields of Ifugao, and it was in their belly that this dance was born and made.

Field: Land is the belly of man addresses the ways in which humans have become increasingly detached from agrarian lifestyles, their mother tongues, and more traditional ways of living. Perhaps the words "belly of man" in the show's title refer to one's center of gravity as a metaphoric connection to one's homeland and nature itself. Tolentino succeeds in representing the struggles not only of the Filipino farmers but also of those around the world who witness environmental degradation. *Field: Land is the belly of man* makes use of accessible and almost pedestrian vocabulary, even though the choreography is decidedly grounded and labor intensive. The use of swinging arms, bent knees, and motions of plowing and tilling the soil are reminiscent of Ted Shawn's earliest works that explored male archetypes and the gestures associated with labor.

The dramatic quality of the show is heightened as the audience follows the rice farmer—albeit transformed into a dancing figure—through a non-linear journey that unfolds in rhythmic and unexpected ways. The simple use of a straw hat conjures images of another time and place, and yet the world of the rice paddy as seen on the video is juxtaposed with highly theatrical and modernist elements. James Proudfoot's lighting is minimal yet effective. He lights areas on the stage in rectangular boxes with clearly defined edges, which act as playing spaces and corridors for Tolentino to travel within. The lighted areas also invite the audience to look for a particular kind of critical engagement with the work. Similar to Bertolt Brecht's *verfremdungseffeckt*, more commonly known as alienation or estrangement effect,[41] the fabrication and artifice of the stage is apparent so that audiences relate to the rice farmer on emotional and critical levels, as well as empathizing while questioning his plight and his struggle. The show provides a gentle reminder about the mass industrial machinations that often create unbearable working conditions in less-developed countries while impacting natural landscapes and the environment.

In many ways, the dance provided by Tolentino is politically intertwined with identity politics. In the past, he has been deliberate in ensuring that his Filipino identity foregrounds his dance creation, revealing that audiences are also curious about the relationship. As he states, "There's a great interest among the public as to how this gay man-of-colour can and has contributed to the Western art world while sustaining his Asian heritage and working on political and contemporary issues." Interested as he is in his Asian roots, Tolentino believes that "the next decade will be a time for artists to defy issues of gender, ethnicity, and disciplinary boundaries."[42] Taking into consideration the intersectionality of culture, ethnicity and gender can inform how a reading of Tolentino's dance can be directly linked back to his homeland.

Yutian Wong describes how literary studies and its methods have affected readings of the dancing body—the latter reconfigured as *texts* that can be *read*—and yet she gestures toward the shortcoming of literary studies to deal adequately with the evaluation or execution of corporeal technique."[43] While my reading of the choreography provides a "reading" of the concept embedded in *Field: Land is the belly of man*, the corporeal text itself must be understood within the larger schema and politics of multicultural funding in Canada. In essence, why is it so important to have a dancing Asian farmer as the featured character onstage? To complement Yutian

Wong's problematizing of corporeal technique, it could be useful to think about the *matter* inherent in bodies, or the fact that "the materiality of the body is not to be taken for granted, for in some sense it is acquired, constituted, through the development of morphology."[44] Further to this idea, Butler suggests that "within Lacanian view, language, understood as rules of differentiation based on idealized kinship relations, is essential to the development of morphology."[45] Tolentino's dancing body must then be understood in relation to the manner in which it materially manifests onstage as well as the manner in which it manifests as a socially constructed identity.

The fact that Tolentino's dance practice is supported through the multicultural values and racial rhetoric of the Equity Office of the Canada Council; the fact that the choreographer is a self-described "gay man of colour"— intersecting with the politics of the Filipino rice farmer's plight—provide additional meaning to the material, dancing body. Thus any reading of the dance must be understood by the literal morphology that precedes it. In essence, the gravitas of the dance creation stems from the fact that land is central to the lives of rural, rice-farming peoples. By gesturing toward his homeland, Tolentino conjures not only nostalgia but also the complicated agricultural program implemented by President Ferdinand Marcos through the work at the International Rice Research Institute (IRRI) in Los Banos. This is inextricably linked to issues of mass production, food export, and Third World economies.[46] The latter become revealed in the First World as Canadian multicultural arts funding supports the preservation of cultural heritage and artists such as Alvin Tolentino take up the challenge.

The practice of Jay Hirabayashi of Kokoro Dance and Alvin Tolentino of Co.ERASGA can be seen as a part of a growing field of study broadly construed as "Asian Canadian studies." In particular, this chapter has attempted to position Asian Canadian dance as a heterogeneous field that manifests in different forms and aesthetics, and yet the works examined here seem to share a preoccupation with the relationship between body, geography, and place. For Jay Hirabayashi, butoh becomes a self-referential form from which to examine the Japanese internment and the displacement of bodies during World War II. Additionally, *Rage* contributes to a politically charged Asian Canadian "cultural activism" that provides a counterpoint to beautiful young or idealized bodies, temporarily transcending the abjected status of Japanese Canadians in search of "bodies that matter."[47] The show places the Japanese body and the postmodern butoh aesthetics in service of social justice. For Alvin Tolentino, the exploration of migration and sense of self in relation to the broader society has always been a preoccupation. *Field: Land is the belly of man* is an extension of state-sanctioned, multicultural policies and funding. By taking up the challenge of representing himself as Filipino Canadian, he is able to bring attention to a homeland where agrarian lifestyles are simultaneously being tested, protected, and revered. His works become conflated with his racialized and sexualized identity, elements that complicate the reading of his material body.

Kokoro Dance and Co.ERASGA Dance are two of the many Asian Canadian dancer companies that contribute to and benefit from the unique and heterogeneous multicultural Canadian dance scene. At this time, it seems premature to overly determine or cluster such artists into one particular category simply because of their cultural heritage, although it has become clear that personal, familial, and cultural identity often intersect with notions of geography, land, and place. In closing, Hirabayashi and Tolentino are contemporary dance artists, first and foremost, whose somatic and artistic practice allows them to explore issues related to their cultural heritage. Partly spurred by multicultural policies and by proximity of Vancouver as the gateway to the Asia Pacific, their work gestures to the cultural and economic ties between Asia and North America, potentially expanding and challenging the limited view of contemporary dance as a European or Euro-American construction. The work of Jay Hirabayashi of Kokoro Dance and Alvin Tolentino of Co.ERASGA Dance reveals the somatic possibilities of expressing the trauma and resilience of the displaced body and the potential nostalgia that results from sharing the history of agrarian lifestyles and traditions with twenty-first-century audiences.

NOTES

1. Recent scholarship includes Eleanor Ty, *Unfastened: Globality and Asian North American Narratives* (Minneapolis: University of Minnesota Press, 2010); Roy Miki, *In Flux: Transnational Shifts in Asian Canadian Writing* (Edmonton: NeWest Press, 2011); and Larissa Lai, *Slanting I, Imagining We: Asian Canadian Literary Production in the 1980s and 1990s* (Waterloo: Wilfred Laurier University Press, 2014).

2. Su-Feh Lee of battery opera, Wen Wei Wang of Wen Wei Dance, rising independent Jung-Ah Chung, and Ziyian Kwan of dumb instrument Dance are some of the most active Asian Canadian dance artists working in Vancouver. Peter Chin of Tribal Crackling Wind, Emily Cheung of Little Pear Garden Collective,

and Denise Fujiwara of Fujiwara Dance Inventions are some of the most active artists in Toronto.

3. Multiculturalism was initiated as official policy by Prime Minister Pierre Elliott Trudeau in 1971, included in Section 27 of the Canadian Charter of Rights and Freedoms in 1982, and enacted as the Canadian Multiculturalism Act in 1988 by Prime Minister Brian Mulroney.

The Canada Council for the Arts was established in 1957 as the nation's federal funding body for the arts. It is a Crown Corporation of the government of Canada. The Equity Office of the Canada Council began in 1991, with a particular mandate to support artists of Asian, Latino, and African descent.

4. For a definition of "abjection," see Karen Shimakawa, *National Abjection: The Asian American Body Onstage* (Durham, NC: Duke University Press, 2002), 8–11.

5. I am suggesting that choreographers such as Mary Wigman, Martha Graham, Ruth St. Denis, and Ted Shawn are part of a lineage that often positions modern dance as a strictly European or Euro-American construction even though many of these artists borrowed from Asian or "Oriental" sources. Arguably, their fame is partly due to their rootedness within large urban centers with cultural capital: New York or LA or Berlin. See Joseph H. Mazo, *Prime Movers: The Makers of Modern Dance in America* (Hightstown, NJ: Princeton Book Co., 2000).

6. Jay Hirabayashi, interview by the author, May 25, 2012.

7. Founded in 1986, the company takes its name from the Japanese word *kokoro*, which translates into "soul," "spirit," or "heart." See Kokoro Dance, http://www.kokoro.ca.

8. In addition to his tasks as butoh choreographer, dancer, and teacher, Jay Hirabayashi produces the Vancouver International Dance Festival, which began as the Vancouver International Butoh Festival in 1998.

9. Experimental Dance and Music (EDAM), "About EDAM," http://www.edamdance.org/pages/aboutedam.html, accessed February 5, 2015.

10. *Hirabayashi v. United States*, 320 U.S. 81 (1943), U.S. Supreme Court, http://supreme.justia.com/cases/federal/us/320/81/case.html, accessed February 15, 2015.

11. Ibid.

12. Roy Miki, *Redress: Inside the Japanese Canadian Call for Justice* (Vancouver: Raincoast Books, 2004), 2.

13. Ibid., 9.

14. Gordon Hirabayashi, quoted in Miki, *Redress*, 174.

15. Canadian Multiculturalism Act, Government of Canada, R.S.C., 1985, c. 24 (4th Supp.), http://laws-lois.justice.gc.ca/eng/acts/C-18.7, accessed February 15, 2015.

16. Andrea Monike Fatona, "'Where Outrage Meets Outrage': Racial Equity at the Canada Council for the Arts (1989–1999)" (PhD diss., University of Toronto, 2011), 104.

17. Xiaoping Li, *Voices Rising: Asian Canadian Cultural Activism* (Vancouver: University of British Columbia Press, 2007), 2.

18. There is not much left in old Japantown, due to forced evacuation during World War II. As of 2014, few shops remain, although the Vancouver Japanese Language School and Japanese Hall (1906) is still operating. The description of *Rage* is based on its premiere at the Firehall Theatre in 1986.

19. Jay Hirabayashi, quoted in Eury Chang, "Canada's First Generation of Butoh: Kokoro Dance Celebrates 25 Years as Contemporary Butoh Pioneer," *Ricepaper/Asian Canadian Arts and Culture* 16, no. 1 (Spring 2011): 35.

20. Shimakawa, *National Abjection*, 10.

21. Ibid.

22. Yutian Wong, *Choreographing Asian America* (Middletown, CT: Wesleyan University Press, 2010), 16.

23. Shimakawa, *National Abjection*, 13–15.

24. Butoh is said to have evolved in post–World War II Japan, partly in response to the American bombing of Hiroshima and the growing disinterest in emulating Western or traditional Japanese forms such as Noh. Kazuo Ohno and Tatsumi Hijikata are credited as its founders. In 1993 Jay Hirabayashi and Barbara Bourget saw Kazuo Ohno and his son Yoshito perform *Water Lilies* at the Moore Theatre in Seattle. Two years later, Hirabayashi traveled to Tokyo to study with the father-and-son team.

25. Foucault, quoted in Judith Butler, *Bodies That Matter: On the Discursive Limits of "Sex"* (New York: Routledge, 1993), 33–34.

26. Butler, *Bodies That Matter*, 35.

27. Jay Hirabayashi, "In Memory of Kazuo Ohno," *Ricepaper/Asian Canadian Arts and Culture* 15, no. 3 (Fall 2010): 52–53.

28. Samantha Mehra, "Heart, Soul and Spirit: An Ethnography of the Kokoro Dance Body" (paper presented at the annual meeting of the Canadian Society for Dance Studies, St. John's, Newfoundland, June 17–21, 2008), 3, http://www.csds -sced.ca/English/Resources/SamanthaMehra.pdf, accessed August 15, 2014.

29. Interview with Jay Hirabayashi and Barbara Bourget, January 26, 2011.

30. Before meeting her future dance partner and husband Jay Hirabayashi, Barbara Bourget trained as a scholarship student at the Royal Winnipeg Ballet and then danced professionally in Montreal with Les Grands Ballets Canadiens.

31. Co.ERASGA, "About Us," http://www.companyerasgadance.ca/en/about _us/about_the_company/, accessed February 5, 2015.

32. Alvin Tolentino's Co.ERASGA Dance has toured its repertoire within Canada and to France, Venezuela, Philippines, Singapore, and Belgium. The company has received support through Canada Council for the Arts (Equity Office, Dance Section) and the Department of Foreign Affairs to embark on tours abroad.

33. Tolentino, quoted in Li, *Voices Rising*, 234.

34. Canadian Multiculturalism Act.

35. Fatona, "Where Outreach Meets Outrage," 34.

36. "About the Equity Office," http:// http://canadacouncil.ca/equity-office /about-the-equity-office, accessed February 5, 2015.

37. Between 2004 and 2007 I worked as the general and tour manager for Co.ERASGA Dance Society, writing all the grants and preparing budgets for three levels of government. During this time, we received money from the Dance Section and the Equity Office of the Canada Council, BC Arts Council, City of Vancouver, and the Department of Foreign Affairs.

38. "Rice Terraces of the Philippine Cordilleras," UNESCO, World Heritage List, http://whc.unesco.org/en/list/722, accessed February 5, 2015.

39. During a year-long "artist-in-residence" stint at Scotiabank Dance Centre, Alvin Tolentino performed *Field: Land is the belly of man* to public and critical acclaim. The fundraising show in collaboration with the Philippine Women Centre of BC—titled "The Purple Rose Campaign"—helped raise money to bring awareness to and stop the trafficking of Filipina women and children. Co.ERASGA subsequently was invited to Singapore in May 2012 to participate as the only Asian Canadian dance company during the Asian Arts Mart. I attended as a delegate representing Co.ERASGA Dance. *Field* remains the most widely toured dance in the company's repertoire.

40. The following paragraphs document my observations of *Field: Land is the belly of man* (performed on May 12 and 13, 2005, at the Scotiabank Dance Centre—Canada's flagship dance facility located in Vancouver) and the subsequent video of those performances.

41. Bertolt Brecht, "Alienation Effects in Chinese Acting," 1935, in *Theatre/ Theory/Theatre*, ed. Daniel Gerould (New York: Applause Theatre & Cinema Books, 2000), 457.

42. Tolentino, quoted in Li, *Voices Rising*, 236.

43. Y. Wong, *Choreographing Asian America*, 22.

44. Butler, *Bodies That Matter*, 69.

45. Ibid.

46. Luis H. Francia, *A History of the Philippines: From Indios Bravos to Filipinos* (New York: Overlook Press, 2014), 244.

47. Judith Butler speaks of "bodies that matter" in her book of the same name; she uses feminist theory to build a case about marginalized bodies: i.e., gay people, women. Here, I use the term to refer to a once marginalized, but increasingly active and politicized, Asian Canadian body that has become *one that matters*.

4

"Started in the Streets . . ."

Criminalizing Blackness and the Performance of
Asian American Entrepreneurship on America's
Best Dance Crew, *Season 1*

BRIAN SU-JEN CHUNG

> I don't think it's too outlandish to suggest that MTV might have
> manipulated the results so the battle could have a certain "look." Two
> (mostly) Asian American crews killing it all the way, then making it to
> the finals? Perhaps MTV thought America wasn't quite ready for it.
> —Angry Asian Man, "Crazy for Kaba Modern"

Up until the penultimate episode of the first season of *Randy Jackson Presents America's Best Dance Crew (ABDC)*, a reality gamedoc where hip-hop
dance crews battle for a grand prize of $100,000, Asian American journal-
ists, bloggers, and fans anticipated a finale between the two Asian American dance crews, the Jabbawockeez and Kaba Modern. Throughout the
first season, Asian American fans discussed online their excitement of seeing two Asian American crews being acknowledged week-to-week by the
judges for their comprehensive knowledge of hip-hop dance styles and for
their proficiency in executing choreographed dance routines. This public
acknowledgment of the two crews as "good dancers" and their advancement
throughout the show appealed to Asian American fans because it held the
national promise of meritocracy and national healing. Prior to *ABDC*, Asian
Americans had appeared as contestants and judges on Fox Broadcasting
Company's popular reality show dance competition, *So You Think You Can
Dance*, wherein dancers are tested on their knowledge of American and
international dance styles. Similarly, *ABDC* tested the proficiency of dance
crews based on expectations of professional hip-hop dancers—athleticism,

entertainment value, comprehensive knowledge of hip-hop dance styles (as seen in hip-hop music videos of the past and present), and the ability to dance in unison to choreography. Fan interpretation of the transformative potential of *ABDC* was further emphasized by the diversity of U.S. hip-hop dance scenes while honoring an ongoing legacy of African American culture as national culture in weekly challenges. Together, the show's pluralism and the critical mass of Asian Americans on the show made it appear as if Asian American excellence in hip-hop dancing was the embodied proof of national progress.

The elimination of Kaba Modern during the penultimate episode, however, opened up new conversations regarding Asian American viewer excitement and celebration over their recent national visibility. In contrast to the weekly response to Kaba Modern, Status Quo was a black crew from Boston who were, at times, criticized by the judges for performances that lacked precision or for being overly reliant upon "stunts" (flips). In response to Asian American fans of *ABDC* who flooded his inbox with possible conspiracies over the dismissal of Kaba Modern, Angry Asian Man (real name Phil Yu) of the popular Asian American–interest blog of the same name, questioned the show's judgment of which hip-hop crews deserved to compete in the finale given the consistent success of the two Asian American crews.[1] Angry Asian Man responded by inviting the readership of his popular blog to consider whether MTV purposely rigged the finale to feature an Asian American crew and a black crew in order to suggest that emphasizing the racial authenticity of hip-hop culture as black, urban, and poor in the season finale would generate better ratings despite the merits of Kaba Modern.[2] What does it mean however, to critique MTV for selectively placing Asian American and African American racial difference in tension without extending this critique to also include an analysis of how the African American subject is used to enforce the myth of meritocracy and Asian American "equal participation" on the show? As black cultural critics such as Nicole Fleetwood and Uri McMillian have argued, such national and visual narratives of meritocracy rely on antiblack discourses produced by national public policies and the use of black performers to give meaning to such policies.[3] With that said, what happens if we were to read Angry Asian Man's comment as positioning blackness as a form of "entitlement," an injury against the meritocratic pathway toward Asian American national belonging?

I open with this vignette to discuss how *ABDC* is an important site for exploring how reality television mediates the cultural meanings of hip-hop dance as it relates to neoliberalism and antiblack discourses that enable, but also constrain, an existing Asian American politics of citizenship—a constantly contested question of national belonging that takes place upon a cultural terrain.[4] In response to claims made that Asian American interest in hip-hop culture is a form of "blackface," scholarship on Asian Americans and hip-hop culture argues that hip-hop music's reflections on African American oppression serves as political knowledge for Asian Americans to politicize their own racial identity through real or imagined solidarity and coalition building with black communities.[5] This chapter considers Asian American and African American relations within hip-hop cultural consumption, but through the lens of reality television and the neoliberal cultural logics its narrative conventions impart upon our knowledge of hip-hop dance and blackness. I argue that the winner, the subject of "the best," is a discourse of meritocracy centered specifically on the racial logics of work ethic and proficiency associated with professionalism. The liberal multicultural ethos that shaped the desires of Asian American fans in seeing two Asian American crews in the finale—a demand for the respect, inclusion, and "equality" of cultural differences—represents a much larger and worrisome desire driven by the idea that hip-hop dance is a career and that hip-hop dancing is a set of skills to be used for capitalist production in the marketplace. If hip-hop culture represents a counterhegemonic space for the assertion of politics and belonging, then Asian American fan responses to Kaba Modern's elimination encourages a more nuanced reading of antiblack discourses that pervade Asian American antiracist politics through hip-hop cultural practice even when Asian Americans claim their social and political equivalences to racial blackness.

Reflections such as these by Asian American journalists, bloggers, and fans demonstrate how the reality television show genre can circulate hegemonic meanings and discourses of race, citizenship, and national belonging for audiences. As a popular format of television programming, reality television is a "fusion of popular entertainment with a self-conscious claim to the discourse of the real."[6] Scholars of media studies suggest that reality television is not so much a mirror of real life but rather a genre with a narrative structure that reflects and produces political and economic imperatives such as the political rationality of neoliberal citizenship. Focusing on the format of makeover TV, Laurie Ouelette and James Hay emphasize how narrative conventions of "popular instruction" centered on "rehabilitat(ion)" and the "reform" of individuals follow neoliberal subject formation that paints people in need, such as welfare recipients, as possessing "poor and self-destructive behavior" (e.g., the myth of the black welfare queen) and as merely requiring "privatized services of self-care to help them remake themselves into self-sufficient citizens."[7] Neoliberal policies of reducing state aid for social welfare in favor of expanding military spending and corporate sponsorship, the deregulation of industry, and the public–private partnerships of governance produces a political rationality that citizens should bear responsibility for their own actions, of which "a mismanaged life, the neoliberal appellation for failure to navigate impediments to prosperity, becomes a new mode of depoliticizing social and economic powers."[8] Black feminist scholars and critical race theorists have demonstrated how this ongoing history of welfare reform policies, the criminalization of black reproductive health, and neoliberal citizenship is constituted through "killing the black body" and the constitution of blackness against the nation and its independent, tax-paying citizenry.[9] Thus, a specific racial logic supports the "self-improvement," meritocratic "bootstraps" throughout *ABDC*'s dramatic national narratives and brings forth the need for scholarship to analyze further how the show, as a specific genre of the cultural production of dance, participates in reproducing neoliberal antiblack narratives.

Although the contestants selected for *ABDC* are prescreened as proficient hip-hop dancers before they can even appear on the show, every episode dramatizes scenes wherein mental and physical rigor must be overcome to become a professional dancer in the commercial dance industry. The logic of the "makeover" pervades the first season of *ABDC*'s racial representations and constitutes and is constituted by the show's careful staging of hip-hop history as the rehabilitation of poor African American communities with a strong capitalist work ethic and entrepreneurial initiative. This is the dominant dramatic lens through which the "best" dance crew of America is decided, and a multicultural "imagined community" is attached to this notion of not only who can dance but also who can be a productive worker of commercial dance. This singular narrative of hip-hop history and culture defined by transforming black leisure into black enterprise is invoked by Asian Americans who express their own national belonging through a universalized neoliberal narrative of work ethic and individual empowerment—nowhere do we see another history of hip-hop.

ABDC's lessons on race and citizenship may come as no surprise. The theme of "social responsibility" has been part of MTV's mantra and integral to its programming. Beginning in the late 1980s and 1990s, MTV branded itself through countercultural and youth rebellion discourses as evidenced by its liberal political content of its news reporting, support for humanitarian and domestic social issues, and irreverence for social mores of public television broadcasting.[10] MTV's *The Real World*, a reality television show focused on the lives of seven strangers living in a home together, impressed upon audiences the network's brand as socially engaged. Jon Kraszewski writes that the show staged "real" conflicts and resolutions among the participants around racism and homophobia, albeit through liberal discourses of individuality that avoided altogether discussing structural racisms.[11] *ABDC*'s "teaching moment" on U.S. race relations lies in its instruction of minority inclusion made possible through the subjection of oneself to the normative cultural conduct of neoliberal citizenship, which in this case is expressed through the meritocratic language of (dance) professionalization. Although appearing as an abstract goal of finding gigs as a backup dancer or choreographer to a recording artist or learning what it takes mentally and physically to "make it" as a dancer in the commercial dance industry, professionalism, here, discursively exists as a cultural narrative of not only what it means to be black but also what it means to be an American, where demanding capitalist discipline becomes a cultural norm for racialized liberal multicultural inclusion.

On *ABDC*, the public memory of hip-hop dance is entrenched within normative discourses of neoliberal citizenship. Stripped of any reference to black intellectual and political discourse of black social dance, the conditions of possibility for hip-hop dance's blackness on *ABDC* are structured by a neoliberal narrative where African Americans become productive citizens by turning leisure into a billion-dollar entertainment industry.[12] With each dance performance and evaluation process, *ABDC* restages this scene of black inclusion through the rhetoric of professionalism wherein African American judges lend authenticity to their evaluation of what qualifies as dance while providing instruction and proof of black inclusion through a desire for capitalist discipline. It is this particular antiblack discourse that shapes the propriety that Asian American audiences address in their quest for citizenship.

The first part of this chapter examines how neoliberal logics of citizenship criminalize blackness. Second, I describe how the structure of the *ABDC* show—the challenges, the judges, and the evaluation process—shapes audiences perception of the show as "teaching moments" and follows MTV's existing programming. Third, I explore antiblackness discourse where blackness signals both "crime" and "meritocracy." This seemingly contradictory theme is a part of the same antiblack logic that reproduces black stereotypes that constitute normative neoliberal citizenship. Lastly, I show how these logics are present in the discursive practices of Asian American journalists' and bloggers' characterization of Asian American politics of national belonging. In doing so, I propose an investigation of antiblack discourses that emerge in Asian American politics of citizenship. There is urgency for this work as state violence in black life produces the discourses of "freedom" in our understandings of citizenship.

NEOLIBERALISM, NORMATIVE CITIZENSHIP, AND THE CRIMINALIZATION OF BLACKNESS

We can locate *ABDC*'s politics of racial inclusion within a broader political context of neoliberalism, which characterizes citizenship through and against the criminalization of blackness. Neoliberal political and economic policies, such as "welfare reform" and state subsidies to support business growth, present themselves as "neutral, managerial precepts of good government and efficient business operations,"[13] when, in fact, the aims of reducing the social safety net are directly tied to the expansion of corporate profits and increasing the vulnerability of poor and working-class people of color. In turn, an entitlement discourse constitutes normative citizenship within neoliberal regimes as "personal responsibility" and "independence" from state aid. The Personal Responsibility and Work Opportunity Reconciliation Act (1996) and Temporary Assistance for Needy Families (TANF) program (1996) generated workfare programs with the intent of ending reliance upon welfare. Lisa Duggan argues that these workfare programs, however, were connected to state subsidies aimed at increasing corporate growth through the expansion of the low-wage job market, into which welfare recipients were funneled. These reductions of government social costs were inextricably tied to increasing corporate accumulation and declining wages, job stability, and benefits. Welfare recipients, particularly poor women of color, are constructed within public debates on welfare reform as committing crimes against the nation for receiving and, allegedly, taking advantage of state aid. In spite of figures that demonstrate that black women do not disproportionately receive state aid in comparison to white women, stereotypes such as the black "welfare queen" persist in framing black women as a significant source in the nation's ongoing budgetary crisis.[14]

Crime is not just a metaphor to describe how anti-welfare discourse reproduces and reflects existing black stereotypes of "cultural pathology"; it also exists as a logic of white supremacy that maintains black motherhood requires state surveillance, intervention, and control. As feminist of color scholarship has shown, the War on Drugs and neoliberal welfare reform have sought and implemented punitive measures to punish black mothers who use drugs. The law professor Dorothy Roberts points out several cases where dozens of black women were criminally prosecuted by law enforcement for allegedly infecting their children with crack cocaine prenatally.[15] Roberts questions the criminal justice system's interest in protecting black children by asking to what extent the state has shown a commitment to providing safe prenatal health care for black mothers. Furthermore, she provides ample figures to show how drug and alcohol consumption prenatally, which is not racialized as black (read=white), is less likely to be treated as an issue that requires criminal justice intervention.[16] More recently, different proposed amendments to TANF, such as denying public assistance—housing, employment, education, and voting rights—to drug users and mandatory drug testing, reveal the extension of these logics that assume black criminality and the subsequent unconstitutionality of subjecting black bodies to the state surveillance.[17] INCITE, a national activist feminist of color organization, connects the criminalization of blackness to neoliberal citizenship by showing how these proposed bills construct tax payers as normative citizens against black drug users, who are seen as a financial drain on society and who require punishment to be remade into productive citizens.[18] Taken together, neoliberal citizenship is equated with white behavior, deliberately made distant to blackness, stereotyped as if these black bodies were receptacles of pathological behavior. *ABDC* portrayals of blackness, the performative visibility of black desire for rehabilitation, are discursively embedded within the show's historical narrative of hip-hop culture, performances of hip-hop dance, and politics of liberal multicultural inclusion. Work ethic and professionalism serve as metrics for how national inclusion and national healing are achieved.

INTRODUCING STREET DANCE AND *ABDC's* TEACHING MOMENTS

ABDC first aired in February 2008 and was not renewed by MTV after its seventh and final season in 2012 due to declining ratings.[19] Each season the show brought eight crews to compete in what was billed as a "street battle" competition for a grand prize of $100,000 and the title and trophy of "America's Best Dance Crew." Week-to-week, dance crews were given a thematic challenge to create original choreography to perform. The challenges were often based on knowledge of past and present dance trends (often, but not exclusively, black social dances) but also included incorporating narrative structures or a physical stunt (e.g., creating a human pyramid or incorporating an illusion or exercise) somewhere in their weekly choreography. The crew's precision during their performance, how in sync they were with each other, was also an important metric that judges used to evaluate a crew's skill. These gimmicks were phased out in favor of challenges based around performing choreography to the hit music of contemporary or legendary artists (e.g., Janet Jackson and Michael Jackson) or mimicking choreography as seen in their music videos.

During each show, *ABDC* provided a short montage of each remaining crew, updating audiences on how the contestants were physically and emotionally coping with challenges. The montages were filled with jump cuts of crews struggling to learn the choreography within the week timespan, feeling uncomfortable with unfamiliar dance styles, and dealing with ongoing personal issues, such as poverty, injuries, and family. Here, audiences are introduced to hip-hop dance as a career. Amateur dancers are shown learning to manage the rigors and expectations of commercial hip-hop dance. Through narrations by *ABDC*'s backstage correspondent and contestants themselves, contestants and audiences alike are treated to an inside look at the work ethic required of commercial hip-hop dancers who must persevere through (inter)personal drama in order to achieve their goal of being "America's Best Dance Crew" and the potential job opportunities that may follow. The authenticity of the show's portrayal of hip-hop and its pedagogical lessons are further impressed upon audiences and contestants by the panel of judges. In the first season, the African American hip-hop choreographer Shane Sparks, most notable for his choreography in the film *You Got Served*; the African American hip-hop recording artist Lil Mama; and the white recording artist and songwriter J. C. Chasez, of the multiplatinum-selling boy band 'N Sync, served as "native informants," with authority to evaluate the "cultural authenticity" and industry standards of the performances. Sparks and Lil Mama appear genuinely thrilled to see black crews performing black social dances, such as variations of booty popping (thrusting one's pelvic area and hips quickly in a forward and back motion), acrobatic flips, and body contortions, which they celebrate as part of the creativity and traditions of street dances that are not acknowledged as dance within the choreographic expectations of commercial hip-hop dance performance seen in music videos. While providing a space to showcase these moves is central to the show's narrative of liberal multicultural tolerance and exchange, judges evaluated its significance secondary to each crew's ability to "hit their steps" and choreograph preset routines as seen in music videos and live performances. The crews who received the least amount of audience votes per week are up for elimination in the following episode. Ultimately, the panel of judges had the final say in which of these two crews, based on their performance for that week and their final "dance-off," would no longer return to the competition.

The show's talent scouts held auditions in four major cities—Los Angeles, New York, Atlanta, and Chicago—to find the best talent from the four regions—West Coast, East Coast, Midwest, and South—that made up the show's geographic impression of America. In the first season, several of the chosen crews possessed their own twist on hip-hop dance that was loosely based on their regional affiliation. For example, Live in Color from Miami specialized in choreographing a regional variation of "booty dancing." ICONic, from New Jersey, were known for incorporating Broadway musical and choreographic aesthetics into their routines because of their proximity to New York City. From the same season, judges marked the all-white female crew representing the Midwest representatives as bringing "femininity" to hip-hop, but lacking "edge," an ambiguous term judges used to normalize hip-hop dance as black, urban, and, most importantly, nonwhite. Judges did not question the authenticity of the Asian American crews, but frequently lauded them for the precision in their hip-hop choreography involving intricate hand and arm moves, such as tutting.[20] All in all, "diversity," not just in terms of race and ethnicity but also gender, sexuality, geography, disability, or nation, was a consistent element that established the show's premise of multiculturalism throughout its seven-season run.

The show presented itself as an authentic portrayal of both underground hip-hop dance scenes and real-life experiences but also as a culturally transformative experience for audiences to learn about black expressive cultures and the reality of becoming a professional hip-hop dancer. For instance, J. C. Chasez was surprised by the diversity. Chasez notes, "When you look up on the stage, you see so many backgrounds. Even though we're getting exposed to the dance culture, we're also watching personal stories."[21] Chasez's claim reflects Sasha Torres's interpretation of Jane Feuer's conceptualization of the "ideology of liveness."[22] Television's proposed "immediate access and transmission of the real," Torres warns, mean that blackness can only find meaning in "the live," absent of "history and futurity."[23] *ABDC* gives the impression that the show is pushing the boundaries of existing reality television formats not only in its instruction of new cultural phenomena among young people but also its function as a history lesson and an unmediated presentation of a living culture. I would add that the "liveness" of this hip-hop history lesson demonstrates how "professionalism" becomes synonymous with a normative conduct of neoliberal citizenship.

When Karen and Howard Schwartz, the original creators of the show and most notably known for being global promoters of fitness and dance, developed the idea for *ABDC*, their only interest was to introduce hip-hop dance to a wider audience on television. Although the show was originally titled *World Moves*, slated for the public television network National Broadcasting Channel (NBC), Howard claims that they struggled for over five years to get the show on air because "people get it confused with all the bad elements that hip-hop present."[24] Although Howard does not qualify that statement further, we can presume that by "bad elements," Howard is referring to the conservative pundits that claim black youth, particularly the black rap artists on the radio, impart upon American audiences homophobic, misogynistic, and criminal behavior as if they were "unauthorized imports."[25]

Together, the show's judging process, the makeup of its contestants, and its presence on MTV make it a weekly teaching moment for an American audience on the possibility and pathways toward racial and social harmony. Hip-hop dance serves as an allegory and an everyday practice in the making of a multicultural America. The presence of a variety of regional dance styles alludes to a liberal multicultural ethos of tolerance and respect for diversity. But the challenges paint hip-hop dance styles as a common corporeal vernacular that everyone can master and that this mastery is evidence of the nation's willing inclusion of difference without assimilation into whiteness. This discursive unity is made possible by the fungibility of blackness in becoming a universalizing narrative of American meritocracy expressed through themes of individual initiative and the performance of one's desire to labor.

America's Best Dance Crew, SEASON 1: HIP-HOP ORIGINS NARRATIVES AS A TALE OF BLACK ENTREPRENEURSHIP AND SELF-SUFFICIENCY

In the first season, *ABDC* sets out to provide a historical lesson of hip-hop culture for audiences, which serves as an allegory for citizenship when framed solely as a performance of labor. The show depicts the pathways to liberal multicultural equality through contestants' willing subjection to the professionalization of hip-hop dance, framed as the meritocratic triumph of African Americans over what is portrayed as their own self-induced poverty. For instance, the opening montage during the "Live Audition" and the "Evolution of Street Dance Challenge" of the penultimate episode are important to analyze given that these episodes bookend the show and authoritatively impress upon audiences a triumphant national narrative of black economic mobility through entrepreneurship. This satisfying narrative is enabled through the depiction of black laboring dancing bodies on full display in both episodes.

At the beginning of the "Live Audition," a previously recorded clip of Jackson introducing street dance history, past and present, makes equivalent the history of hip-hop production and consumption, multiculturalism, and neoliberal citizenship. After Jackson describes his interests in giving exposure to dancers much the way he has with musicians, what follows are various clips of hip-hop dance with Jackson authoritatively narrating hip-hop's history: "Street dance is an incredible phenomenon. And it's not just in the clubs anymore. It's in music videos. It's on the big screen. It's on the web. Everywhere. But it started in the streets with crews battling against each other."[26] These representations of hip-hop commercialization visually depict a racially diverse and harmonious America that gradually over time is joined together through music, dance, and style. In the opening montage, there are stock clips of people dancing at night clubs and bars, video footage of hip-hop dance competitions and showcases, and then a clip from a music video starring multiplatinum-selling R&B recording artist Usher. When Jackson says, "it started in the streets with crews battling each other," the next several images show several men (most of whom are black) dancing. These images position hip-hop dance as originating in black communities. The visual portrayal of the black body in "the streets," however, sets up Jackson's linear narrative of the inevitable global and national commercial circulation of hip-hop culture and national unification. What is particularly problematic about this mediated narrative as historical record is that the signification of "America" relies upon excluding any meanings hip-hop may have within black and brown communities. The viewer's attention is focused on black experience as contained to "the live" and how the entrepreneurial development of one's cultural capital into a global commodity serves as a national teleology of equal access toward upward mobility and national belonging.[27]

My point in bringing up these representations is not to question the history of hip-hop's commercialization.[28] Nor is it to make any claims to what is "authentically" hip-hop based on categories of race or commercialization. Instead, my focus is on how the selective disclosure of black experiences and hip-hop dance in these montages reflect and affirm the cultural logics of neoliberal citizenship. On *ABDC*, hip-hop dance is neither a source of social meanings nor bodily movements that archive everyday black social and political experience. Hip-hop dancing is framed as the celebration and instilling of "proper" conduct associated with becoming a productive citizen: independence, personal responsibility, and work ethic. This time, *ABDC* constructs a linear narrative of the movement of black culture and black people from "the streets" to the mainstream through growing commercialization within entertainment industries. In the "Evolution of Street Dance Challenge," *ABDC* returns to the history of hip-hop told in the "Live Audition." The three remaining crews must perform their own rendition of the "iconic [dance] styles from the last thirty years."[29] Not only does each crew have to perform all the dance styles, but they also have to dance to the same music. Here, street dance evolution is reduced to three eras: popping, locking, and break dancing of the 1970s to the early 1980s; New Jack Swing of the late 1980s and early 1990s; and white boy bands at the turn of the millennium, as represented by the multiplatinum-selling 'N Sync.

The montage begins showing a grainy clip of a black male break-dancing outdoors and quickly moves to the first "evolution," visually represented by a brief clip from the music video of Salt-N-Pepa's "Push It." The music video "does the talking" as it shows Salt-N-Pepa performing and dancing on stage in front of fans. The quick shift from break dancing on the streets to performing on stage sets to public memory that hip-hop dance is a narrative where black leisure can easily become black enterprise. The movement of African Americans into mainstream American popular culture, the achievement of black national acceptance, occurs through their willingness, if not desire, to become professional, productive, laboring bodies. The shift away from hip-hop as black leisure, or nonproductivity, discursively crystalizes through the desirability of *ABDC*'s portrayal of hip-hop's multicultural present, featuring the five white men of 'N Sync in the final evolution of hip-hop dance: the music video to "Bye Bye Bye" from their 10x platinum album *No Strings Attached*.[30] The success of the album signaled a turning point in the evolution of the group's sound, in which they deliberately sought out the tempo and heavier bass lines of rhythm and blues and hip-hop.[31] *ABDC*'s bookending of hip-hop's present with 'N Sync, five white men whose musical and life "maturation" occurs through their engagement with black culture, provides an exceptionalist celebratory national narrative of cultural exchange and respect. This feel-good multiculturalism becomes common sense as it is articulated through the visibility of these financially successful white dancing bodies and the sounds that these bodies transmit. The montage and this challenge reiterate the expectations of the contestants to restage neoliberalism's antiblack discourse by continuously performing the event of black "personal responsibility" and productivity.

This desired outcome is echoed among the judges and the contestants, particularly the African American crews. The African American crews hail from urban cities—New York City, Boston, and Miami—but are depicted as experiencing the same circumstances of poverty tinged with a sentiment of despair. In the video clip about Status Quo, the crew from Boston, E-Knock, the official spokesperson of the crew, shares with audiences that they have "nothing at home" and that they "ain't trying to go back."[32] For them, dancing is a means of transcending poverty, and *ABDC* provides the professionalization to make that possible. In the "Crews Choice Challenge" episode, their longer introductory montage of their city shows the group taking the bus, in which an identifiable member quips, "We broke!" E-Knock describes their area of Boston as "not the best," and the camera then pans over an empty snow-covered street full of old brownstones. E-Knock narrates, "We don't have no money, we don't have no cars," and the crew playfully joins him in chiming, "but we have each other!"[33] These representations of blackness as destitute and nomadic to the point of literal disappearance from the urban landscape is captured by their retelling of the death of their good friend murdered randomly at a restaurant with a gunshot sound effect added for emphasis.

In sharp contrast, the judges frequently laud Kaba Modern and the Jabbawockeez, the eventual champions, for already possessing the range of techniques required to be professional dancers. On several occasions, Sparks and Chasez direct audience attention to Kaba Modern's and Jabbawockeez's extensive knowledge of hip-hop dance, past and present, and their ability to adapt to challenges that require them to learn new dance styles outside of their comfort zone, if not completely opposite of what they specialize in. In the "Live Audition" episode, Shane Sparks said it was as if Kaba Modern took "elements of each crew on the show and made it better." Chasez ecstatically endorsed Kaba Modern's identity as a group by their labor: "What I absolutely love about what you just did is the precision. You showed that you don't have to do a back flip to show how athletic you are. You don't have to do a back flip to blow people away. You just have to hit your steps."[34] In addition to describing their expansive dance repertoire, judges frequently talked about their precision—dancing in unison—and the intricacy of their dance steps as seen in their ticking, a series of sharp and jerky body movement in footwork, arms, and hands.

Whereas the African American crews express their feelings of gratitude and indebtedness to *ABDC* for the opportunity to transform their hobbies into economic opportunities, Asian Americans appear as self-evident dancers. The African American crews serve as a living tribute and history of the history lesson of hip-hop culture mentioned earlier. Their backstories frame and reduce African American failure and social and economic ghettoization to their own criminality. This "reality" of death and required "surveillance" of black communities is then translated on the show as the judges remind them that their athleticism and stunts—flips and gymnastics—will only get them so far if they cannot show that they have a wide enough repertoire of dance styles and techniques in their tool box necessary for a career in dance. For instance, Lil Mama warns all the crews, "Take this show and take advantage. Don't take it as they hate us. Oh, they're trying to get rid of us. Think of it as they're trying to help you grow, because you guys are dancers. Grow Everyday. Grow. Everyday."[35] Lil Mama's pep talk, once again, emphasizes the need to treat hip-hop dance not just as hobby but as a career that requires hard work. When this discourse of "performing responsibility" encounters the black crews on stage, "the spectacularity of the performance elides the unrepresentability of these subjects in such a context unless their abjectness is being used to discipline others into normativity."[36] Crews like Status Quo are shown explaining their desire to develop the proper work ethic to transcend poverty, a universal "achieve your dreams" discourse that erases the neoliberal austerity and its criminalizing logics that shapes conditions of black poverty.

As professionalism serves as a cultural metric and cultural narrative for whether a group will succeed on the show, Asian American national belonging is constrained by this meritocratic discourse and buttressed by the antiwelfare discourse that constitutes Status Quo's life story. The professionalism of the Asian American crews combined with the myths of black lawlessness and black desire for capitalist discipline reveals the normativity of neoliberal citizenship that produces conditions of possibility for how Asian American audiences understood the elimination of Kaba Modern. The show's emphasis on the labor of hip-hop dance encourages the staged performances of one's identity as a productive and self-made citizen of society.

ASIAN AMERICAN DANCERS, SELF-DISCIPLINE, AND ENTREPRENEURSHIP

After being named "America's Best Dance Crew" on the inaugural season of *Randy Jackson's America's Best Dance Crew*, the Jabbawockeez went on to star in their headlining show in Las Vegas called *MUS.I.C* (pronounced Muse-Eye-See). The media updates on their professional careers following *ABDC* celebrate the growing national acceptance and arrival of Asian Americans within entertainment industries from which they have been historically excluded on the basis of race and racial stereotypes. In the October 2011 issue of *PacificCitizen.org*, the web version of a semimonthly newspaper published by the Japanese Americans Citizens League, Nalea J. Ko reports that the Jabbawockeez extended *MUS.I.C* at the Monte Carlo

Resort and Casino through spring 2012. Debuting in October 2010 at the MGM Grand, *MUS.I.C* is a ninety-minute "audio-visual story of inspiration brought to life through the harmonization of sound and movement."[37] Ko makes space in her article to discuss the perks of being Las Vegas headliners, such as the Jabbawockeez's infinite access to Red Bull energy drinks and the Monte Carlo steam room and sauna. Ko concludes the article by highlighting how the Jabbawockeez have capitalized on their unique style of hip-hop dance, homegrown in a racially and ethnically diverse southern California upbringing, to establish their national and global brand, which they have already developed through merchandising their signature and customizable masks purchasable on their website.[38]

Throughout the duration of *ABDC*'s seven-season run, Asian American journalists, bloggers, and Asian American–interest media outlets mimicked the antiwelfare discourse of *ABDC* in their coverage of the show and the career arcs of Asian American crews following participation on *ABDC*. Articles such as the aforementioned feature in *Pacific Citizen* draws equivalences between the Jabbawockeez's branding of themselves to other globally recognized brands, like Red Bull and the Monte Carlo hotel (part of the MGM Resorts International group), as an index of America's acceptance of Asian Americans as unequivocally "American." Upon closer examination, Ko's praise for the Jabbawockeez invokes neoliberal logics as a pathway toward Asian American empowerment. From being the darling of the first season to becoming a Las Vegas headliner, the Jabbawockeez, as Ko suggests, made sound financial decisions about how to monetize themselves and their quirky regional aesthetics. These responses to *ABDC* are significant as they demonstrate how "culture (and its meanings and pleasures) is a constant succession of social practices; it is therefore inherently political, it is centrally involved in the distribution and possible redistribution of various forms of power."[39] Ko's comments do not exist in a vacuum but must be located within a larger constellation of discourses and a genre of television that shapes knowledge and discursive practices of citizenship. These Asian American writers find equivalence to hip-hop's blackness as the promise of a multicultural Americanness when it discursively expresses free market logics promoting open and inclusive competition within a hip-hop marketplace (e.g., professionalism).

Many of these articles follow the same narrative conventions, in which writers describe the transformations of Asian American crews from model minority stereotypes to being "American" in the entertainment industry based on their creative labor. As these stories go, writers mention that Asian Americans gravitate toward hip-hop dance because they believe that Asian Americans, like African Americans, experience forms of disenfranchisement and social marginalization on an everyday basis. But these writers then make the leap to say that hip-hop dance provides a common ground for Asian Americans, African Americans, and the rest of the country to "move beyond race." The "Americanness" of blackness lies in its signification of professionalism that holds the promise for Asian Americans to also "move beyond race."

In *Hyphen* magazine's online blog post "Asian America's Best Dance Crew," contributor Mic Nguyen asks, "What is it about an art form that started in the 1970s in New York by disenfranchised African American youth that resonates with Asians and APIs the world over?"[40] But Nguyen's identification with blackness as politics morphs into a set of generic cultural codes, like "the hip-hop swag, or the raw expression" that Asian Americans can perform to prove they're "not the studious model minority." Nguyen further evacuates race, namely blackness, of historic context to legitimize the place (or lack thereof) of Asian Americans within hip-hop "mainstream success:" "It's clear hip-hop as a *culture* goes beyond race, which is part of the reason why it's so powerful in the first place."[41] The move to framing hip-hop dance as "mainstream success" as opposed to, say, politics (e.g., "disenfranchised black youth") suggests that Nguyen articulates the performance of Asian American identity through the logic of economic productivity. But this marketplace of freely competing ethnic and racial identities is constituted by discursive impossibility of blackness to be anything but a universalized narrative of black enterprise. In "Jabbawockeez, Unmasked," *Asian Week* contributor Tina Tsai praises *ABDC* because it was "not about ethnic heritage or race—it's about dancing." Then, Tsai connects "break(ing) down . . . those enslaving model minority walls" to Asian American futures in "the field of arts and entertainment."[42] These writers are not making explicit claims to a distinct Asian American hip-hop dance culture with its own kinds of dance styles and techniques. Instead, these narratives demand a universal pathway toward "equality" based on neoliberal citizenship discourse via a career as commercially viable and economically self-reliant hip-hop dancers.

Elise Shin, a contributor to *Asian Week*, makes a similar move when she writes, "ballet is for blonde wasps" and "break dancing is black Americans."[43] In her recap of the first season, Shin commends *ABDC* for its encouragement of pluralism for "representing all parts of the nation." She later contends that Asian Americans are drawn to the "living-on-the-edge-mentality" of street dancing.[44] Like Nguyen, Shin addresses how Asian American dancers challenge stereotypical ideas of Asian American professions of doctors, engineers, grocers, and laundry workers. To be sure, Shin and Nguyen are drawn to the particular oppositional narratives of hip-hop dance because it offers a site for understanding the stereotypes and social construction of their own racial difference. But both abandon discursive constructions of blackness as a possible structural critique of race, inequality, and marginalization in favor of a multicultural America reminiscent of *ABDC*'s neoliberal logics of self-improvement and entrepreneurial enterprise as a pathway toward "good" citizenship. Knowledge of "disenfranchised African American youth" is produced by and circulates through a neoliberal discourse, which appears to shape how these writers imagine Asian American "equality" through their freedom to enter the marketplace as consumers and producers and to be recognized as such. Their transcendence of blackness from politics to culture explicitly occurs through the circulation of the antiblack discourse that poses black poverty as lacking and in need of capitalist discipline, such as developing the proper cultural aptitude for personal responsibility and hard work.

Another popular narrative structure that writers utilize is the investigative, biographic sketch of Asian American crews. As a means of recovery, these pieces tell the backstory behind the group's formation to its current form and their struggles to gain recognition within the dance industry dominated by African Americans. The writers focus their attention on Asian American interest in dance and their struggles to pursue hip-hop dance as a career. This commonly features a quote or two from their informants who claim that the hip-hop dance industry assumes only African Americans can dance. These stories then move to describing the dedication and work ethic that Asian American dancers put into their craft. In a *Hyphen* magazine article titled "Dance, Dance Evolution," Maveric Vu quotes Arnel Calvario, a Filipino American dancer and founder of Kaba Modern, who cites "a culture of discipline and respect" as the "secret weapon" for Asian American dancers.[45] Vu quotes Calvario further, "When you put together discipline, respect, and sense of family, that's really a foundation for a successful group."[46] In the *OC Weekly* article titled "Kaba Modern Created a Dance Dance Revolution," Michelle Woo also relies on similar tropes of

Asian American work ethic but also resourcefulness in Kaba Modern's gradual move from college phenomenon to national (and paid) stages. Woo
writes that former college dancers, such as Elm Pizarro, created network-
ing opportunities for Asian Americans to gain a foothold in the professional dance world. "The barriers have come down," says Pizarro, cited in
Woo's story."[47] In an *Audrey* article titled "From Subculture to Popular
Culture: The New Rhythm Nation," Teena Apeles quotes Calvario citing
dance gamedocs as gradually changing the audience in the dance industry
to becoming more inclusive of Asian Americans: "Shows such as *America's
Best Dance Crew*, *So You Think You Can Dance* and even *Dancing with the
Stars* all had many, inspiring talented dancers and choreographers, which I
believe has really diversified the face of hip-hop dance past the previous
perceptions that it was an art dominated by just one race."[48] Under the
subheading "Hip Hop Hooray," what Apeles finds celebratory of these
shows for Asian Americans is the growing appreciation among national
audiences, particularly Asian Americans, of hip-hop dance as a viable career.
Apeles quotes Calvario again to make this argument: "[*ABDC* and *So You
Think You Can Dance?*] brings 'parents and youth together in dialogue and
in joint respect of urban street dance as premier entertainment.'"[49]

   In these narratives, the hip-hop dance industry neither recognizes nor
rewards Asian American "work ethic" since blackness, when seen here
impeding upon Asian American free market capitalism, is an act of anti-
Asian racism. Treated as "entitlements," this logic of black criminality as
a national injury finds its way in these discourses about Asian American
discrimination. These writers frame liberal multiculturalism as resolving
an unofficially regulated dance industry favoring black bodies. Asian American writers, through their informants, reproduce discourses of belonging
through their submission to neoliberal rationalities of free markets, open
competition, and "freedom" of choice. In contrast, black dancers are framed
by an "entitlement" discourse as if unworthy or unskilled. In these instances,
these writers identify with hip-hop's blackness only as a neoliberal, "post-
welfare" discourse when it constitutes Asian Americans as good citizens
by virtue of their resourcefulness, entrepreneurship, work ethic, and Asian
cultures of "respect" in their approach to hip-hop dance cultures as a career
("premier entertainment"). Thus, *ABDC*'s pedagogical lessons of black
personal responsibility and submission to market logics can be found in
these writers' expressions of Asian American national belonging. Asian

American hip-hop dancing—a performance of self-management—brings Asian American and citizenship into discursive equivalence for which they are finally rewarded. Multiculturalism and neoliberalism construct blackness as a signifier of America as it supports, while also obscuring from view, the economic and political power and polices that produce race and class inequalities. This discursive construction of blackness, as presented on *ABDC*, constrains the political possibilities that these writers assume to be transformative pathways toward citizenship and national identity.

Conclusion

During season 4 of *ABDC*, judge and recording artist Lil Mama apologized to black transgender performer Leoimy Maldonado, a member of the openly gay crew Vogue Evolution (VE), and the LGBTQ community through GLAAD (Gay and Lesbian Alliance Against Defamation) for the following comments she had directed at Leoimy following VE's Bollywood challenge performance:

> Leiomy, come on. Your behavior . . . it's unacceptable. I just feel that you always have to remember your truth. You were born a man and you are becoming a woman. If you're going to become a woman, act like a lady. Don't be a bird, like 'Oh my god, I'm not doing this!' You know what I'm saying? It gets too crazy and it gets confusing. You're doing this for America. Even though you're the face for transgenders, you're the face of America right now with this group and it's not about anybody else.[50]

The behavior that Lil Mama referred to was an outburst by Leiomy, who was shown in the weekly recap videos as visibly frustrated by expectations of the competition. In response to what they witnessed on *ABDC*, *Racialicious*, a blog about "the intersection of race and pop culture," printed a two-part roundtable discussion among Robin Akimbo, Alaska B, Michelle Cho, and Elisha Lim. Collectively, this group of African American and Asian American artists argued that Lil Mama's comments were racist, homophobic, and transphobic in the way that it positioned black transgender identities and culture as deviant to the "universal" American gender norms espoused by Lil Mama.[51] They added that Lil Mama invoked a cultural discourse of "bad behavior" to stigmatize and discipline Leiomy's transgender "outburst" as unprofessional and irrational, which they felt produced a snowball effect

on audience approval ratings in their future performances and their eventual elimination soon after. These panelists further critiqued Lil Mama's
signification of "America" as connected to the deliberate silencing of the
queer histories and cultural politics produced through the House/Ballroom
scene that VE is originally known for and to which it sought to expose
national audiences when trying out for the show.[52] These panelists were
critical of not only the identities excluded from Lil Mama's gender normative depiction of America but also how America signified multicultural and
international inclusion of difference strictly within the priorities of capitalist production and consumption. That is, the notion of American national
unity rests upon the value of difference as aesthetics to be commodified
and sold, while effacing the racial and sexual politics that could undermine
these capitalist and exploitative conditions.

I conclude my discussion with this roundtable held between black and
Asian artists for the way that it invites a critical inquiry to the representations of blackness and black expressive culture on display. In this particular
case, the inclusion of Bollywood as a representation of *ABDC*'s multicultural and (inter)national "imagined community" of America signals how
cultural representations, such as dance, are where Asian American diasporic
subjects and African American subjects are relationally produced and dis-
ciplined within national neoliberal politics.[53] The idealized Asian American and African American subjects of *ABDC* provide another possibility
for interrogating black–Asian relationships, specifically in the context of
hip-hop culture, by extending it to a discussion of reality television, neoliberal policies, antiblackness, and the cultural logics of citizenship. The
verbal discipline and eventual dismissal of VE reflect and encourage neoliberal cultural logics that affirm policies targeting and stigmatizing specific
race, class, and gendered subjects while also legitimatizing the inequalities
produced in its wake. As these different articles covering *ABDC* demonstrate, blackness is not only central to the production of the show but also
serves a pedagogical function of reality television in providing for audiences specific scripts of what it means to be a good citizen. As the *Racialicious* roundtable points out, *ABDC* is not an exception to antiblackness or
homophobia but, in fact, clearly representative of it. Their analysis of Lil
Mama's comments allude to the ways that *ABDC*'s cultural narratives of
"America" are entrenched within neoliberal politics, discourses, and cultural
politics and its racializing effects. These articles reveal the shortcomings of

such triumphant narratives that these Asian American writers consume from watching the show. These writers desire to identify with blackness, but this desire must be detached from the neoliberal discourses and its multiculturalism that offers this seductive illusion of sameness. Antonio Tiongson Jr.'s warning of postracial discourse among Filipino American DJs seems particularly apt: "a level of equivalence is assumed in which difference is acknowledged only to be reconfigured as part of a colorful mosaic that is hip-hop."[54] Like Filipino American DJs who invoke their popularity based on skills to legitimize their claims to being "hip-hop," these Asian American writers similarly run the risk of "displac(ing) issues of race and power, rendering questions of social and cultural identity benign."[55] On *ABDC*, Asian American national belonging is made possible by neoliberalism's antiblack discourse. We should be wary of the ease and seductiveness by which these pathways toward recognition have been reconfigured within and beyond reality television.

NOTES

1. Created by Phil Yu, Angry Asian Man is a popular website dedicated to Yu's coverage of Asian American issues. His site offers regular updates on popular culture, politics, public policy, social work, and social justice issues.

2. In this instance, I define hip-hop culture the way that *ABDC* and Asian American responses refer to it as a commercially mediated expressive culture consisting primarily of rap music and dance. I recognize that hip-hop culture consists of additional elements, including dj-ing, graffiti, and also fashion, which can signify various different meanings. I focus primarily on the way that these shows and their audiences emphasize and choose to narrowly see hip-hop's history as a narrative of economic accumulation, of which rap and dance are two elements that have garnered many economic opportunities in the entertainment industry.

3. Nicole R. Fleetwood, *Troubling Vision: Performance, Visuality, and Blackness* (Chicago: University of Chicago Press, 2010); Uri McMillian, "Mammy-Memory: Staging Joice Heth, or the Curious Phenomenon of the 'Ancient Negress,'" *Women & Performance: A Journal of Feminist History* 22, no. 1 (2012): 29–46.

4. Here, I use citizenship to draw attention to the ways that culture produces ideas of citizenship beyond legal parameters. I follow Lisa Lowe's interpretation of the relationship between national culture and the politics of citizenship: "It is passing by way of this terrain of culture that the subject is immersed in the repertoire of American memories, events, and narratives and comes to articulate itself in the domain of language, social hierarchy, law, and ultimately, political representation. In being represented as a citizen within the political sphere, however, the subject

is 'split off' from the unrepresentable histories of situated embodiment that contradict the abstract form of citizenship. Culture is the medium of the present—the imagined equivalences and identifications through which the individual invents lived relationships with the national collective—but it is simultaneously the site that mediates the past and through which history is grasped as difference, as fragments, shocks, and flashes of disjunction. It is through culture that the subject becomes, acts, and speaks itself as 'American.'" Lisa Lowe, *Immigrant Acts: On Asian American Cultural Politics* (Durham, NC: Duke University Press, 1996), 2–3.

5. Oliver Wang, "These Are the Breaks: Hip-Hop and AfroAsian Cultural (Dis)Connections," in *AfroAsian Encounters: Culture, History and Politics*, ed. Heike Raphael-Hernadez and Shannon Steen (New York: New York University Press, 2006), 146–64; Oliver Wang, "Rapping and Repping Asian: Race, Authenticity, and the Asian American MC," in *Alien Encounters: Popular Culture in Asian America*, ed. Mimi Thi Nguyen and Thuy Linh N. Tu (Durham, NC: Duke University Press, 2007), 35–68; Nitasha Sharma, *Hip Hop Desis: South Asian Americans, Blackness, and a Global Racial Consciousness* (Durham, NC: Duke University Press, 2010).

6. Susan Murray and Laurie Ouelette, "Introduction," in *Reality TV: Remaking Television Culture*, ed. Susan Murray and Laurie Ouelette (New York: New York University Press, 2004), 3.

7. Laurie Oullette and James Hay, "Makeover Television, Governmentality and the Good Citizen," *Continuum: Journal of Media & Cultural Studies* 22, no. 4 (2008): 475.

8. Wendy Brown, *Edgework: Critical Essays on Knowledge and Politics* (Princeton: Princeton University Press, 2005), 42–43.

9. Dorothy Roberts, *Killing the Black Body: Race, Reproduction, and the Meaning of Liberty* (New York: Vintage, 1997).

10. Andrew Goodwin, "Fatal Distractions: MTV Meets Postmodern Theory," in *Sound and Vision: The Music Video Reader*, ed. Simon Frith, Andrew Goodwin, and Lawrence Grossberg (New York: Routledge, 1993), 53–54.

11. Jon Kraszewski, "Country Hicks and Urban Cliques: Mediating Race, Reality, and Liberalism in MTV's Real World," in *Reality TV: Remaking Television Culture*, ed. Susan Murray and Laurie Ouelette (New York: New York University Press, 2004), 179–196.

12. I follow Thomas F. DeFrantz's definition of black social dance as containing "dual transcripts of 'public' and 'private' meaning." Drawing on the black intellectual traditions, particularly W. E. B. DuBois's concept of "dual consciousness" to describe black subject formations within and without white supremacist U.S. society, DeFrantz frames black social dances as a form of communication that contains private meanings of protest, critique, and social discourse often misread

by whites who read the bodily movements as erotic and physical pleasure. For more on the pleasure, politics, and formation of identity and community around hip-hop dance cultures, see Jeff Chang, *Can't Stop Won't Stop: A History of the Hip-Hop Generation* (New York: St. Martin's Press, 2005); Joseph Schloss, *Foundation: B-boys, B-girls and Hip-Hop Culture in New York* (Oxford: Oxford University Press, 2009); and Tricia Rose, *Black Noise: Rap Music and Black Culture in Contemporary America* (Middletown, CT: Wesleyan University Press, 1994).

13. Lisa Duggan, *Twilight of Equality: Neoliberalism, Cultural Politics and the Attack on Democracy* (Boston: Beacon Press, 2004), xiii,

14. Roberts, *Killing the Black Body*, 150–201.

15. Ibid.

16. Ibid., 177–179.

17. Ibid., 150–201.

18. New Orleans–based Women's Health & Justice Initiative, "Stereotypes, Myths, & Criminalizing Policies: Regulating the Lives of Poor Women," *Incite!* blog, July 19, 2011, http://inciteblog.wordpress.com/2011/07/19/stereotypes-myths-criminalizing-policies-regulating-the-lives-of-poor-women/, accessed June 11, 2014.

19. MTV brought back *America's Best Dance Crew* for a six-episode run in summer 2015, which featured winning crews from five previous seasons and one crew made up of contestants from crews across different seasons. Titled *America's Best Dance Crew: Road to the VMAs*, VMA referring to the annual MTV Video Music Award show, this special season appeared to serve as an extended promotion for the VMAs. MTV has not indicated that additional seasons of *ABDC* are scheduled for production. See Andy Denhart, "Big Changes Ahead for America's Best Dance Crew," *Hitflix.com*, July 13, 2014, http://www.hitfix.com/news/big-changes-ahead-for-americas-best-dance-crew, accessed October 15, 2015; Cate Meighan, "A Rebooted 'America's Best Dance Crew' Will Return More Than 2 Years After Being Canceled by MTV," *MusicTimes.com*, January 11, 2015, http://www.musictimes.com/articles/24102/20150111/rebooted-americas-best-dance-crew-return-more-than-2-years-canceled-mtv.htm, accessed April 19, 2005.

20. Tutting refers to a style of dance where dancers manipulate their bodies to create shapes, such as boxes, through movements of bending their arms and legs at 90-degree angles. The visible form is meant to mimic imagery of ancient Egyptian reliefs.

21. J. C. Chasez, quoted in Jevon Phillips, "Making All the Right Moves," *Los Angeles Times*, August 21, 2008.

22. Naomi Bragin, "Shot and Captured: Turf Dance, YAK Films, and the Oakland, California, R.I.P. Project," *TDR: The Drama Review* 58, no. 2 (2014): 101.

23. Ibid.

24. "Dance Interview: Howard Schwartz," *DancePlug*, August 8, 2008, http://www.danceplug.com/insidertips/interviews/howard-schwartz, accessed December 8, 2011.

25. Tricia Rose, *The Hip-Hop Wars: What We Talk about When We Talk about Hip-Hop—And Why It Matters* (New York: Basic Books, 2008), 8.

26. "Live Auditions," *Randy Jackson Presents America's Best Dance Crew*, MTV, January 26, 2008 (Burbank, CA: Warner Bros.).

27. My point here is not about hip-hop authenticity but rather the constrained idea of what hip-hop culture is and its value—culturally, socially, and politically (or lack thereof) to those who participate in hip-hop culture, even within the entertainment industry. For more, see Imani Perry, *Prophets of the Hood: Politics and Poetics in Hip-Hop* (Durham, NC: Duke University Press, 2004).

28. For a detailed social history that aims to challenge origins narratives by showing hip-hop's pioneers as always entrenched within capitalist production, see Daniel Charnas, *The Big Payback: The History of the Business of Hip-Hop* (New York: New American Library, 2001).

29. "Evolution of Street Dance Challenge," *Randy Jackson Presents America's Best Dance Crew*, MTV, March 20, 2008 (Burbank, CA: Warner Bros.).

30. Ibid.

31. Brian Hiatt, "'N Sync Descend on Times Square for In-Store Appearance," MTV.com, March 21, 2000, http://www.mtv.com/news/819908/n-sync-descend-on-times-square-for-in-store-appearance/, accessed June 12, 2014.

32. "Crews Choice Challenge," *Randy Jackson Presents America's Best Dance Crew*, MTV, February 7, 2008 (Burbank, CA: Warner Bros.).

33. Ibid.

34. "Live Auditions," *Randy Jackson Presents*.

35. "Michael Jackson's Thriller," *Randy Jackson Presents America's Best Dance Crew*, MTV, March 6, 2008 (Burbank, CA: Warner Bros.).

36. Elizabeth Ault, "Nightmares of Neoliberalism: Performing Failure on Hell Date," *Spectator* 31, no. 2 (2011): 50. For more on reality television and the persistent invoking of blackness as instructive of good and bad citizenship, see E. M. Drew, "Pretending to Be 'Postracial': The Spectacularization of Race and Reality in TV's *Survivor*," *Television & New Media* 12, no. 4 (2011): 326–346.

37. Nalea J. Ko, "The Jabbawockeez Unmasked," *Pacific Citizen* (Los Angeles, CA), October 7–20, 2011, 9.

38. Ibid.

39. John Fiske, *Reading the Popular* (New York: Routledge, 1989), 1.

40. Mic Nguyen, "Asian America's Best Dance Crew," *Hyphen*, March 6, 2009, http://www.hyphenmagazine.com/blog/2009/03/asian-americas-best-dance-crew, accessed December 4, 2011.

41. Ibid., original emphasis.

42. Tina Tsai, "Jabbawockeez, Unmasked," *Asian Week*, March 13, 2008, http ://www.asianweek.com/2008/03/13/jabbawockeez-unmasked/, accessed March 13, 2008.

43. Elise Shin, "JabbaWockeeZ Wins! America's Best Dance Crew Recap," *Asian Week*, March 27, 2008, http://www.asianweek.com/2008/03/27/americas-best -dance-crew-asian-jabbawockeez-finale-winner-week-7/, accessed March 27, 2008.

44. Ibid.

45. Maveric Vu, "Dance, Dance Evolution: Asian Americans Pop, Lock and Break Their Way into Hip-Hop Dance Culture," *Hyphen*, no. 21 (Fall 2010), http:// www.hyphenmagazine.com/magazine/issue-21-new-legacy/dance-dance-evolu tion, accessed November 29, 2011.

46. Ibid.

47. Michelle Woo, "Kaba Modern Created a Dance Dance Revolution: Pop- ping and Locking with UC Irvine's Dance Crew and the Movement It Helped Create," *OC Weekly*, January 19, 2012, http://www.ocweekly.com/2012-01-19/cul ture/kaba-modern-irvine/, accessed January 19, 2012.

48. Teena Apeles, "From Subculture to Popular Culture: The New Rhythm Nation," *Audrey*, July 2010, 33.

49. Ibid.

50. "Bollywood Challenge," *Randy Jackson Presents America's Best Dance Crew*, MTV, August 30, 2009 (Burbank: Warner Bros.).

51. Thea Lim, comp., with Robin Akimbo, Alaska B, Michelle Cho, and Eli- sha Shim, "Vogue Evolution Forever Part 1: The Racialicious Roundtable on *America's Best Dance Crew*," *Racialicious—The Intersection of Race and Pop Culture*, September 16, 2009, http://www.racialicious.com/2009/09/16/vogue-evolution -forever-part-1-the-racialicious-roundtable-on-americas-best-dance-crew/, accessed May 28, 2014.

52. Ibid.

53. Grewal argues that Bollywood narratives and the representations of gender reflective of the cultural logics of normative Indian American diasporic subject formation must be considered within the context of postcoloniality, modernity, and a U.S. neoliberal state. Grewal's work is useful here as it draws attention to the relationship between the consumption of cultural narratives of race, class, and gender and the position of diasporic Indian Americans within U.S. neoliberal projects. For more, see Inderpal Grewal, *Transnational America: Feminisms, Dias- poras, and Neoliberalisms* (Durham, NC: Duke University Press, 2005), 111–120.

54. Antonio Tiongsen Jr., *Filipinos Represent: DJs, Racial Authenticity, and the Hip-Hop Nation* (Minneapolis: University of Minnesota Press, 2013), 61.

55. Ibid., 60.

Part II

Choreographing Aesthetics

5

Mediated Meditations

Choreographies of Shen Wei and Kun-Yang Lin

ELLEN V. P. GERDES

Shen Wei and Kun-Yang Lin are two prominent Asian-born American choreographers whom critics have heralded as cultural ambassadors because their work ostensibly communicates universal sentiment and embodies intercultural and multicultural harmony. About Kun-Yang Lin, the Philadelphia dance critic Steven Weisz writes: "Our need to connect and transcend is still ever present. What Kun-Yang does so well as a choreographer, artist and individual, is allow us through his artistry to view this need."[1] Similarly, *Washington Post* writer Sara Kaufman assigns to Shen Wei the burden of producing cultural harmony, describing Shen as "a man who has handled the bruising clash of his culture and ours with composure and a powerful renewal of purpose."[2] The title of this chapter, "Mediated Meditations," references how the belief in the possibility that peaceful coexistence, harmony, and spiritual truth can be achieved via the consumption of Asian American dance forms is reinforced in a closed loop between live performance and online interactions among viewers, choreographers, and critics. Asian American choreographers navigate and at times exploit the relationship between the desire to draw upon Asian aesthetic forms or thematic content and the essentialist expectations of critics and audiences. By focusing on Shen Wei Dance Arts and Kun-Yang Lin/Dancers as case studies, this chapter investigates the effects of Orientalizing and auto-Orientalizing discourses on the creation, reception, marketing, and circulation of contemporary Asian American dance in the twenty-first century.

The practice of casting Asian American artists in the role of cultural ambassadors is oftentimes done as a multicultural maneuver. Expected to provide a bridge between the seemingly insurmountable gap between two disparate cultures, Asian American artists are imagined as conduits who share, reach out, and model tolerance and acceptance. The gap, the space of the conduit, is imagined as unknown and mysterious, a leftover of the legacy of Orientalism in the United States. Although Edward Said's work has been critiqued as overly binary, the concept of Orientalism remains useful in exploring how Shen Wei and Kun-Yang Lin operate internationally within the contemporary dance scene in New York City and Philadelphia, respectively. To borrow a theatrical metaphor, Said set the stage for thinking through the Western projections of desire and anxiety onto the Middle East and Asia and the prevailing representation of the imagined geography of the East as static and ancient.[3] John Kuo Wei Tchen applies Orientalism to the specific American cultural context and contends that white identity formation depended upon the exchange of Chinese goods, ideas, and people, especially during 1776–1882. This was accomplished in three ways: first, patrician social Orientalism conferred status on society's elite who possessed ideas and consumer goods from the "Orient," which eventually resulted in marketplace shifts; second, commercial Orientalism opened up access to an urban public to experience the "Orient" through things and spectacles, including performances for P. T. Barnum's circus; and third, political Orientalism placed Chinese laborers at the center of debates about assimilation into the United States, where nineteenth-century Chinese immigrants were viewed as a threat.[4]

The logic of Asian American cultural ambassadorship in the twenty-first century continues to operate within this rubric. The consumption of material goods and experiences deemed Chinese by white Americans is a practice that increases cultural capital while assuaging (white) anxiety over cultural conflict. Dance scholars have contended with Orientalism and auto-Orientalism, but in the context of popular journalism, the good feeling of appreciation still operates as a stand-in for critique. Orientalism as a framework remains relevant because it undergirds the distance between the critique of aestheticized multiculturalism that has gone out of favor in scholarly circles and its continued presence in practice.[5]

A year after earning a MacArthur "Genius" Award in 2007, Shen Wei became one of the most visible Asian American choreographers in the United States when he was propelled into the international spotlight for his choreography at the opening ceremony for the 2008 Olympic Games in Beijing.[6] The lesser-known Lin has found success touring extensively both nationally and internationally with the support of competitive funding through the USArtists International Mid Atlantic Arts Foundation. Since 2000, Shen and Lin have choreographed a number of works that address similar themes—calligraphy, Tibet, travel to Asia, and Asian philosophy— to which critics have responded by praising the works for their innovation, aesthetic beauty, and a contagious sense of spirituality. This chapter pairs the work of Shen and Lin to compare how the two choreographers deploy the themes of spirituality and harmony in their choreography and promotional materials, and how the critical dialogue among dance critics about Shen's and Lin's work has been limited to the discourse of cultural appreciation as the sincere effort to learn about another culture. The goal of this analysis is to question and move beyond the earnest sincerity of cultural appreciation by examining how Shen and Lin thrive in a dance ecosystem that still exoticizes Asian American artists.

East Already Knows West

Asian American dance is often promoted and funded in much the same manner as World Dance. The scholar Marta Savigliano argues that performance venues and the academy primarily schedule dance that is deemed "traditional" as World Dance, yet the current concept of World Dance also includes dances that "retain the signature elements of cultural difference."[7] For example, in the summer of 2014, Kun-Yang Lin/Dancers performed for the Outdoor at Lincoln Center program on a bill with a Bharatanatyam company and a Chinese folk dance/opera company. It is not unusual for World or "ethnic" dance concerts to group dance companies based on geographic regions rather than thematic content such that geography doubles as theme. Programming an evening of Asian dance regardless of genre often suffices as acceptable curatorial decision making. In an attempt to impart a more progressive multicultural agenda, "fusion," "hybrid," and "cross-cultural" become operative words that neglect the cultural and aesthetic overlap already present throughout dance history.

In the promotion or review of Asian American performance, readers are bombarded with headlines of "East Meets West" as if it were a first date.[8] The dance critic Alistair Macaulay for the *New York Times* employs the words as a catchall phrase to describe Shen's biography and Lin's aesthetic.[9] He writes, "Everything about the choreographer Shen Wei's story says 'East meets West,'" and "Kun-Yang Lin/Dancers, from Philadelphia, danced two

East-meets-West excerpts." Shen's and Lin's works are most often perceived as an East/West fusion while audience and reviewers alike exoticize the supposedly Asian components in the mix. For example, one critic uses the familiar metaphor of the multicultural melting pot to make note of Lin's "exotic spices blended into the stewpot of today's modern dance."[10] American multiculturalism is rendered palatable in the language of food—stews, pots, and salads.

Savigliano cautions against the multicultural harmony proposed by institutional and curatorial practices that fall under the rubric of World Dance. She argues, "World Dance reframes difference as a political resource" and "is a territorial expansion coded as aesthetic discovery."[11] Asian philosophy in particular is often cited as the inspiration for harmony embodied by World Dance even if a form is presented in highly commercialized and spectacle-oriented formats. The Montreal-based entertainment company Cirque du Soleil has marketed its Chinese-themed *Dralion* as a fusion of Chinese acrobatics and Cirque de Soleil's multidisciplinary style that "draws its inspiration from Eastern philosophy and its never-ending quest for harmony between humans and nature."[12] All Cirque de Soleil productions incorporate Chinese acrobatic traditions, but out of the nineteen current shows on tour, *Dralion* is the only one framed as a representation of a specific culture. *Dralion* presents Chineseness through an acrobatic lion dance act and a balancing bamboo act performed by men dressed in rust-red costumes that are vaguely reminiscent of Buddhist monks' robes. This harkens back to nineteenth- and early twentieth-century American Orientalism in which one could experience the "Orient" through commercial objects and spectacles such as P. T. Barnum's circus acts.[13] While the marketing team for *Dralion* promotes the idea of Eastern philosophy for highly accessible circus acts, Shen and Lin make similar claims about the role of Asian philosophy as an influence on their work within the realm of contemporary dance.

Shen and Lin exemplify this supposed harmony through what Yutian Wong calls the trope of the nonwhite "international artist," who is at once exotic and familiar, visibly different and socially legible.[14] Wong further emphasizes that this trope "is often used to gloss the political exigency of racial, ethnic, gender, and class difference suggested by the term artist-of-color."[15] In Shen's and Lin's promotional materials, neither choreographer uses the term "artist-of-color" to describe himself. During interviews with news correspondent Geoffrey Fowler, Shen identifies himself as a "New

York international artist"[16] and notes his desire to communicate with his audience members regardless of their cultural background.[17] The company is also referred to as an international company in its mission statement.[18] A fund-raising video similarly stresses the importance of Kun-Yang Lin's global perspective, his multicultural sources, and his work's universal appeal.[19] On its website and promotional postcards, respectively, Kun-Yang Lin/Dancers is cited as "internationally acclaimed" and marketed as "Philly's most lauded international dance company."[20] Lin is referred to on promotional materials as a Taiwan-born artist who "probes at the limits of national identity."[21] Both artists, therefore, embrace this idea of the international artist, at once held in high esteem and universally relevant.

As an example, in *ONE—Immortal Game* (2013), Lin utilizes the cliché metaphor of a chess game to express conquest, conflict, and an ultimate hope for pluralistic unity. The dancers perform atop a black vinyl dance floor overlaid with a white checkerboard pattern (not unlike Shen Wei's checkerboard floor for *Rite of Spring*). In the opening section, two dancers sit facing one another and perform a series of dueling, sharp, and sweeping arm movements. Jessica Warchal-King, a white professional dancer with serious ballet training, has danced with the company since 2010. Mo Liu joined the dance company in 2012 from the Beijing Dance Academy, where he majored in Chinese classical dance. Both are highly skilled in executing modern dance technique. Later, two large groups of six dancers separate to either side of the stage, facing one another as if they are chess opponents. Their movement has a strong sense of attack, linearity, and sudden energetic shifts. Moments of partnering involve daring leaps and lifts as the rest of the cast freezes in stillness. The multiracial cast and the juxtaposition of multiple genres function as a promotion of multicultural harmony. Toward the end of *ONE—Immortal Game*, Mo Liu enters wearing one Chinese silk dance sleeve. Liu's body traces curvilinear patterns while swirling the silk sleeve. He tosses the sleeve into the air as he leaps over one of the life-size dice pieces on stage.

Kun-Yang Lin/Dancers performed *ONE—Immortal Game* as part of a show titled *ONE: Gifts from Afar*. This title's auto-Orientalist sentiment is reminiscent of patrician social orientalism of the nineteenth century, during which Americans sought out Asian consumer goods as a sign of social status.[22] The promise of multicultural harmony is the gift that comes from afar. The program notes describe the dance as "a gateway to recognize and embody the oneness in each of us," and the viewer is addressed directly using therapeutic language: "you all come from different backgrounds and places and bring singular strengths and gifts. . . . The light in me sees the light in you." The folklorist Nancy Watterson contributed additional program notes, which include an optimistic entreaty for the audience to envision peace, inclusivity, and connectivity in the performance.[23] The free-floating spiritual language of generalized difference stands in contrast to Lin's repeated statements about being an immigrant and therefore sensitive to racial tensions in the United States. His studio, CHI Movement Arts Center, is located in the historically Italian American neighborhood of South Philadelphia just one block from the famous Geno's Cheesesteaks. Geno's has displayed an anti-immigrant sign reading: "This is America, when ordering, please speak English" in its front window.[24]

My purpose here is not to tease apart Asian and American aesthetics but rather to discuss how Shen and Lin are read through the trope of the international artist and to pose questions about their contributions to an essentialized view of Asianness. By analyzing their use of similar content (calligraphy, Tibet, Asian travel as inspiration, and mandalas) and similar technique (*qi* awareness), I hope to demonstrate some challenges Asian American artists face within an audience-consumer structure that upholds narrowly constrained expectations about Asian American dance. In the mission statements of each company, I see the choreographers' hopes to cross cultural borders and to move beyond boundaries of difference, commodified by venues and audiences. In their mission statements, both choreographers employ the verb "transcend." On its website, Shen's company markets its purpose as the following: "Transcending East and West, Shen Wei Dance Arts fuses these disparate forms to forge a startling new hybrid form of dance."[25] Lin's company online mission statement likewise reads: "The company creates and presents uncommon works that, while inspired by the traditions and aesthetic of Eastern Asia, transcend cultural boundaries and speak to the universality of the human experience."[26] The choreographers both promote their work as partially sourced from Asia ("traditional Chinese culture and arts" for Shen Wei Dance Arts and "traditions and aesthetic of Eastern Asia" for Kun-Yang Lin/Dancers) while making claims for a universal artistic product in fulfillment of their roles as international artists.

Also evident in their mission statements are their goals for innovation, which is a quality often ascribed to Western modern and postmodern dance.[27] Notably, Kun-Yang Lin/Dancers is said to improve upon Western contemporary dance via an "Asian American cultural perspective."[28] In this way, these choreographers attempt to subvert the Orientalist stereotypes that relegate Asian cultural practices to the past even as Orientalism features prominently in modern dance history. Ruth St. Denis imagined Asian dances; Martha Graham created seated spiral positions modeled after yoga; John Cage formed his improvisational structures from ideas set forth in the I-Ching and Zen Buddhism; and Steve Paxton based contact improvisation technique in principles of Aikido. Ted Shawn and Ruth St. Denis toured with Denishawn dancers to Asia as early as 1925. In 1955 Martha Graham and her company toured Asia on a U.S. State Department tour. Ananya Chatterjea contends, however, that references to these influences can reproduce the modern West/traditional East binary by suggesting that postmodern dance recycled static traditions from Asian cultures to create innovation.[29] As an example, Wong observes that when critics parse apart the Asian and American components of Asian American choreography, full-bodied dancing is often attributed to an American source, while minimal, austere, or still movement is often attributed to an Asian aesthetic without an acknowledgment of early appropriations of Asian dance.[30]

HISTORICAL AND BIOGRAPHICAL CONTEXT

A brief look at the trajectory of dance in Taiwan (Republic of China) and China (People's Republic of China) for the past century demonstrates the shifting landscape of dance as fundamentally shaped by the state. Under the Japanese occupation of Taiwan between 1895 and 1945, some dancers studied ballet and modern dance abroad in Japan.[31] As the Communist Party gained control in China (1949), the party sponsored the codification of *gudianwu* or classical dance constructed from folk dance, Chinese opera, and ballet technique.[32] When the Kuomintang (KMT) party was defeated by the Communists in 1949, the KMT escaped to the island of Taiwan and utilized *minzu wudao* (folk dance) to legitimize its culture as authentically Chinese both culturally and politically.[33] In the 1950s, China resisted post–World War II American expansionism by creating dance forms that seemed progressive to the nation without mirroring American modern aesthetics.[34]

While the leaders of the Cultural Revolution (1966–1976) in China attempted to expel all things of feudal origin by promoting propaganda ballets, such as the *Red Detachment of Women* (1964) and the *White Haired Girl* (1965), Taiwan began experimenting with modern dance. Lin Hwai-Min, who studied at the Graham school in New York City, formed the Cloud Gate Dance Theatre in 1973, which is now known the world over. Because Lin Hwai-Min served as an adviser to many high school and university dance programs in Taiwan, Graham technique is still a staple in Taiwan dance conservatory education.[35] Therefore, Graham's approach to physicalizing inner psychology might be understood as a strong *Taiwanese* influence on Kun-Yang Lin.

Shen moved to New York in 1995 and Lin in 1997, so they became contemporaries in the New York dance scene. Shen grew up studying Chinese opera in Hunan Province during its revival after the Cultural Revolution. He later switched to modern dance as a founding member of the Guandong Dance Company and as a member at the Nikolai/Louis Dance Lab. Lin studied acting, folk dance, ballet, and Graham technique in Taiwan. He then graduated with an MFA from NYU Tisch School of the Arts and toured with the Martha Graham Company, Doris Humphrey Repertory Dance Company, and Mary Anthony Dance Theatre, among others.

Conceptualizing Asian American Dance

The conversations about African American dance in Thomas DeFrantz's *Dancing Many Drums* can be easily extended to Asian American dance. First, dance critics have historically imposed a binary of Art dance versus Black Vernacular dance just as many Asian dance forms are treated as mere community dance practice in the United States.[36] Second, many artists utilize the term "black dance" to signify political mobilization or collective self-identification.[37] Yutian Wong similarly frames Asian American performance "as a social space in which Asian American artists are grappling with questions of form, content, and process as markers of identity."[38] DeFrantz's declaration of black dance as "several discursive spaces" versus a "singular idiom" can also be extended to thinking about Asian American dance as a pluralistic set of practices.[39] The term "Asian American" originated during the late 1960s on the heels of the black civil rights movement to express a shared experience of systemic and historically rooted racism: "Asian to emphasize race, American to emphasize non-foreignness."[40] Asian Americans have been racialized as foreign or foreign immigrants regardless of citizenship status due to the legacy of American policy and political Orientalism.[41] One of the most invisibilized results of this racialization is Japanese internment during World War II.[42] Karen Shimikawa, in her analysis of Asian American theater's potential to interrogate an Asian American experience of *national abjection*, formulates her argument based on the simultaneous legal exclusions of Asian Americans and the inclusive tone of multiculturalism/diversity discourse.[43]

Dance critics often use language that racializes Asian Americans as foreign. Writing for the *Dance Journal* in Philadelphia, Merilyn Jackson states that Wen-Chun Liu, a new dancer (Taiwan-born and MFA-educated at SUNY Purchase) to the Kun-Yang Lin/Dancers company, explored her "newness to the company and to the country" in rehearsal to suggest that Asian American dance is an obvious space in which to make adjustments to national identity.[44] Furthermore, Mo Liu's status as a Chinese national makes him a likely candidate to represent multicultural harmony in Kun-Yang Lin's *ONE—Immortal Game*. In fact, Kat Richter, a dance anthropologist and journalist, problematically equates Mo's body with commodified Chinese silk: "Mo's hands gestured so quickly that they seemed to be made of silk and not muscles and bone."[45] Here, Mo's material body is not even permitted its muscles and bones. He is otherworldly.

Finally bringing dance into Asian American performance studies, Wong asserts, "The political potential of Asian American performance depends upon a refiguring of the ideology under which Asian bodies are visually perceived."[46] According to Wong, a number of stereotypes based on the historic racialization of Asian Americans affect the viewing of Asian American dance, including the double effeminization of dance and Asia, the model minority, the Oriental dancing girl, Asianness as spiritual, and Asian American as foreign.[47]

Wong also identifies the tendency of critics to either focus solely on the sections of Asian American choreography that express "overt sociological analysis" or complain that the dance is only aesthetic, rendering the form of the choreography invisible.[48] She departs from the germinal study on Asian American theater by Josephine Lee by allowing established forms of choreography to be considered as Asian American—form, content, and process as dialogic—rather than requiring social consciousness.[49] I draw from Wong's work, however, with marked difference—both companies of my analysis performed with all-white or nearly all-white companies between 2008 and 2012, during the time of this research. The Asian Americanness of both of these companies lies in the form, content, and authorship (Asian American as choreographer), not the performers' identity.[50]

What is at stake when Asian American choreographers are "grappling with form, content, and process as markers of identity" through white bodies?[51] For Shen's *Re* trilogy (2009) and *Connect Transfer* (2005) and Lin's *Mandala Project* (2011) and *From the Land of Lost Content* (2000), both choreographers trained their dancers in meditative and martial arts practices to present Asian topics and images alongside white dancing bodies. In effect, the training, the themes, and the images authenticate the performances as a partially Asian experience. Choreographing on white bodies reinforces the concept of the international artist working toward universal understanding. Due to the claims of hybrid, intercultural, or multicultural aesthetics, and because the choreographer is Asian American, the work is not critiqued under the rubric of white appropriation of Asian material. Audiences, however, read Asianness differently on Asian American and white bodies.

Even though the New York–based H. T. Chen is a self-identified Asian American who tends to apply more obvious symbols of Chineseness in his work than either Lin or Shen,[52] SanSan Kwan's analysis of H. T. Chen is relevant to this discussion. Kwan argues that familiar components of Chinese dance such as flexed feet and red ribbons in Chen's work are read as novel rather than as part of an ongoing aesthetic conversation within American concert dance. She finds the multiracial cast the key to the success of *Apple Dreams* (2007) in its representation of Chinatown's role in a post-9/11 New York City. Audiences and reviewers, however, were uncomfortable seeing non-Asian bodies. The generic Asian symbols in Chen's choreography were deemed more natural on the Asian American dancers in the company.[53] Likewise, one audience member told me that she could not stomach Lin's choreography on white bodies and felt relieved when she watched an Asian American dancer perform the same movement. These reactions conflate race and training, which reasserts the universalism of modern dance by defining a subset of movement that Asian American bodies should be performing.

Calligraphy Dances: *Qi* and Ink

Public knowledge of a choreographer's racial identity and the identity of the bodies dancing on stage influences the perceived Asianness of a work.

The dancers in Shen's *Connect Transfer* (2004) act as full-body calligraphers on panels of canvas laid out on the floor of the stage or performance area. Shen choreographed three different versions of this piece, and the second version was part of the opening ceremony of the 2008 Olympic Games in Beijing. In a spectacular display of nationalism, the opening ceremony showcased many Chinese movement forms such as *gudianwu* and *tai qi* in addition to Shen's calligraphy dance from *Connect Transfer*. His border crossing as an American citizen back to China helped support China's image as a country that is modern and innovative while inspired by "ancient" fundamental values and power. He says, "I want to show China today, the modern China. We don't only want to see dragons and lanterns, but want to meld modern culture with Chinese traditions."[54] Unlike the first version of *Connect Transfer* (2004), performed by a predominantly white company, the second version was performed by a visibly all-Asian cast of Chinese citizens.

The special-effects designer of the opening ceremony, Shen's press materials, and the *China Daily* make vague references to his use of Eastern philosophy.[55] While I find the Chinese aesthetic and philosophical concept of *wuwei* in the work, there is little evidence that Shen actively draws upon Chinese philosophical authors.[56] Dai Jian, a former Shen Wei Dance Arts company member, observes that Shen emphasizes a cultivation of *qi* energy awareness from his dancers but does not speak otherwise of philosophy.[57] Like many teachers of postmodern dance technique, Shen cautions against tensing muscles, but instead he advises dancers to allow movement to flow from breath. Kun-Yang Lin's technique classes (called "CHI awareness technique"[58]) also highlight a cultivation of *qi* as an impetus for movement and emotionality. In rehearsals, he calls out percussive vocalizations to inspire musicality, such as "Sa, Sa, Huh."

According to Shen, the dancers in *Connect Transfer* explore cumulative energies as they use their bodies to create a large-scale painting.[59] As the dancers paint with paint-laden mitts, they manage to fold easily at their joints. The effect seems anatomically impossible, which is a somewhat ironic manifestation of a form described as a "natural body technique"—a common legitimizing claim made by modern/postmodern choreographers that can be traced back to Isadora Duncan.[60] Shen's dancers swirl paint in spirals, swipe their arms and legs, and invert. In an adaptation of a Chinese opera step, they skitter across the canvas like a flock of birds directing one another.[61] An aesthetic of flow can be seen in the choreography's ever-present actions.[62] The current scholarship on Asian American dance has not sought to identify specific Asian aesthetics in American dance to the extent that scholars have identified Africanist aesthetics, but the aesthetic of flow versus geometry pervades traditional East Asian arts.[63] The Taoist text *Tao Te Ching* extols least resistance or softness as powerful: "The world's softest thing tramples the world's hardest. . . . Therefore I understand the benefits of not-acting."[64] This concept of not-acting or *wuwei* encompasses mind-body unity, which is thought to lead to artistic mastery and transcendence.[65] *Connect Transfer* is not position oriented; dancers neither pose nor hit certain body shapes. Shen refers to the transference of energy as an "ancient *tai chi* idea."[66] Practitioners of *tai qi chuan* explore physical flow as it is thought to circulate *qi* throughout the body.[67]

As the dancers paint, their relentless continuation of physical pathways produces a sustained energy dynamic. Although I view this as an active stillness of sorts, I do not mean to strip them of agency. In fact, the audience sees them in the act of art making, effecting change in front of us. The dance simultaneously presents process and product, a self-reflexive goal characteristic of much postmodern dance. Even though I have found an aesthetic representation of *wuwei* corresponds with Shen's embrace of *qi*, the version of *Connect Transfer* performed at the Olympic stadium in Beijing was not overtly spiritual. For starters, the canvas lay atop one of the largest LED screens in history with artificial images of nature. Given the scale of the stadium, the audience could not see the "tracing of the dancers' energy," as Shen defines it.[68]

In the intimate space of Judson Memorial Church in New York, a section in which a dancer flopped around covered in black paint like an oiled seal looked like a visually kinetic gimmick rather than a deeply spiritual exploration of Chinese philosophy. Shen's solo drew me in more than other sections of the dance because of its small scale and specificity set atop the chaotic swirls and smudges of paint. He circled his hands while keeping his wrists touching and then outstretched his arms into a diagonal, intently tracking his gaze from one hand to the other. At the end of the piece, squares of the painted canvas were auctioned off to support the company. This auction encouraged me to think about the painting, however thrilling, as a funding mechanism for the dance, not as an archive of the dancers' kinetic and spiritual energy.

Although Shen gained international recognition for his body calligraphy, the topic of calligraphy or ink is not a unique one for Asian American choreographers. Many consider the art of calligraphy a kinesthetic and spiritual practice, like *tai qi*, making it a likely partner for dance.[69] It would be too simple to say that Asian Americans are merely attracted to this content because it is also what audiences will support.[70] In 2006 Yin Mei performed a solo on paper with ink first titled *Cursive*, which was later shown as *Ink/Paper/Body/Scent* in New York art galleries. In Eiko & Koma's *Hunger* (2008), their two Cambodian collaborators utilized ink and brush to paint a large image of birds on a large paper backdrop hanging from the ceiling of the stage. Taiwan-based Cloud Gate Dance Theatre has toured *Cursive* (2003) as a kinetic presentation of writing in the United States at venues such as the Brooklyn Academy of Music in New York City. Most recently, Nai-Ni Chen Dance Company premiered *Calligraffiti* (2015).

Lin's calligraphy piece *Traces of Brush* (2005) involves no actual ink or paper but does call attention to *qi* energy.[71] Inspired by Buddhist texts and contemplative practices, Lin's "CHI awareness technique" promotes harmony.[72] Lin says, "'Chi' or universal life source, transcends all forms and the many 'boxes' some people like to inhabit and put others in. Cultivation of 'chi' is essential to creating and embodying our work because doing so allows us to explore spaces and dialogues between false opposites such as 'traditional' and 'contemporary,' 'visible' and 'invisible,' 'East' and 'West.'"[73] In preparation for remounting *Traces of Brush*, Lin recruited Hsu-Hui Huang, a member of Cloud Gate Dance Theatre, to teach *tai qi*, meditation, *qi gong*, dance, and calligraphy workshops to the company members. Huang functioned as the messenger of Asian forms, perhaps seen as more authentically Asian than Lin himself. In Lin's choreography, the dancers paint through the air with pointed fingers, outstretched arms, and high leg extensions. As a group, they swirl and blend. They do not read as people but rather as abstract forms that expand like drops of ink. The dancers' breath punctuates the lively movement, which contrasts the recorded spoken text of a lifeless poem about calligraphy. Lin stresses to the dancers that they must tap into a sense of observation, listening to the breath and weight of their bodies, always aware of their internal energy.[74]

In this piece, Lin performs a compelling solo where he holds a black Chinese dance fan in his teeth, the fabric of the fan spilling out like the hairs on a paintbrush.[75] Here, he reappropriates a Chinese folk dance prop to extend beyond his kinesphere and obscure his face. With his chest bare and a long silk black skirt, he collapses suddenly into his hip and skitters upstage. In one moment, he holds the fan closed in his hand and quickly writes his name in both English and Chinese characters in the air, symbolizing pluralistic identity. In 2010 *Traces of Brush* was included as part of an evening of work titled *Autumn Skin: Journeys of East/West*, where Lin intended to take a jab at the false dichotomy between East and West by presenting this work as equally Eastern as it is Western.[76] The title reveals his dependence upon dichotomy rather than the integration. His marketing materials for the concert distribute the quote "his distinctive blend of traditional and Western dance has the dark, bold force of a woodcut print. *New York Times*, 2007," which reifies a Western component as contemporary. It becomes difficult to imagine alternative readings within the loop between the exoticism practiced by critics and the auto-Orientalism practiced by the choreographer.

Dancing for Tibet, Breathing Deep, and Making Mandalas

Both Shen and Lin also draw from their own travels in Asia as inspiration for choreography. Shen's *Re* trilogy (2009) presents his response to travel in China, Cambodia, and Tibet. Lin's *Mandala Project* (2011) is inspired by his trips to Indonesia. Lin connects the idea of travel to his position as an international choreographer, saying, "And in order to become a global citizen, particularly in dance, we travel through our work. We travel through our vision."[77] Although both choreographers address Tibet as a theme, Lin bases his piece *From the Land of Lost Content* (2000) on readings and music, whereas Shen directly responds to his travels in Tibet from 2005 to 2006. Shen writes, "*Re-(Part 1)* is broadly based on the feeling of the land, the people, the religion and the culture of Tibet that I gained from my recent journey there."[78] The movement initiates from breath deep in the lower back, initially improvised by the dancers in the dark. In the original version, a quartet of dancers—dressed in red long-sleeve shirts, black pants, and red socks—glides through an elaborate confetti mandala. The dancers' arms and torsos curl in toward their centers before releasing into the distal reaches of their body. Tibetan chanting plays in the background. Dai Jian and Sara Procopio's movements are seamless as they easily gather their strength before shifting off balance and propelling themselves across the mandala to blur its design. In Deborah Jowitt's words, "Nothing changes for good. There's no destination, just the hypnotic beauty of the path."[79] The words "hypnotic" and "mesmerizing" are employed repeatedly by critics to undertake a meditative reading of Shen's work. A Google search of "Shen Wei" yields five pages of references to his work as "hypnotic" and eight pages for "mesmerizing." Despite Jowitt's claim that nothing changes, the mandala does change. By the end of the piece, the colors of the confetti mandala are mixed together, and the shape is reconfigured in much the same way that a Tibetan sand mandala is dismantled after it is completed. Re-(Part 1) is not didactic; Shen provides visual imagery, breath-like musicality, sinuous movements, and spreading confetti.

The Re trilogy completed in 2009 does not address the subject of the Chinese occupation of Tibet in direct terms, but it might offer sympathy for the erasure of Tibetan culture and political self-determination by placing Re-(Part I) alongside works about China and Cambodia. Dance critics have not questioned Shen's subject position as a former Chinese national making work about Tibet. Moreover, his public comments about Tibet to China have centered on characterizing Tibet as more spiritual, quieter, and less materialistic than China and have avoided the topics of international conflict and human rights.[80] Shen draws from his experience returning to Beijing in 2008 after his travels on the China Silk Road in 2007 for Re-(Part III). His program notes refer to a consideration of East/West conceptualizations of the collective and of the individual.[81] The movement is repetitive and, at times, militaristic. A small group of dancers swing their arms at their sides in perfect synchronicity as one dancer whirls and spirals, trapped inside the group. This third section could be read as a choreographed critique of Chinese imperialism in relation to Re-(Part I) even if this is not the advertised intent of the work. The critic Robert Johnson responds to Shen's choreographic illustrations of the Silk Road with an allusion to imagined impending conflict between China and the United States.[82]

Shen aims to develop visual images to elicit a feeling for the audience,[83] whereas Lin choreographs a much more specific version of Tibet. The exile of the Dalai Lama inspired Lin's From the Land of Lost Content (2000). In the first section, called "Pilgrimage," six dancers—three women standing in front of three men—fall to the floor on their knees in canon. They bow their hands forward to the ground, stand up, clap their hands in a prayer position over their heads, then move their mouths as if whispering. They contract toward their center, pulling their arms toward their stomachs,

then release their arms upward in a plea. The men lift the women in a spi-
raling pas de chat. Their costumes are the same color red as Tibetan Buddhist monks' robes. Both men and women wear loose wrap pants, while
the men are bare-chested and the women wear halter-tops that show their
bare shoulders. In a duet titled "Compassion," Elrey Belmonti and Jillian
Harris execute a series of soaring lifts and weight sharing. In one moment,
Harris helps Belmonti walk by lifting his legs from behind; in another, he
catches her neck as she falls in a backbend, chest parallel with the floor. Lin
connects the motifs of extension, compassion, and resonance in the choreography to Buddhism and Nirvana.[84] When I first saw this duet performed
by Lin and Harris without any projections on the scrim, I felt most engaged
by the intense focus and synchronicity of the pair.

In the 2009 revised version, Lin coupled *From the Land of Lost Content*
with projections of smiling Tibetans and Tibetan landscape photographed
by his friend.[85] Here, the pictures, like the slideshow of Amerasian children
from Vietnamese orphanages in *Miss Saigon*, attempt to evoke sympathy in
the viewers.[86] The leaping non-Tibetan bodies seem to exploit the actual
humanitarian crisis in Tibet. The Tibetans are somehow larger than life in
front of us but cannot speak for themselves. During intermission, the dancers lay bowls with water and flower petals on the marley flooring and then
exit the stage.[87] The program notes by the folklorist Nancy Watterson com-
mend Lin for his capacity to employ dance as a mode for "cultivating peace
for all sentient beings" and mediate the interpretation of this concert.[88]

Many remarked that they felt a part of a ritual or meditative experience.
Deni Kasrel observed that "Friday night's crowd sat rapt throughout, and
who could blame them? . . . Much of the movement and music draws on
group ritual and meditative states of consciousness. The collective energy
emanates around the room, and if you let yourself go with his flow, you
don't just watch it, you feel it, too."[89] An e-mail sent out after the show to
the company's listserv included quotes from audience responses proclaim-
ing, "It was truly a meditative experience. I felt my body carry the experience
inside. I was not a spectator, but a participant" and "Inspiring, powerful and
spiritual. The space felt sacred. The performance was transforming, magical."[90] This e-mail feedback mediates the audience's experience even after
everyone has left the theater and impresses upon the reader the importance
of spirituality to Lin's work. While I do not doubt people's sincerity in
their desires for spiritual fulfillment, I argue that the audience was eager

to consume a sacred experience from an Asian American choreographer. Even though Lin is not Tibetan, he offers an "Asian experience," perceived as authentic by the audience. Multiple newspaper previews on the training process and the program context reassure the audience members that they are not merely watching Asian kitsch. By feeling close to Lin through his choreography, the audience can feel relieved about East–West power dynamics—both the anxiety of China's rise in economic power and the concern over U.S. multiracial harmony.

Merilyn Jackson, a frequent dance reviewer for the *Philadelphia Inquirer,* writes that *From the Land of Lost Content* "hooked me on his work for good," and that she craves mystical performances, which Kun-Yang Lin/ Dancers delivers. Jackson asks, "They look very different from other companies in Philadelphia, and for me the question is: Why?"[91] Could it be because Lin looks visibly Asian? She goes on to say that "he exudes a spirituality that's matchless in the local dance scene."[92] Although he is not the only Philadelphia-based choreographer to work with spiritual underpinnings, comments such as these ask Lin to be the model minority, guiding the audience to beauty and mysticism. Kun-Yang Lin/Dancers also acts as a guide. Kat Richter in 2014 reports that Lin's concert titled *Be/Longing: Light/Shadow* even involved a guided meditation for the audience. She writes that at first the audience appeared hesitant, but ultimately felt included in the meditative experience and the technical choreography, a manifestation of Lin's "selflessness" and "love."[93] Moreover, the company sometimes adapts the Orientalist language of critics; Jackson's above quote about Lin's unrivaled spirituality landed on promotional postcards for a fund-raising event.[94]

In 2011 Lin presented *From the Land of Lost Content* alongside the *Mandala Project*, which Jackson praised as a "masterwork of art, spirituality, and stagecraft."[95] Inspired by the Borobudur Temple in Java and Lin's sense of the sacred role of dance in Indonesia, the choreography and light gobos depict circular forms.[96] In the first section of the dance, titled "Earth Mandala," coached by the Chinese American puppet artist Hua Hua Zhang, the piece opens on the company of nine dancers, who are initially obscured from view. They move slowly across the stage shrouded by large sheets of wrinkled paper. Next, they begin to spin and toss the paper in the air, catching the wind like sails. After picking up speed and slowing again, they join one another in a clump, creating a nonhuman breathing organism. During the section titled "Unity—Returning to the Circle" the company of dancers, now all in red mandarin collar long-sleeve shirts and red pants, reminiscent of martial arts silks, count aloud as they expand and shrink a circular formation with stepping side-to-side. Lin thinks of this section as a clock, a symbol that represents impermanence. He relates the mainte-nance of this circle to the practice of spiritual awareness.[97] The dancers then take turns making loud vocalizations as they strike the air with legs and arms, collapsing into a heap together. To train for the piece, the company studied meditative practices with Hsu Hui Huang and Tibetan sacred ritual dance with the venerable Losang Samten, who is a former Tibetan monk to the Dalai Lama and current Philadelphia resident.

During the section titled "Mandala Offering," Lin emerges from the audience to dance a short solo in a flowing red robe-like costume, with excess fabric like wings. To the sound of recorded Tibetan throat singing, Lin begins spinning with his eyes closed. When a gong sounds, Lin stops in place and quickly drops his weight into a low squat. He traces a circle as his hands move inward and outward; then he sits in a raised seated medita-tion position with his eyes closed and pointer fingers touching thumbs. Like an orchestra conductor, he weaves his arms quickly and forcefully in the air, the fabric rippling in the light. He ends hands folded in a prayer position in front of his chest and then looks out, extending his arms toward the audience. This solo clearly represents meditation and focus. Lin clarifies that he feels that he meditates as a choreographer, working on the non-judgment of his dancers' performance.[98] Although the *Philadelphia Inquirer* critic Nancy Heller positively reviewed *Mandala* as "thrilling" and "theatri-cal magic," she complains of the literal nature of Lin's prayer gesture. She writes, "But it was a shame when Lin's otherwise elegant and inventive solo veered off into cliché, as he lowered his eyes and pressed his palms together, a posture soon copied by the other dancers. As the spiritual quality of the work had already been established, this was unnecessarily literal." Here, she applauds the spiritual reading of the work yet expresses a preference for spirituality conveyed via a particular kind of abstraction to strengthen its choreographic merit.[99]

FRAMING AND FUNDING ASIAN AMERICAN DANCE

In 2011 Kun-Yang Lin/Dancers collaborated with Hua Hua Zhang for a show at the University of Pennsylvania's Annenberg Center for the Arts. *Two Hands: Hua Hua Zhang's Visual Expressions* promised to "encourage the audience to distinguish between Western and Asian values and how the two can contrast with and embrace each other."[100] This statement mirrors Savigiliano's thoughts about harmonizing as sentimentalized empathy in which unspecified conflict (real or imagined) is supplanted by the equally unspecified unifying effects of World Dance. Audience reaction is often favorable to the illusion of harmony. Although the content of *Two Hands* featured predictable signifiers of Asia—dancers depicting emperors and dragons—Janet Anderson raved about the piece on behalf of the audience, which "exploded in enthusiasm for such an enthralling presentation that was pure magic from beginning to end."[101] She also incorrectly wrote that Lin hailed from Indonesia, not Taiwan. No one wrote a letter to the editor to correct this error, but Hua Hua Zhang did write a thank-you note for the review.

In the face of such a publicly positive response, Peter Price published a review on *thINKingDANCE* that criticized the piece's commodification of Asian culture and lack of interdisciplinary collaboration. His review was met with great hostility from members of the dance community as well as Kun-Yang Lin/Dancers' executive director. Unfortunately, some dismissed the review entirely because Price's writing style came across as mean-spirited and disorganized. The author and editors quickly amended the title "One from Column A" because of the criticism that it associated the performance with a Chinese takeout menu. The first paragraph addressed the idea of "glocalization," so I understood the title as a challenge to superficial collaborations and buffet-style multiculturalism. Price's review critiques Western romanticization of fusion and appropriated practices from cultural margins, but the backlash squelched this conversation.

Besides the title, one of the most controversial lines of the review reads as follows: "Although Lin advertises his work as a fusion of American and Asian influences, he is first and foremost a modern dance traditionalist and with every taste of traditional Chinese dance, Tai Chi or martial arts comes a full helping of Martha Graham (not everyone's cup of tea)."[102] In his letter to the editor responding to Price's review, Kun-Yang Lin/Dancers' executive director Ken Metzner balks at the terms "fusion" and "modern dance traditionalist," calling these words meaningless labels that Lin would not choose to use about his own work. Metzner also criticizes the lack of research conducted by Price about the intentions behind the performance, the presumed lack of editorial oversight by *thINKingDANCE*, and the subjective negative tone of the review. He deploys heated language to portray his belief in the prejudicial nature of the review: "Readers expect a critic to offer her/his own opinion based on objective investigation. To speak on behalf of unnamed others (as in 'not everyone's cup of tea') in a public forum dedicated to 'upping the ante on dance coverage and conversation' is unacceptable at best. At worst, it is a form of public lynching."[103] Throughout the letter, Metzner asserts a conventional definition of a dance review and calls into question the possibility of negative reviews for professional artists who work hard to develop their craft. While I agree that Price should not have written the phrase "not everyone's cup of tea," I see why he refers to Lin as a "modern dance traditionalist." I think this judgment stems from Lin's attention to inner psychology during his creative process, the training of the company in his specific technique, and his investment in proscenium stage productions. Metzner also clarifies Lin's influences are Taiwanese, not Chinese, which is likely more offensive than calling Lin Indonesian due to the tense cross-strait relations between Taiwan and the People's Republic of China. In addition to this letter to the editor, several other online comments called Price's review racist. A few others wrote in to defend the review, but the opportunity for productive dialogue about the politics of multiculturalism and collaboration was lost as many respondents focused on the tone of Price's review.

Many more of us in the dance community discussed the review's content and the controversy offline. Lin himself did not respond on- or offline, which unfortunately meant that his voice was buried by the online hostile conversation. At the time, I was also writing for *thINKingDANCE* and noted that many writers, including myself, felt nervous about making public critiques of local artists. The lack of negative reviews for both Shen and Lin exemplifies a crisis in Asian American cultural critique identified by Yutian Wong, "whereby the necessity of supporting and claiming the existence of one's community collides with the practice of offering honest or useful criticism."[104] In my opinion, some in the Philadelphia dance community responded to a critique of cultural essentialism by naming it racist, thus demonstrating the need for further public conversation about Orientalist and auto-Orientalist manifestations in dance. The above example shows that Savigliano's corrective to World Dance—*neighboring*—could also remedy the tendency toward Orientalist choreographing, producing, and marketing of Asian American dance. Neighboring allows for "instances of proximity—which do not constitute an idyllic relationality, but rather a permanent negotiation based on the encounters among others, without (and outside) the 'same' as an identitarian foundation."[105] This conception that permits conflict could disrupt the choreographic content, the audience reception, and the expectations of critical response by critiquing the Asian American internationalist dance market that continues to reproduce essentialist notions of Asian difference.

Metzner states that the author's use of the word "advertises" trivialized Lin's artistry. Nevertheless, in this funding climate all artists must advertise in order to sustain their creative work. Whether directed by their executive directors, publicists, or grant writers, they must advertise their work to performance venues and academic departments, all currently invested in multiculturalism. Metzner's letter seems to criticize Price's review for speaking about Lin's work in a way that goes against its branding. Most choreographers find their niche in terms of funding through branding. As Ann Daly writes, "A brand tells them how you are relevant to their lives, and how you are different from other dance companies. In short, a brand suggests to the world how to perceive your work before they've even experienced it for themselves and—even more—prompts them to want to experience it for themselves."[106] Daly places into business terms Susan Leigh Foster's acknowledgment that the beginning of the interpretation of dance occurs with the framing by the promotional materials that first announce the event.[107]

The business practices around producing dance works set up an understanding of choreography before the actual audience experience of attending a performance, thereby impeding any process for undermining Orientalizing stereotypes. Like Daly's advice to all dance companies, Asian American dance companies also face the challenge of claiming their uniqueness through branding in a competitive funding climate. At the time of this writing, both companies thrive. Kun-Yang Lin/Dancers is preparing to take *Mandala Project* to the tenth International Tanzmesse in Germany and Shen Wei Dance Arts is reviving *Connect Transfer* for the first time in six years for its China and Russia tour.

CONCLUSION

Throughout the course of researching these two choreographers, I have realized the extent to which their companies and the discourse surrounding their choreography exist online and not in academic texts. I have had trouble keeping up with the numerous e-mails that market the companies' upcoming performances or fund-raising efforts in addition to all the content on the web. The countless promotional videos, Facebook posts, quotations, reviews, and previews demonstrate that much of the information about dance is produced by fans, critics, and the artists' websites. When I wrote for *thINKingDANCE*, I never anticipated the emotional desire for positive reviews. Did the reviews really affect an artist's image or ticket sales? After all, the audience would form its own opinion of the work. I began to understand that reviews served not only as fodder for funding applications but also as sound bites for programs and websites. Although reviews in newspapers and online blogs have seemingly little influence over an artist's success, I cannot underestimate the capacity of the language in such material to determine how the audience experiences the dancing bodies onstage.

After an embodied performance, reviewers' words then appear on company websites and Facebook sites as endorsements. Journalists, dance critics, and the companies repeatedly deploy quotes such as "'deeply spiritual, remarkable'—*Dance Magazine*" to define Shen and Lin's work.[108] A Google search for the aforementioned *Dance Magazine* quote yields four pages of results, all of which mention Lin and none of which are linked directly to *Dance Magazine*. A search on the *Dance Magazine* site itself produces no results. This search, of course, exposes the more general problems of access and citation on the Internet; like a Facebook graphic, everyone seems to be sharing the same information without understanding its context. I have read the same words recycled by dancers, choreographers, fans, and critics without knowing who said them first. Furthermore, the choreographers might not write their Facebook posts, e-mail messages, or any other promotional materials themselves.

Within this authorless discussion, then, Orientalist rhetoric is circulated via the Internet without context and without the contributions of Asian Americanists working in dance studies who have repeatedly asked questions about dance and representation. Oftentimes, the language surrounding the choreographers' intentions comes to stand in for the analysis of the piece. This phenomenon neutralizes any tensions between the choreographer's intentions and what the audience perceives. In this way, little dialogue or healthy debate ensues. Instead, the fans "like" posts and join events while the dancers provide online testimonials. Auto-Orientalist content emerges within this endless feedback loop. It is difficult to begin a dialogue of *neighboring* and multiple perspectives in the face of such generalized language and without named authors. Due to the recent emergence of the scholarly field of Asian American dance studies, it is especially important for scholars to consider the ways that online media mediates Asian American dance and to intervene in the conversation.

NOTES

1. Steven Weisz, "Review: Kun-Yang Lin/Dancers—Beyond the Bones Revisited," *Dance Journal*, April 1, 2012, http://philadelphiadance.org/blog/2012/04/01/review-kun-yang-lindancers-beyond-the-bones-revisited/, accessed April 1, 2014.

2. Sara Kaufman, "From China by Way of New York, a Cultural Revolution," *Washington Post*, October 24, 2005.

3. Edward W. Said, *Orientalism* (New York: Random House, 1978).

4. John Kuo Wei Tchen, *New York before Chinatown: Orientalism and the Shaping of American Culture, 1776–1882* (Baltimore: Johns Hopkins University Press, 1999).

5. See Yutian Wong, *Choreographing Asian America* (Middletown, CT: Wesleyan University Press, 2010), for a discussion of aestheticized Orientalism.

6. For a complete list of Shen Wei's awards and commissions, refer to his website, Shen Wei Dance Arts, "About Shen Wei," http://www.shenweidancearts.org/about-shenwei/, accessed August 21, 2014.

7. Marta Elena Savigliano, "Worlding Dance and Dancing Out There in the World," in *Worlding Dance*, ed. Susan Foster (New York: Palgrave Macmillan, 2009), 176.

8. At the time of writing, a quick Google search with "east meets west" and the choreographers' names yields a page of approximately ten reviews/previews with the term for each choreographer.

9. Alistair Macaulay, "A Trilogy of Asia, Conceived in Motion," *New York Times*, July 10, 2009; Alistair Macaulay, "Woody Guthrie, Choreographer's Muse: Downtown Dance Festival at Battery Park," *New York Times*, August 17, 2012.

10. Guillermo Perez, "Wide Vistas from Intense Movement," *Fort Lauderdale Sun Sentinel*, April 6, 2004.

11. Savigliano, "Worlding Dance," 166, 168.

12. Cirque du Soleil, *Dralion*, July 19, 2013, https://preprod-www.cirqueduso leil.com/en/shows/dralion/show/about.aspx, accessed October 13, 2015.

13. Tchen, *New York before Chinatown*.

14. Yutian Wong, "Artistic Utopias: Michio Ito and the Trope of the International," in *Worlding Dance*, ed. Susan L. Foster (New York: Palgrave Macmillan, 2009), 150.

15. Ibid., 144.

16. Geoffrey Fowler, "At Lincoln Center: Shen Wei on Choreography Style," *Wall Street Journal*, July 7, 2009.

17. Geoffrey Fowler, "East Meets West on New York's Upper West Side," *China Real Time* (blog), *Wall Street Journal*, July 2, 2009.

18. Shen Wei Dance Arts, "About the Company," http://www.shenweidancearts .org/aboutswda/, accessed August 18, 2014.

19. "The Philo Project: Kun Yang Lin Dancers—Germany Appeal," YouTube video, 3:59, posted by The PHILO Project, March 21, 2014, https://www.youtube .com/watch?v=0RyQzNzkLVQ#t=55, accessed August 18, 2014.

20. Kun-Yang Lin/Dancers, "About the Company," http://kunyanglin.org /About1.htm, accessed August 18, 2014; Kun-Yang Lin/Dancers, *Mandala Project: A World Premiere*, February 2011, promotional postcard.

21. Kun-Yang Lin/Dancers, "About the Company."

22. Tchen, *New York before Chinatown*.

23. Kun-Yang Lin/Dancers, *ONE: Gifts from Afar*, program, 2013.

24. "'Speak English' Signs Allowed at Philly Shop," NBC News, March 19, 2008.

25. Shen Wei Dance Arts, "About the Company."

26. Kun Yang Lin/Dancers, "Mission," "History," and "Neighborhood," http:// kunyanglin.org/, accessed April 1, 2014.

27. Ananya Chatterjea, *Butting Out: Reading Resistive Choreographies through Works by Jawole Willa Jo Zollar and Chandralekha* (Middletown, CT: Wesleyan University Press, 2004), 108; Y. Wong, *Choreographing Asian America*, 45; Susan L. Foster, "Worlding Dance—An Introduction," in *Worlding Dance*, ed. Susan Foster (New York: Palgrave Macmillan, 2009), 6.

28. Kun Yang Lin/Dancers, "Mission," "History," and "Neighborhood."

29. Chatterjea, *Butting Out*, 128.

30. Y. Wong, *Choreographing Asian America*, 53.

31. Wen-Chi Wu and Yin-Ying Huang, "The State of Dance Research in Taiwan, Republic of China," *Dance Research Journal* 31, no. 1 (1999): 130–136.

32. Emily Wilcox, "Han-Tang *Zhongguo Gudianwu* and the Problem of Chineseness in Contemporary Chinese Dance: Sixty Years of Creation and Controversy," *Asian Theatre Journal* 29, no. 1 (Spring 2012): 206–232.

33. Cheng Kuang Yu, "The Transition of Nation Identity in Taiwan and the Politics of Exporting *Minzu Wudao*," *in Dance, Identity and Integration: Conference Proceedings, Congress on Research in Dance, International Dance Conference Proceedings, Taiwan, August 1–4, 2004*, ed. J. LaPointe-Crump (Cambridge, MA: Congress on Research in Dance, 2004), 80.

34. Emily Wilcox, "Against American Imperialism: The Forgotten Legacies of Third World Leftism" (paper presented at the annual Congress on Research in Dance/Society of Dance History Scholars Conference, Riverside, CA, November 14–17, 2013).

35. Ellen V. P. Gerdes, "Hard-Working Dance Students: Lessons from Taiwan" (EdM thesis, Temple University, 2009).

36. Thomas F. DeFrantz, *Dancing Many Drums: Excavations in African American Dance* (Madison: University of Wisconsin Press, 2002), 13; Y. Wong, *Choreographing Asian America*, 33.

37. DeFrantz, *Dancing Many Drums*, 11.

38. Y. Wong, *Choreographing Asian America*, 38.

39. DeFrantz, *Dancing Many Drums*, 16.

40. Angelo N. Ancheta, *Race, Rights, and the Asian American Experience* (New Brunswick: Rutgers University Press, 2001), 128.

41. See *People v. Hall*, *Fong Yue Ting v. United States*, Immigration Acts of 1917/1924/1964, and *Terrace v. Thompson*.

42. Angelo N. Ancheta, *Race, Rights, and the Asian American Experience*, 67–69.

43. Karen Shimakawa, *National Abjection: The Asian American Body Onstage* (Durham, NC: Duke University Press, 2002), 9.

44. Merilyn Jackson, "Hua Hua Zhang Puppetmaster," *Dance Journal*, December 4, 2010, http://philadelphiadance.org/blog/2010/12/04/hua-hua-zhang-puppet master/, accessed April 1, 2014.

45. Kat Richter, "Review—ONE Gifts from Afar," *Dance Journal*, March 26, 2013, http://philadelphiadance.org/blog/2013/03/26/review-one-gifts-from-afar/, accessed August 18, 2014.

46. Y. Wong, *Choreographing Asian America*, 40.

47. Ibid.

48. Ibid., 30.

49. Josephine Lee, *Performing Asian America* (Philadelphia: Temple University Press, 1997).

50. Both Lin and Shen occasionally dance in their own works or perform solos, and the racial diversity of their casts has fluctuated over the years. During 2013–2014 Lin showed a commitment to a multiracial cast. In 2014 Shen's company was composed of primarily white dancers.

51. Y. Wong, *Choreographing Asian America*, 38.

52. Chen Dance Center, "Our Repertoire," http://www.chendancecenter.org /index.php/the_company/repertoire/, accessed August 18, 2014.

53. SanSan Kwan, *Kinesthetic City: Dance and Movement in Chinese Urban Spaces* (New York: Oxford University Press, 2013), 116–118.

54. Maria Staub, "Shen Wei's Olympic Moves," *New York Sun*, June 9, 2008.

55. Zhao Xu, "Dancing in the Spotlight on Opening Night," *China Daily*, August 6, 2008, http://www.absolutechinatours.com/news/Dancing-in-the-spot light-on-opening-night-503.html, accessed August 18, 2014; Julie Bloom, "Before the Games Begin, He Has to Make Moves," *New York Times*, July 6, 2008.

56. Kuang-Ming Wu, "Chinese Aesthetics," in *Understanding the Chinese Mind: The Philosophical Roots*, ed. Robert E. Allinson (New York: Oxford University Press, 1989), 237.

57. Dai Jian, conversation with author, 2009.

58. Kun-Yang Lin/Dancers, CHI Movement Arts Center Schedule: "The class focuses on how, through modulation of breath, weight and weightlessness can co-exist simultaneously and energy can seamlessly transition among explosive bursts of rapid, expansive phrase work, and absolute stillness. Lin's vocabulary is dynamic, contemporary and global, drawing on Eastern philosophy to explore dance as the ultimate integration of 'body, mind and spirit.'" See http://kunyanglin.org/School -p2.htm, accessed October 15, 2015.

59. Shen Wei Dance Arts, *Connect Transfer II*, program notes, December 3, 5, 6, and 7, 2009.

60. Ann Daly, *Done into Dance: Isadora Duncan in America* (Middletown, CT: Wesleyan University Press, 2002).

61. "Olympics Opening Dancing Beijing 2008," YouTube video, 6:53, posted by Jerry Widjaja, August 11, 2008, https://www.youtube.com/watch?v=7scUIT 7z23Y, accessed October 13, 2015.

62. See Ellen V. P. Gerdes, "Shen Wei Dance Arts: Chinese Philosophy in Body Calligraphy," *Dance Chronicle* 33, no. 2 (2010): 231–250.

63. K.-M. Wu, "Chinese Aesthetics."

64. Lao Tzu, *Tao Te Ching: A New Translation*, trans. Sam Hamill (Boston: Shambhala, 2005), 150, 111.

65. Yu, "The Energy Flow," 258.

66. Xu, "Dancing in the Spotlight."

67. Jin-Wen Yu, "The Energy Flow of the Human Being and the Universe: Tai Ji Philosophy as an Artistic and Philosophical Foundation for the Development of Chinese Contemporary Dance" (PhD diss., Temple University, 1994), 150.

68. Lewis Segal, "That'll Leave a Mark: Shen Wei Dancers Will Turn the Disney Hall Floor into a Painted Canvas," *Los Angeles Times*, June 20, 2007.

69. John Hay, "The Human Body as a Microcosmic Source of Macrocosmic Values in Calligraphy," in *Self as Body in Asian Theory and Practice*, ed. Thomas P. Kasulis, Roger T. Ames, and Wimal Dissanayake (Albany: State University of New York Press, 1992), 183.

70. Shen is now working with dancers as installation. *Folding* was presented at the Temple of Dendur at the Metropolitan Museum of Art, New York; Limited

States Body Painting was presented by American Dance Festival; *Undivided Divided* is currently being toured.

71. Kun-Yang Lin/Dancers, *Autumn Skin: Journeys of East/West*, March 2010.

72. Lin's studio in South Philadelphia now offers a children's dance class: CHI Dance Mindfulness through Movement for Children. This class is advertised on its flier as a blend of modern dance and creative movement that will teach children "imagination, creativity, self-discipline and inner peace."

73. Sammy Lim, "The Dance Enthusiast Asks Kun-Yang Lin about Chi, His Mandala Works, and What He Would Do If He Were Not a Dance Artist," *Dance Enthusiast*, August 2, 2014, http://www.dance-enthusiast.com/features/view/kun -yang-lin14, accessed August 18, 2014.

74. Kun-Yang Lin, interview by author, August 2011.

75. Yin Mei actually manipulates a fan the same way in her */Asunder* (2001).

76. Kun-Yang Lin, interview by author, February 2010.

77. "The Philo Project," YouTube video.

78. Shen Wei Dance Arts, *Re-(Part 1)*, program notes, Kimmel Center, Phila-delphia, February 15, 16, 17, 2008.

79. Deborah Jowitt, "Dance: Springing into Action," *Village Voice*, September 26, 2006.

80. Paul Hodgins, "Acclaimed Dance Troupe Comes to Costa Mesa," *Orange County Register*, April 13, 2010.

81. Shen Wei, *Re-(Part III)*, program notes, Lincoln Center, New York City, July 9, 10, 11, 2009.

82. Robert Johnson, "East Meets West in Shen Wei's Brilliantly Imaginative Dance Trilogy," *Star-Ledger*, July 10, 2009, http://static.squarespace.com/static/538 ce592e4b0c9ce3db3bf4c/t/53c40ae3e4b07557fac24c14/1405356771963/Review_Re _II%20and%20III_2009.07.10_The%20Star%20Ledger.pdf, accessed August 20, 2014.

83. Anna Kisselgoff, "Dance; With His Heart in His Imagery," *New York Times*, June 24, 2001; Shen Wei Dance Arts, "Metropolitan Museum of Art, Temple of Dendur, 20th Annual Conference Gala Awards Dinner Performance: Shen Wei Dance Arts," YouTube video, 7:05, posted by committee100, July 8, 2011, http:// www.youtube.com/watch?v=brmvN83E5sA, accessed March 1, 2012.

84. Kun-Yang Lin, interview by author, November 1, 2008.

85. Shen has also used tourist photography as a backdrop to his choreography. For *Re-(Part II)*, dancers pose like sculptures in front of photographic images of tree roots that grow into ruined temples in Ankor Wat, Cambodia. During the intermis-sion of *Re-(Part I)* at the Kimmel Center in Philadelphia, Shen Wei Dance Arts staff sold books of Shen's photography of Tibet as a benefit for a Tibetan charity. Like Lin's Tibetan photographs, these images cite the Asian source of the choreography.

By displaying this photography, Shen and Lin further assume the authority to represent Tibet and Cambodia.

86. Y. Wong, *Choreographing Asian America*, 213.

87. In March 2013 I saw Kun-Yang Lin/Dancers at a larger venue, the Mandell Theatre at Drexel University. There was no intermission "ritual," and the distance from the proscenium stage made the choreography seem more presentational as an aesthetic experience.

88. Kun-Yang Lin/Dancers, *Mandala Project: Entering the Circle*, program, 2011.

89. Deni Kasrel, "Spirited Away," *Philadelphia City Paper*, February 16, 2011.

90. Kun-Yang Lin/Dancers, e-mail communication with author, February 28, 2011.

91. Merilyn Jackson, "Kun-Yang Lin's Quest: Connecting Body to Soul," *Broad Street Review*, September 4, 2010, http://www.broadstreetreview.com/dance/kun_yang_lins_quest_connecting_body_to_soul, accessed April 1, 2013.

92. Merilyn Jackson, "In Search of Honest Generosity: A Backward Glance at the Dance Season," *Broad Street Review*, June 26, 2010, http://www.broadstreetreview.com/dance/the_dance_season_nine_nighlights, accessed April 1, 2013.

93. Kat Richter, "Review—Be/longing: Light/Shadow," *Dance Journal*, March 29, 2014, http://philadelphiadance.org/blog/2014/03/29/12881/, accessed June 1, 2014.

94. Kun-Yang Lin/Dancers, promotional postcard, *Kun-Yang Lin/Dancers First Fundraiser*, October 2010.

95. Merilyn Jackson, "Spiritual Movement: 'Mandala' Is a Masterwork of Art and Stagecraft," *Philadelphia Inquirer*, February 12, 2011, http://static1.squarespace.com/static/52dec4c5e4b00bfdc05d604e/t/52eff2c8e4b03c2851db81d3/13914569 68717/20110212-phila-inquirer-review.pdf, accessed October 13, 2015.

96. Kun-Yang Lin, interview by author, July 3, 2013.

97. Ibid.

98. Ibid.

99. Nancy Heller, "Kun-Yang/Lin Dancers Program Marred by Repetition," *Philadelphia Inquirer*, March 25, 2013.

100. "Hua Hua Zhang's Visual Expressions," Annenberg Center Live, University of Pennsylvania, October 2011, http://www.annenbergcenter.org/event/hua-hu-zhangs-visual-expressions-181, accessed October 13, 2015.

101. Janet Anderson, "'Two Hands' at Annenberg: Magical Moments," *Broad Street Review*, October 18, 2011, http://www.broadstreetreview.com/dance/two_hands_at_annenberg1, accessed August 18, 2014.

102. Peter Price, "'Two Hands' from Hua Hua Zhang's Visual Expressions," *thINKingDANCE,* November 5, 2011, http://thinkingdance.net/articles/2011/11/05/Two-Hands-from-Hua-Hua-Zhangs-Visual-Expressions, August 18, 2014.

103. "Letters from Rev. Ken Metzner, TD and Helen Faller," *thINKingDANCE*, December 4, 2011, http://thinkingdance.net/articles/2011/12/05/Letters-from-Rev.-Ken-Metzner-TD-and-Helen-Faller, accessed August 18, 2014.

104. Y. Wong, *Choreographing Asian America*, 128.

105. Savigliano, "Worlding Dance," 184.

106. Ann Daly, "Defining Your Brand Identity: What Business Are You In?," *Chicago Artists Resource*, http://www.chicagoartistsresource.org/articles/defining-your-brand-identity-what-business-are-you, accessed October 14, 2015.

107. Susan L. Foster, *Reading Dancing: Bodies and Subjects in Contemporary American Dance* (Berkeley: University of California Press, 1986).

108. "Kun-Yang Lin/Dancers," Facebook, https://www.facebook.com/kyldancers, accessed August 8, 2014.

6

An Asian American *Land*

Eiko & Koma Choreograph Cultural Politics

ROSEMARY CANDELARIO

Two figures lie on a stage covered with a canvas that echoes the colors and shapes of the desert: sand, rock, and minerals are evoked in the colors and textures of the massive painting. Curled on their sides facing away from one another at a great distance from the audience, the two bodies slowly draw closer together by minutely opening and lengthening their torsos and limbs until they meet, back to back. One lying atop the other, the pair then crawls downstage at the pace of a desert tortoise, their lower bodies wrapped in skins that camouflage them against their vast surrounds. They arrive only to retreat back upstage side-by-side. Glacial, this local migration is accompanied by two musicians playing a ceremonial flute and drum while hovering downstage of the expanse to participate in calling the space into existence, yet not occupying it. Watching Eiko & Koma's *Land*, I am transported to another space that is both here and not here. It is not another place that I could travel to on my own, but we are, collectively, somespace else.

≈

I want to think about dance as generating space, not only phenomenologically but also politically. I want to think about the ability of dance to tell us something about the place where we live, and how it has been formed, and continues to be formed through concerted human activity. I want to think about how the space of a dance has the ability to describe the larger space we inhabit.

When the dancers Eiko & Koma moved to New York City from Tokyo in 1977, they settled in the United States as the country underwent a major demographic shift in the wake of the Immigration and Nationality Act of 1965 and a concomitant political shift in response to identity-based movements such as the Third World Strike. They made *Land* in 1991, at the culmination of the Cold War and just a few short years after the passage of the Civil Liberties Act of 1988 granted reparations to Japanese Americans interned during World War II. It was created at a time when multiculturalism was attempting to acknowledge and manage the increasing diversity of the nation while American Orientalism continued to hold Asians apart as "model minorities."

In what follows, I argue that reading *Land* from a critical Asian American perspective has significant implications for theorizing spatial formation. By using the term "spatial formation," I am referencing Michael Omi and Howard Winant's theory of racial formation, which proposes that racial identities and categories are socially constructed on both micro and macro levels.[1] Race is therefore not fixed but fluid, influenced and enforced by social, economic, and political relations. The idea of "spatial formation" adds space to the list of relations that work to construct race. Scholars such as Steven Hoelscher and Laura Liu have pointed out that processes of racialization and geographic concentration are mutually implicated.[2] For example, what we imagine about a place extends to how we think about the people who live there, and conversely our opinions about the inhabitants of an area largely define that locality. SanSan Kwan suggests that because this interdependent relationship between race and place is not fixed, it needs to be constantly reinforced, and that performance is an effective means of doing so.[3] In other words, performing bodies have the ability to intervene in the race-place relationship as well as to reinforce it, and may even do both at the same time.

However, such a reading of *Land* has not been possible because of the occlusion of Eiko & Koma as Asian American subjects. In what follows, I identify the sources and impacts of this occlusion. In the second section, I theorize the spatial formation choreographed by *Land*, what I call "spaces apart," and in the final section I examine how these "spaces apart" function in relation to diaspora and Asian America. Throughout, Eiko & Koma's choreography serves as both object of analysis and a theoretical model of contemporary Asian America. Although I focus here in depth on a work from 1991, I contend that Eiko & Koma's body of work over the last four decades aids in the understanding of post-1965 Asian American spatial formation by demonstrating how and why contingent, multiple, and dia-sporically mobile "spaces apart" are generated.

A Multicultural *Land*

Eiko Otake (b. Tokyo 1952) and Takashi Koma Yamada (b. Niigata 1948) grew up in postwar Japan, in the midst of rapid industrialization, signifi-cant rural to urban migration, and unprecedented economic upswing. They both joined the massive student protest movement in the late 1960s, rally-ing against U.S. military bases in Okinawa, the Vietnam War, and govern-ment control of education. From the streets, each found their way to *butoh* cofounder Hijikata Tatsumi's Asbestos Hall in 1971, where despite a lack of dance experience, they were able to live and participate in his avant-garde cabaret shows, which were performed in Tokyo theaters and generated in-come to support Hijikata's studio and work. After only a few months, the pair left Asbestos Hall together. They began to create their own cabaret shows and happening-like performances and took workshops with Ohno Kazuo, *butoh*'s other key figure. By the end of 1972, they left Japan for Europe, intending to support their travels by performing. In Germany they made contact with Manja Chmiel, a noted soloist and the former assistant to Mary Wigman. Chmiel entered Eiko & Koma in an important choreog-rapher's competition in Cologne, where to their surprise they were selected as one of three finalists. The competition brought the duo much acclaim and further performance and teaching opportunities in the Netherlands and Tunisia. They returned to Japan two years later, and after a further year of study with Ohno, they made their U.S. debut at the Japan Society in 1976. They relocated to New York City the following year and quickly became critically acclaimed members of the American avant-garde and post-modern dance scene. Awarded the MacArthur "genius grant" Fellowship in 1996 and Doris Duke Performing Artist Awards in 2012, Eiko & Koma are celebrated for their slow-moving dances grounded in elemental con-cepts, such as *Grain* (1983), *River* (1996), and *Mourning* (2007), their favor-ing of nontraditional performance spaces, and their use of a style that employs subtle shifts of movement over time.

Eiko & Koma premiered the seventy-five-minute *Land* in 1991 at the BAM Next Wave festival.[4] The dance was a collaboration with the Taos Pueblo musician Robert Mirabal and the New York–based artist Sandra Lerner. Mirabal composed the Bessie Award–winning score for flute, drums, rattles, and voice, which he and Reynaldo Lujon performed live, and for which Mirabal later won a Grammy.[5] Lerner contributed the dance's environment: a massive backdrop and floor cloth. As part of the process of creating the piece, Eiko & Koma visited Mirabal in New Mexico, and the artists then traveled together to Japan, visiting Hiroshima and presenting a work-in-progress showing of *Land* at the Hiroshima City Museum of Contemporary Art.

While the title *Land* is decidedly broad, the opening moments of the dance establish specific references within which the term is meant to be understood. The lights come up on Mirabal and Lujon standing center stage in ceremonial Taos Pueblo dress. Their position center stage places them at the heart of a Southwest environment evoked through the colors and textures of Lerner's set cloths and indicates that the land of this dance is precisely theirs. As the two proceed solemnly downstage, stopping just short of entering the audience to take up their instruments, they seem to usher in a ritual space. It is only after the musicians have begun their flute, drum, and sung score that our attention turns to Eiko & Koma, lying almost

FIGURE 6.1. Robert Mirabal (flute), Ben Sandoval (drum), Eiko (*top*), and Koma in *Land* (photo © 2015 by Johan Elbers)

immobile upstage. Wrapped in supple leather, the two have choreographed themselves as creatures inextricable from this indigenous landscape.

It is possible to view *Land* as a multicultural production that romanticizes a Native American interconnection with the earth and suggests parallels to a mythic Japanese relationship to nature.[6] Indeed, reviews of the dance by leading and local dance critics alike focused heavily on the Native American aspects of the performance, understandably so given the distinctive staging, score, and costuming that differed from Eiko & Koma's previous works in their specific and striking references to Pueblo landscape and culture. Furthermore, the dance was viewed as an intercultural collaboration between the avant-garde and the traditional, again a justifiable impression in light of Eiko & Koma's reception as avant-garde dancers upon their arrival in the United States. It is important, nonetheless, to acknowledge the assumptions that underlie this reading of the dance, and what those assumptions authorize or occlude. For example, the *New York Times* dance critic and long-time Eiko & Koma reviewer Anna Kisselgoff seemed confused that *Land* was not the spiritual "ode to the earth" she expected. Her review focused largely on how the dance did—or did not, as was largely the case—celebrate the land or portray a spiritual connection to it. This led the critic to observe, "A culture that is at one with nature, like that of the American Indian, will hardly lose its essence, even when it is, as in this case, sophisticated. How a sophisticated civilization can reach back to such a culture is another matter."[7] It is unclear from Kisselgoff's review whether "sophisticated civilization" is meant to refer to Eiko & Koma's Japanese heritage, their status as international artists, or their membership in the New York high art scene.[8] It also glosses Mirabal's status as a decidedly contemporary artist and subsequent Grammy winner. Kisselgoff's intent of one or the other meaning is ultimately unimportant because in each case the end result is the same: Eiko & Koma's "sophistication" is seen to enable universalist messages about the environment or the spirit world. Not only does such a reading play into long-standing appropriations of Native American dance by American modern dance, but it also precludes other possible readings of this dance that pay attention to Eiko & Koma as Japanese Americans.[9]

Eiko & Koma's failure to live up to Kisselgoff's expectations for *Land* evidently did not signal to the reviewer the necessity for a different approach to reading the dance, one that takes into account the causes for the friction she saw in place of the celebration she anticipated. This is not surprising, given the prevailing pattern in American modern dance of Asian Americans being misread and even effaced. Yutian Wong points to the pervasive and ongoing Orientalism in and of American modern and postmodern dance that not only impacts the reading of choreography and dancing bodies but also has functioned historically and continues to function today in complicity with national legal and political discourses that maintain Asian Americans as perpetually other, even within the nation.[10] Wong's emphasis on a contemporary and nationally specific Orientalism is helpful in understanding the ways the performance of "modern" (as opposed to "traditional") Japan in the form of an avant-garde movement practice such as Eiko & Koma's dances can still read in Orientalist terms. However, it is not only a problem of Asian American dancers being "unseen and misrecognized" due to Orientalism.[11] In fact, the flip side is often the case: bodies constructed by Orientalism are often *hypervisible* to such an extent that they erase from view the individual bodies or alternative narratives being staged.[12]

If the hypervisibility of Orientalism erases specific subjects, multiculturalism selects and holds up certain individuals as proof of the ability of the nation to incorporate difference. A 2005 *Dance Magazine* special issue on race demonstrates how dominant multiculturalism is in structuring discussions of race in the mainstream dance world. In the article "Asian Dancers, a Balancing Act," Maura Nguyen Donohue quotes the Asian American choreographer Minh Tran in order to highlight the very real ways Orientalism and multiculturalism impact choreographers and dancers:

> "I can assure you that Stephen Petronio wouldn't have blinked an eye at me if I hadn't been Asian and male.[13] I was a rare and exotic commodity. . . . When I got my first commission at Oregon Ballet Theatre I was really young and unknown and suddenly sharing a platform with Bebe Miller, Donald Byrd, and Paul Taylor. What was I doing there?"[14]

Tran clearly articulates the ways that Petronio's Orientalist gaze and the Oregon Ballet Theater's multicultural commissioning project functioned to make his self-described "fusion of traditional Asian and contemporary western techniques" a hypervisible, and thus desirable, commodity.[15] His query "What was I doing there?" is part incredulity at being made equivalent

with older, established choreographers, and part rhetorical question pointing out the ways he as an Asian male dancer—"rare and exotic"—has been
selected (to stand) for inclusion in American dance. Donohue follows Tran's
question with the observation that although "considered by some to be
mere tokenism, this openness to Asians has worked to the benefit of many
dancers," pointing to the fact that for Asian Americans already subjected to
the model minority trope, multiculturalism can sometimes serve to under-
line a discourse of exceptionalism that can translate into career-advancing
opportunities.[16]

What I am trying to demonstrate here is how Orientalism and multiculturalism work together to triangulate the location of contemporary Asian
American dance and determine how it is viewed, whether that dance draws
from traditional Asian, avant-garde, or modern movement vocabularies.
Certainly, Eiko & Koma have benefited from multicultural programming
practices of organizations such as the American Dance Festival, a frequent
presenter and commissioner of their choreography, and the MacArthur
Foundation, which honored them with a fellowship in 1996, to name but
a few. Their dances are widely praised and honored by the mainstream
dance press, albeit often through an Orientalist lens. Yet Lisa Lowe claims
that Asian American cultural politics is an oppositional force that operates
as a countersite to American national culture, even when it appears to be
fulfilling hegemonic functions. How can we reconcile these seemingly contradictory perspectives? That is, can dances function on a register of Orientalism and multiculturalism while at the same time effecting a critique
of those systems?

Returning our attention to the choreography, what happens if we
approach the staging of *Land* not as grounds for universalist messages but
as the specific site of engagement between Japanese Americans and Native
Americans? What happens if we examine the specificities of the land on
which these four artists meet? In the next section I home in on Eiko &
Koma's use of space, their movement vocabulary, and their relationship to
the music(ians), in order to suggest another possible reading of the dance,
one that notices how Eiko & Koma use their choreography to tackle ideas
that expand the purview of Japanese American issues beyond internment
to include the nuclear bombing of Hiroshima and Nagasaki and extend
transnational and intranational Asian American solidarity, despite the fact
that their work does not conform to expectations for Asian American

dance to engage narratively or stylistically with Asian American histories and traditions.

CHOREOGRAPHING *Land*, CHOREOGRAPHING SPACES APART

Unlike the cross-continental and international air travel that characterized the creation of *Land*, Eiko & Koma's minimal movements in the dance keep them connected to the ground, and to each other, for the first third of the piece. They seem to not be able to move except in close contact and cooperation with one another. Not only must they support and actuate their own trunks and limbs, but they must sustain the other's as well. Rather than fighting against gravity, they give in to it, pouring their weight into one another and the ground beneath them, at times blurring the boundaries between their bodies and their environment. This approach to movement takes time to initiate and carry out. As we observe their slow progress, attuned to every small shift, we note how Eiko & Koma simultaneously move with the land, become a microcosm of the landscape, and merge with the land itself.

Eiko & Koma's use and understanding of space in *Land* diverges from that of modern and postmodern dance, where exploitation of the entire stage area is imperative. Modern dance was designed for the proscenium stage with a frontal orientation that declares that the center is the most important spot, an orientation I call spatial hierarchy. Early modern dance choreographers such as Doris Humphrey and Martha Graham took it as a given that particular parts of the stage communicated specific narratives or emotions. In this view, a trajectory from upstage right through center to downstage left, for example, conveyed a hero's journey.[17] Postmodern choreographers such as Merce Cunningham, although still working within the constraints of the proscenium, sought to democratize the dance space, rejecting the centered, frontal orientation of modern dance in favor of endless possibilities of spatial patterns and facings. In making all spaces equal on stage, this approach opens up the range of possibilities for movement and for meaning. In contrast to these examples, Eiko & Koma's danced space seems to be very specific and very local. They use only a small part of the large set, as if to imply that their bodies, while materially linked to the land, cannot and perhaps should not occupy it all. Their corporeal argument about *Land* is a spatial one, asking how we move through it, with whom, and to what ends.

Land asks us to think about the local and the specific, with its concentration on where we are at each particular moment, to acknowledge that right here, right now, deserves our full and careful attention. At the same time, the mutual choreography of dancers and musicians continuously reminds us that the local is relational, showing us how the two pairs functioning in different realms nonetheless work toward the same goal. The space of this dance is not established in isolation from others. It is neither secreted from the dancer's body nor formed phenomenologically by humans alone.[18] Instead, it is generated in alliance with the musicians and the set. The music and dance are not synchronized, yet they are in a cooperative relationship with one another. Skin skimming and sinking into the set acknowledges the drum beats that suffuse the space. The floating flute melody observes the bodies below. This is a shared space, generated by both groups. More than that, however, the choreography articulates a particular orientation to space in general and describes—kinesthetically and aurally—a new space, a space apart.

In articulating the spaces apart that are generated by Eiko & Koma's choreography, I seek to push beyond the physical reach of the dancing body to a place where choreography may serve as a nexus of the politics of place, reflecting and constructing a multiplicity of interrelationships among bodies, sites, and technologies. A choreographic practice such as the one I am articulating for Eiko & Koma across their body of work acknowledges a mutual co-construction of bodies and places, in which neither are fixed entities but are both always radically open and contingent.

This is consonant with Eiko & Koma's choreography in general. For Eiko & Koma, space is, in fact, produced by the particular relationship between performing human bodies and their movement vocabulary, the setting, and the technologies—in the broadest sense of the term—used to bring the performance to fruition. In the case of *Land*, the set, the live music, and the musicians themselves all connect together with Eiko & Koma to form something that the dancers could not form on their own. The process of connection does not, however, transcend the specificities of the constituent parts but rather is predicated on existing affinities. This process, I argue, effects the creation of a space apart where alternatives to the dominant society may be rehearsed and entrenched binaries such as nature/culture and east/west may be challenged. Eiko & Koma's constant (if not always discernable) activity suggests that the labor of establishing and maintaining a space apart is a constant process. When the performance is over, the particular space apart dissipates, although its effects may linger in the audience. Spaces apart can be tangible spaces in a way that a utopia can never be.

To define "spaces apart," I favor de Certeau's sense of space as a practiced place, that is, a space that is created through conscious and unconscious uses of a place.[19] For de Certeau, place is delimitable, stable, a locus of power; space, to the contrary, is in motion, practiced. If place is a map, then space is a walking tour. While de Certeau focused on the everyday, often unintentional, actions of humans, I extend this idea to include the impact of improvised and choreographed performance. It is precisely a Certeauian tactical and contingent human activity that can initiate a space apart.

I have chosen the word "apart" for its sense of separateness, but also because, coming from the Latin *a parte*, it etymologically contains a sense of existing alongside. A space apart is both detached from and beside the places from which it is formed. This is crucial because it means that the space may be accessible to people—for example, an audience—beyond those who participate in its generation. It is a space to try out alternatives, especially ones that interrupt established binaries or fixed categories. Not permanent, these spaces are contingent and temporary, existing only for the duration of a particular project.[20] The spaces can, however, be regenerated and may even travel from site to site to be generated at multiple locations. For this reason, I either refer to spaces apart in the plural to indicate their inherent multiplicity, or with an indefinite article to indicate the particularity of a specific space apart.

Spaces apart are contingent, multiple, and diasporically mobile. The spaces circulate within the context of national borders and global flows of capital, people, and culture. Spaces apart are not determined by the locations where they are generated, but they nonetheless come into being at specific time and sites and thus are formed in a larger geography in which history and politics meet. In other words, they respond to their sociopolitical-historical contexts as well as shape them. For example, as Eiko & Koma toured with Mirabal, they repeatedly generated a space apart that questioned how and why these Native Americans and Japanese Americans might share this *Land*.

Spaces apart generated by Eiko & Koma's choreography, including but not limited to *Land*, are not a spatial segregation. Nor are they a phenomenological and aesthetic replication of the dominant U.S. legal, political, and ideological system of racial formation, in which "America" has been defined through the ongoing exclusion of Asians who thus constitute a necessary part of that same identity. This abjection of Asian Americans is both a process and condition of American national identity formation in which Asian Americans are both "constituent element *and* radical other."[21] Instead, spaces apart are a site where Asian American cultural politics, to borrow Lisa Lowe's term, may be practiced and alternates to national U.S. culture may be explored.[22]

Victor Bascara further delineates Lowe's term by breaking it down into its constituent parts. Key for my purposes is how he defines "cultural" as well as "cultural politics": the former is significantly a *process* that produces subjects, whereas the latter in the U.S. context "has meant the infusion of historical materialism and political economy into critiques of . . . racial formations."[23] Asian American cultural politics, then, "sets the terms for describing the process by which Asian difference was and is managed in American culture,"[24] but it also is the process by which that same national culture is challenged. In other words, the production of Asian American subjects is simultaneously a production of the possibility of Asian American agency and critique. Since both politics and the law are tied up in the nation from the beginning, culture becomes the one site where agency can be exercised and critique can emerge because it is "in culture that individuals and collectivities struggle and remember and, in the difficult remembering, imagine and practice both subject and community differently."[25] Memory, remembrance, and forgetting thus become central themes, methodologies and epistemologies of Asian American cultural politics. Remembrance here is not a simple act of uncovering lost histories or of recuperating erased heroes. Forgetting and memory and remembrance are instead critical modes of survival in which the act of imagining, remembering, and narrating the past is very much part of the construction of the present and even the future.

"Asian American cultural politics" is not a discrete product, though it (they?) can be enacted through particular cultural productions. Cultural politics in this sense is a doing, an action, an emergent critique, a *movement*. Indeed, because of the alienated relationship of Asian Americans to state and capital, Asian American cultural productions are oppositional "even and especially when that literature appears to be performing a canonical function."[26] That is, Asian American culture is *inherently* a countersite to American national culture and also increasingly to a globalized commercial culture.

If we view *Land* from this point of view, we see how the choreography of Native American musicians, Japanese American dancers, and a desolate desert landscape creates a space that calls to mind the historical relationship of New Mexico to Japan, and of Native Americans to Japanese and Japanese Americans, which was also echoed in the *Land*'s development process. During the making of the work, Eiko & Koma took Mirabal to Japan after spending time with him in New Mexico, even performing together in Hiroshima at the City Museum of Contemporary Art. The mutual travels of the artists remind us how Hiroshima and the desert setting of *Land* are sites mutually implicated in a nuclear age; nuclear weapon technology was, after all, developed and tested in New Mexico before being deployed in Japan.[27] *Land* generates a space apart, a countersite, where we can ask how Japanese, Japanese Americans, and Native Americans can act in solidarity with one another, calling attention to the fact—surely no coincidence—that New Mexico and other southwestern lands were considered by the American government to be useless, and therefore to be equally useful for containing Native Americans on reservations, interning Japanese Americans, and testing nuclear devices with the intent of using them on Japan.

But *Land* also suggests a way to think about Japanese Americans' relationship to the American continent, acknowledging that the current relationship is deeply implicated with the history of race, racism, and racialization in the United States, beginning with the genocide and forced relocation of Native Americans. It is a meditation on the connection between humans and the land they occupy that casts its attention across continents and back and forth across history. Persistent inequities, however, mean that interned Japanese Americans received reparations from the government as part of the Civil Liberties Act of 1988, but reparations for Native Americans have not been forthcoming. Victor Bascara argues that the Civil Liberties Act enabled the United States' narrative about Japanese Americans as model minorities at the very moment when it needed to justify the dismantling of welfare programs in its shift from Keynesian to neoliberal economic policies.[28] Native Americans offered no such strategic use under neoliberalism. *Land* presents these multiple meanings and inequities together on one stage, holding them together without attempting to resolve them.

Land in Diaspora

As I have discussed, for the first third of *Land* Eiko & Koma remain in full bodily contact with each other and with the ground, all of their attention directed toward forming linkages with their immediate material and aural surrounds. The space apart that forms as a result—a space for exploring historical and environmental relationships among Native Americans and Japanese Americans—becomes upright and mobile in the second two-thirds of the dance. The transition from one section to the next is ushered in by a young boy who purposefully walks the center line of the stage, downstage to up, never turning to face the audience.[29] His shoulders draped in a cloak, he is utterly alone in the dim light, save for the high notes of Mirabal's flute that accompany him on his travels.

When first Eiko and later Koma return to the stage, they repeat the child's migration, albeit in different directions. Often their trajectories follow a straight line, but sometimes the clarity of the path is lost, and the figures seem to wander. After the close communion of the first section, Eiko seems lost on her own. Yet when Koma rushes to join her, their brief interaction is full of joints jutting at awkward angles, and she soon departs, leaving Koma to languish as if disoriented or unrooted. Kisselgoff calls them "dislocated creatures"; her reading is unable to register more than the mere fact of dislocation because multiculturalism erases historical and material differences in favor of portraying an equalizing portrait of American incorporation. But if we think about Eiko & Koma as Japanese immigrants, and as Japanese Americans, we can understand this dislocation as a sort of diaspora in which one's relationship to the *Land* is not fixed, nor does it flow uninterrupted from one generation to the next. Rather, the space is in motion, across generations.

Normally when we think of diaspora it is linked to the image of dispersal, of a people leaving their homeland behind for a new life in a new land. Such a view of diaspora, traced through ancestry and immigration, could be expressed choreographically as a journey along the diagonal from upstage right to downstage left, a one-way trajectory not dissimilar from those favored by Doris Humphrey, across which a protagonist moves from the darkness of the past into the bright promise of the future. This approach to diaspora underscores a multicultural understanding of the United States, in which immigrants leave behind a previous life in order to be incorporated into the American dream.

Eiko & Koma's choreography in the second two-thirds of *Land* suggests another model that argues against this normative definition of diaspora. Instead of a straightforward, unidirectional path, we witness a multitude of crossings that challenge us to think beyond ideas of origin and destination— spatially or temporally—in favor of more complex notions of relationality. More specifically, if we cast our vision to the margins of the space, or rather if we remember that the aural and kinesthetic, traveling separate routes, have arrived here to form together this local and temporary space, we could see their sharing of this *Land* as an attempt to offer a new approach to concep- tualizing Asian America as a relational and dynamic space that is simulta- neously specific, local, and contemporary, even as it acknowledges and grapples with intranational and international history by constructing stra- tegic alliances with others who have shared or intersecting experiences. While offering these possibilities, and responsibilities, *Land* also demon- strates how they may be obscured by the operation of multiculturalism and Orientalism.

We see this when the final moments of *Land* reference the musicians' opening simple walk from upstage to downstage along the center axis. This time, however, it is Eiko who makes the journey, spurred on by Lujon's regular, insistent rattle and Mirabal's floating melody. For minutes she does nothing but hesitantly walk. Tentatively she bends her right knee, its flexion lifting her heel off the ground. Leg muscles somehow coordinate to scooch the ball of her foot forward along the ground before the knee and heel give into gravity and the whole process starts again. Along the way, her footing becomes more assured, her pace more even. Her arms begin to rise to her sides—a tightrope walker nearing the center of her line, a confident head thrown gently back. But symmetry gives way as first one vertebra wavers off center, then suddenly many, sending Eiko's head in a slow-motion deep sideways arc. As her upper arm seeks to restore the balance and right her trunk, her palm turns toward the audience, revealing an object, perhaps a totem, clasped there. For a brief moment of equilibrium, Eiko's eyes pierce the audience, her hand and its contents held insistently aloft. Is it a warn- ing? She collapses before we can fully apprehend her message. Behind her, Koma wends his way forward, while the small boy confidently crosses up- stage. The boy does not engage with the others on stage, as if he cannot see them. It is not a hopeful ending, or even an ending for that matter. The migrations and music continue well after the stage is darkened, suggesting that these diasporic movements are ongoing and that the causes for them are unresolved.

I have attempted to demonstrate here how *Land* makes space—literally and figuratively—for the negotiation of Asian identity in America, as well as the contours of Asian America itself. Through their formal experimentation, Eiko & Koma engage in a discourse that struggles with the forgetting and remembering of histories of war, violence, immigration, and diaspora that link Japan and much of Asia to the United States, histories that are not part of the past but indeed are present and active in Asian American communities. By embodying these linkages and disjunctures, memories and gaps in their dances, Eiko & Koma repeatedly "seize hold of a memory as it flashes up at a moment of danger" and insist that we continue to look at it.[30]

Notes

1. Michael Omi and Howard Winant, *Racial Formation in the United States from the 1960s to the 1980s* (New York: Routledge, 1986).

2. Steven Hoelscher, "Making Place, Making Race: Performances of Whiteness in the Jim Crow South," *Annals of the Association of American Geographers* 93, no. 3 (2003): 657–686; Laura Liu, "The Place of Immigration in Studies of Geography and Race," *Social & Cultural Geography* 1, no. 2 (2000): 169–182.

3. SanSan Kwan, "Performing a Geography of Asian America: The Chop Suey Circuit," *TDR: The Drama Review* 55 (Spring 2011): 120–136.

4. *Land* was cocommissioned by the Next Wave Festival, the American Dance Festival, and the Lied Center at the University of Nebraska. An excerpt of a performance at the University of Wisconsin, recorded by Douglas Rosenberg, is available on the Eiko & Koma website at http://eikoandkoma.org/index.php?p=ek&id=2521.

5. Ben Sandoval replaced Lujon on drums in some performances.

6. Shoko Letton takes care to trace similarities between the Taos Pueblo worldview and Japanese mythology and connect these to particular narrative moments in *Land*. Shoko Letton, "Eiko And Koma: Dance Philosophy and Aesthetic" (MA thesis, Florida State University, 2009).

7. Anna Kisselgoff, "An Indian at One with the Buffalo in Eiko and Koma's Spirit World," *New York Times*, November 7, 1991.

8. Yutian Wong argues that the word "international" "is often used to gloss the political exigency of racial, ethnic, gender and class difference suggested by the term 'artist-of-color.'" Yutian Wong, "Artistic Utopias: Michio Ito and the Trope of the International," in *Worlding Dance*, ed. Susan L. Foster (New York: Palgrave Macmillan, 2009), 144–162, quote on 144. At the same time that these "international"

artists are seen as able to transcend borders in a way their fellow migrants cannot, they are never allowed to be grounded as American, nor is their work deemed capable of engaging in American discourses on race or identity. At best, these artists are seen as producing work with "universal" or transcendent themes that is therefore capable of universal impact. Ultimately, however, the trope of the international is a (failed) attempt to gloss very real material and political conditions with a romantic vision of the artist (usually an artist of color) as able to transcend race, bridge cultural gaps, and heal social wounds. To become international then is to be deracialized, while at the same time remaining susceptible to racist policies.

9. On the relationship between Native American dance and modern dance, see Jacqueline Shea Murphy, *The People Have Never Stopped Dancing: Native American Modern Dance Histories* (Minneapolis: University of Minnesota Press, 2007).

10. Yutian Wong, "Towards a New Asian American Dance Theory: Locating the Dancing Asian American Body," *Discourses in Dance* 1, no. 1 (2002): 69–90.

11. Y. Wong, "Asian American Dance Theory," 86.

12. I borrow the term "hypervisibility" from Preeti Sharma, "The (T)errors of Visibility" (MA thesis, UCLA, 2008). Attention to the hypervisibility of Orientalism resonates with ways that Karen Shimakawa and Celine Parreñas Shimizu have written about Asian American theater and film, respectively. See Karen Shimakawa, *National Abjection: The Asian American Body Onstage* (Durham, NC: Duke University Press, 2002); Celine Parreñas Shimizu, *The Hypersexuality of Race: Performing Asian/American Women on Screen and Scene* (Durham, NC: Duke University Press, 2007).

13. Petronio is a prominent New York–based postmodern choreographer. That he is a white gay man adds an eroticizing component to his already exoticizing and power-filled gaze on Tran, a component I do not have the space to explore further here.

14. Maura Nguyen Donohue, "Asian Dancers, a Balancing Act," *Dance Magazine*, June 2005. *Dance Magazine* is a widely circulated publication targeted at dance professionals and aspiring dancers, primarily but not exclusively in ballet.

15. Minh Tran & Company, http://www.mtdance.org/, accessed June 11, 2009.

16. Donohue, "Asian Dancers."

17. This view of the meanings of stage space, operative in much of modern dance, was famously articulated by Doris Humphrey, *The Art of Making Dances*, ed. Barbara Pollack (New York: Grove Press, 1959). See especially "The Stage Space," 72–90.

18. José Gil theorizes that the dancing body secretes from itself the space of the body, whereas Maurice Merleau-Ponty sees space not as a preformed site but as something that is constantly being created and re-created through the movement of the human body. José Gil, "Paradoxical Body," *TDR: The Drama Review* 50, no.

4 (2006): 21–35; Elizabeth Grosz, "Space, Time, Bodies," in *Space Time and Perversion: Essays on the Politics of Bodies* (New York: Routledge, 1995), 83–102.

19. Many social scientists follow the geographer Yi-Fu Tuan's definition of place as security, home, a felt attachment in the face of an undifferentiated space that, while offering freedom and openness, lacks any sort of individuation or personal identification. Space in this case seems to exist prior to human activity, which particularizes a universal space into a place. Yi-Fu Tuan, *Space and Place: The Perspective of Experience* (Minneapolis: University of Minnesota Press, 1977). Michel de Certeau's approach sees both place and space as constructed and particular, the former by power and the latter by everyday practice. Michel de Certeau, *The Practice of Everyday Life*, trans. S. Rendall (Berkeley: University of California Press, 1988).

20. In this sense a space apart shares some similarities with Edward Soja's concept of Thirdspace, in which space is neither solely material nor symbolic but is contingent and constructed. Edward Soja, *Thirdspace: Journeys to Los Angeles and Other Real-and-Imagined Places* (Oxford: Blackwell, 1996).

21. Shimakawa, *National Abjection*, 3.

22. Lisa Lowe, *Immigrant Acts: On Asian American Cultural Politics* (Durham, NC: Duke University Press, 1996).

23. Victor Bascara, *Model-Minority Imperialism* (Minneapolis: University of Minnesota Press, 2006), xxvii.

24. Ibid., xxviii.

25. Lowe, *Immigrant Acts*, 3.

26. Ibid., 31. Lowe's analysis focuses on literature, but the arguments are applicable to other cultural forms.

27. The Fukushima Daiichi nuclear power plant disaster in Japan on March 11, 2011, once again brought concerns about nuclear power to the fore, in Japan and around the world.

28. Victor Bascara, "Cultural Politics of Redress: Reassessing the Meaning of the Civil Liberties Act of 1988 after 9/11," *Asian Law Journal* 10, no. 2 (2003): 101–130.

29. This role was originated by Eiko & Koma's six-year-old son, Yuta. In later years his younger brother, Shin, took on the part.

30. Walter Benjamin, "Theses on the Philosophy of History," in *Illuminations*, trans. Harry Zhon (New York: Harcourt, Brace & World, 1968), 255.

7

Ambivalent Selves

The Asian Female Body in Contemporary American Dance

MAURA NGUYEN DONOHUE

This chapter focuses on the process by which two dance artists—from within the Asian diaspora—manifest ambivalence as they simultaneously engage and disrupt static and narrow parameters of Asian and Asian American identities. The choreographers Yasuko Yokoshi and Sam Kim perform their own racially different (and thereby perceived as culturally foreign) bodies within an unmarked (white) postmodern dance aesthetic. As dance artists who regularly present their choreography in the experimental "downtown" venues of New York City's contemporary dance scene, Yokoshi and Sam combine seemingly opposite or incompatible performance elements together to create and resist representations of cultural identity.

New York City is home to organizations such as the Asian American Arts Alliance, the Asian American Arts Centre, the Asian American Writers Workshops, and a number of Asian American theater companies that have been instrumental in supporting and developing the careers of Asian American artists working across a wide range of genres including dance, theater, music, writing, and the visual and media arts. These organizations recognized the need to support Asian Americans given the historical dearth of opportunity allowed artists-of-color in the mainstream art world. In addition to supporting the development and production of work by Asian American artists, Asian American arts organizations recognize the Asian American experience, history, and issues affecting Asian American communities as valid subject matter for art making. These politics align and are in conversation with the intellectual trajectory of Asian American studies. The ideals set forth in the Asian American Movement of the 1960s and identity politics of the 1990s have influenced the politics of the Asian American arts scene through the late twentieth and early twenty-first centuries. Asian American artists have benefited from funding and performance opportunities provided by such organizations, but artists such as Kristina Wong have questioned the expectations of what Asian American audiences expect from Asian American artists.

In her 2003 solo performance *Free?*, Wong, of bigbadasianmama and Fannie Wong Miss Chinatown 2nd Runner Up fame, pokes fun at the themes that Asian American artists are expected to address in their work. The opening segment of the show, titled "Checklist," features Wong standing in front of a list of tasks projected on a large screen. The tasks include instructions to "appeal to growing Asian American Hip hop / spoken word demographic . . . reference to foods from homeland or offer snippet of 'mothertongue' . . . and confront the overly exhausted issue of Asian stereotypes." Wong embarks on a five-minute routine in which she fulfills every single task on the list in a rapid-fire manner. Every time she completes a task from the list, a large check mark appears next to each item, the implication being that Wong has satisfied the expectations of an Asian American artist trying to establish a career at the turn of the millennium. This chapter examines the work of Yoshiko and Sam, whose works have not abided by the kinds of expectations that Kristina Wong satirizes in the "Checklist." This is not to say that the choreographers do not engage with politics of otherness in their works, but they do so in aesthetic terms that have not been accounted for within Asian American discourses invested in obvious representations of immigrant or racialized experiences. In doing so, these artists engage the possibility of avant-garde performance as a haven for the ambivalent body.

Through physically intimate presentations of both the familiar and the exotic—as located in their live, performing bodies—Yokoshi and Kim both invite and disrupt readings of otherness. Yasuko Yokoshi is a Japanese transplant who questions authenticity and identity in a mobile and fluid world where the merging of cultures is increasingly prevalent. As an artist she has been called both "unruly" and "enigmatic," revealing the thorny process of assessing her cultural bonds by a public that values appropriate, explicable behavior.[1] The Korean American choreographer Sam Kim's works defy standards of propriety. She actively denies the hegemony of both dance technique and conceptions of cultural alliance. Without making explicit references to Asian American experiences, Kim handles the terrain of public representation by situating herself into spaces dominated by American pop culture references.

Many artists resist disciplinary labels imposed by the producers, curators, funders, and critics who require distinctions between dance, theater, interdisciplinary work, or performance art. Additional labels marking gender (female choreographer), race (Asian female choreographer), and sexuality (queer Asian female choreographer) can further marginalize an artist by limiting the scope of imagining who and what she will speak to. Straddled with the burden of an ever-increasing list of qualifiers, the "Asian female dance artist" expands the potential for an artist to be in conflict with discrete categories.

So, it is no surprise that neither Yokoshi nor Kim call themselves Asian American dance artists. Their work does not tell stories about the experience of immigrating to the United States or the contradictions of citizenship. They do not concern themselves with portraying cross-cultural misunderstandings or racial stereotyping. There is no presence of intergenerational conflict or the pull from an earlier homeland against the lure of the new one. Their work as choreographers has not been overly concerned with proving their Americanness or establishing their Asian credentials. They do not make use of narratives pitting silk ribbons against denim, nor do they bear the external trappings of exoticism to satisfy a curatorial imperative for diversity. Instead, their works are most deeply engaged in formal pursuits and offer examples of the potentially broad scope of aesthetic material available for consideration as Asian American performance.

The tension between the evolving internal identity of an artist and the constraints imposed by external categories of social, political, and aesthetic alignment is always present for artists who are pushing at the edges of their forms. Yokoshi and Kim have purposefully distanced themselves from the Asian American arts community. Theirs is not a new stance. The multidisciplinary artist Ping Chong has often expressed a public ambivalence to be labeled as an Asian American artist. As a native of New York City's Chinatown, Chong is the son of Cantonese Opera performers. His prolific body of work in theater and dance bridges intimate venues and opera houses across the United States, Europe, and Asia. His professional career has been punctuated with two Obie Awards, two New York Dance and Performance ("Bessie") Awards, a Doris Duke Award, and a Guggenheim

Fellowship, and his work has been presented at major venues such as the Kennedy Center, Lincoln Center Festival, Brooklyn Academy of Music, Spoleto USA Festival, Vienna Festival, RomaEuropa Festival, Lille European Capital of Culture, Tokyo International Arts Festival, Singapore Festival of the Arts, and many others.

On the surface, Chong's stature within the avant-garde theater and dance scene would seem to make him an icon within the Asian American arts community, but in Alvin Eng's 1999 collection *Tokens: The NYC Asian American Experience on Stage* he characterizes the problem of classification. He writes:

> I'm not a "professional Asian American" so I've dealt with it in my own personal way. I've never been a joiner of any one group. By personality or choice I've always been Other. People say he's part of the avant-garde, well the white avant-garde never really academically accepted me. Like with Performing Arts Journal, I never really fit into their white theories. Then some Asian American organizations might say, "Oh, he's not really part of the Asian American scene." But then because I have visibility and am needed, then I'm part of the Asian American scene. The funny thing is that sometimes the people who are saying to me, "You're not Asian American," don't even speak their own language. They're completely American pie really and I don't judge that . . . am I supposed to judge them because they don't know anything about their culture? Yet they say to me, "You're not Asian American."[2]

The resulting twofold nature of Chong's ambivalence toward racially identified artistic allegiances results from perceived rejections from dual fronts. Rejected by the Ivory Tower academics whose theorizations of experimental work ignore his contributions and by the *jook-sing* or third-generation members of the Asian American arts community, Chong embraces an outsider position that fuels his creative work.[3]

The scope and reach of Chong's creative work pursuits are expansive. In 2006 he was named to the first class of USA Artist Fellows in recognition of his contributions to American arts and culture. In 1992 he embarked on an oral history project titled *Undesirable Elements*. Based on the oral histories of actors and performers who live in the communities where the work is produced, *Undesirable Elements* has been produced in over forty different communities in the United States and abroad. Although Chong does not draw upon Asian American identity as a singular point of reference, he has drawn upon the collision between Asia and the West as source material for projects such as the *East West Quartet*—a series of works addressing colonial relationships between the United States, Japan, China, and Vietnam. In taking on the role of the outsider to examine major historical issues such as the arrival of Commodore Perry in Japan, World War II, and the U.S. war in Vietnam, Chong utilizes fragmented narratives, cross-racial casting, and experimental staging. His work blurs the lines between text-based theater and technique-driven dance.

The experimental quality of Chong's work is often accused of creating work that is inaccessible as compared to that of his contemporaries in theater who create linear narratives about immigrant experiences. His works do not feature characters that are discernably Asian American and are often confusing to Asian American audiences who are expecting to identify with a recognizable Asian American character. His refusal to concern himself with the expectations of Asian American audiences and the ambivalent nature of his outsider status continues to be important to his artistic practice. Chong came to performance from a background in film and established a name working with the NYC experimental choreographer and composer Meredith Monk. Artists such as Monk, Phillip Glass, Julie Taymor, Robert Wilson, Tan Dun, Blue Man Group, and many other well-regarded innovators had their earliest starts at New York's La Mama Experimental Theater Club. As a resident artist of La Mama, Chong was a recognized figure in a community of contemporary performance that championed the use of the body, sound, and language in new modes of expression. La Mama ETC was founded by Ellen Stewart in a basement in the Lower East Side of Manhattan and maintains its mission to support artistic exploration and experimentation. In addition to Ping Chong & Company, La Mama has housed many influential Asian diaspora organizations as resident companies including La Mama Chinatown (which became Pan Asian Repertory), HT Chen & Dancers, Sin Cha Hong's Laughing Stone Dance Company, Kinding Sindaw, Yara Arts Group, and Slant Performance Group.

It is from venues like La Mama that the idea of a "downtown" arts scene grew, and it is within the downtown arts scene that Chong's work has thrived and Yokoshi's and Kim's work has developed. In a community that values the blurring of categorical divisions and the reduction of traditional modes of presentation, contemporary choreographers have actively supported the shared motivation to develop an original voice in the service of new, boundary-breaking, artistic practice. Within the mandate of innovation for the avant-garde is the need to hone and disseminate art that is different from what has come before and that bears the identifiable and individual stamp of its creator. When Chong explains that he has dealt with Asian Americanness in his "own personal way" and provides details of his conflicts with the white-dominated avant-garde and the artistically conservative Asian American arts community, he articulates the challenge that experimental artists have in developing their own original voice against the larger external demands of social representation. Regardless of whether their works carry or address the influence of an Asian heritage, it becomes easier for modern, diasporic artists in America to avoid allegiance with anything other than their own aesthetic vision.

In Yokoshi's 2006 work *what we when we*, she may seem, at first glance, to be adhering to the perpetuation of stereotypical representations, such as that of the exotic, Asian female. The women in her cast appear muted, affecting a level of gentle restraint in focus and physicality. To an untrained eye this seems easy fodder for latent Orientalist beliefs. Inside Yokoshi's

FIGURE 7.1. *what we when we* (photo by Yasuko Yokoshi)

orchestration of the seemingly exotic, her arrangement of her own and other culturally marked bodies, and the use of an exclusive and traditional Japanese form, we can find her bringing forward ideas from Western dance and American mores. Yokoshi's deliberate presentation of ambivalence to a downtown dance audience reflects her agenda to exploit and alter notions of Otherness.

what we when we is inspired by Raymond Carver's acclaimed collection of short stories, *What We Talk about When We Talk about Love*. Yokoshi has sheltered Carver's spare and fundamentally American short stories within the placid frame of Japanese traditional, Kabuki Su-odori dance. Su-odori is the stripped down form of Kabuki dance, devoid of its intense costume makeup and exaggerated gestures. Yokoshi spent three years training with Masumi Seyama VI, the direct disciple of Kanjyuro Fuji, who is celebrated for refining Su-odori into its own art. "Su" is translated as "bare, fundamental, pure, simple and natural" and "odori" as dance. This "naked dance" maintains a signature style focused on the "refined articulation of ambiguity."[4]

By concentrating her physical and aesthetic schema toward the engagement of a traditional Japanese performing art, Yokoshi voluntarily makes the deeply integrated nature of a Japanese aesthetic explicit in this work. The concern for order, beauty, and a sophisticated type of subtlety is a deeply rooted component of Japanese society. Almost any aspect of daily life can be enacted with conscious grace and can serve as opportunity for aesthetic satisfaction. This integration, called "aesthetic egalitarianism," brings attention to every aspect of even the seemingly most mundane activity. However, when everything can serve as rewarding aesthetic experience, then additional criteria must be employed to develop some valuing of aesthetic achievement. For the purposes of looking at Yokoshi's interest in "refined ambiguity," the blending of concepts of *yojo* (emotional aftertaste in poetry) and *yugen* (mystery and depth) into a specific Japanese aesthetic becomes vital. It brings the appreciation of minimalism and indirect communication to the foreground, highlighting a respect for the spectator's imagination. "A straightforward outpouring of feelings and ideas, while it may provide optimal, unambiguous communication, is considered crude and uncouth, hence aesthetically undesirable."[5] Su-odori, as a technique, physicalizes the deep-seated beauty of ambiguity; and Yokoshi, as an artist, uses this tradition to full effect in *what we when we*, presenting moment after moment of compelling interactions and poetic interpretations of the text that happen against the concrete exposition that a literal and translatable narrative would provide.

However, Yokoshi is not a traditional Japanese artist. Born in Hiroshima, Japan, she came to the United States in 1981 with an extensive background in classical ballet and kendo to study choreography and theater at Hampshire College in western Massachusetts. Over the course of twenty-five years in the United States, her work repeatedly reflected her interest in bringing multiple mediums and cultural elements together. She has authored an autobiographical book, *Once in a Life Time*; directed a documentary video, *Last Sokoshi*, based on her complex family history; and performed works in various museums and alternative performance venues in the United States, Europe, and Asia. Yokoshi is a two-time New York Dance and Performance (Bessie) Award–winning choreographer (the second awarded for *what we when we*) and is the first New York Live Arts Resident Commissioned Artist, which is an invitation-only program that offers a salary, health benefits, a two-year residency, a commission of a new work to premiere at NYLA, and the potential for a fully produced tour. Yokoshi's newest work continues her collaboration with Seyama and her "in-depth research of the parallel aesthetics of traditional and contemporary forms and the authenticity and ownership of culture."[6]

what we when we is constructed on a foundation of sophisticated Japanese minimalism spotlighting the sparest dramatic indications and coloring it with "a very specific tone of grey" that still allows Japanese tradition a home within contemporary America.[7] The dance is not a literal retelling of Carver's modern stories by Kabuki dancers. The dance dwells more on Carver's ambivalent sentiment than on the actual narrative; and the dancers are not Su-odori dancers who have been training for a lifetime. These dancers enact a physical ambivalence by imposing a cultural body onto their own bodies. Yokoshi exerts this resistance against category by placing a group of ethnically Japanese dancer bodies (with contemporary Western dance training) inside a contemporary dance structure (consisting of traditional Japanese movement vocabulary and aesthetic). Here the somatic realness of the dancers (their Japaneseness) comes in contact with the social unrealness of their portrayal of culture (traditional Japanese in a contemporary dance setting).

Yokoshi intentionally arranges time and space to bring the audience closer to a culturally different way of engaging with the work. The pace is calculated to focus our attention on the details and on the smallest and slightest shifts, so as to experience the work with a kinship for Japanese aesthetic egalitarianism. In reality the work takes little over an hour to unfold in the sanctuary of New York City's St. Mark's Church located in the East Village where Danspace Project presents performances. It is possible to feel as though Yokoshi manages to stop time. No movement is wasted, and every act is deliberate. Passion and violence are reduced to a shifting glance, a controlled look, or a controlled motion. Some audience members sit on the red L-shaped carpet on the hardwood floor, creating a setting of physical equality within the performance zone. The dancers Ryutaro Mishima, Kazu Nakamura, Matsuhide Nakashima, Hiromi Naruse, and Yokoshi enter and exit the performance space following similarly angled pathways. When the dancers sit kneeling side by side with their shoulders touching, they are in very close proximity to many audience members.

Yokoshi introduces bits of character play as one way of making her way around explicit narrative. Mishima often pulls our attention, appearing as "something of a world-weary swaggerer, often with a cigarette."[8] He slowly leans in to wrap his arm around Nakamura to take his chin in one hand and try to kiss him. Nakamura pulls away, and later the same exchange is repeated between different dancers. One group sits for a long time pouring one another tea (or sake), pulling cigarettes out of sleeves, and adjusting matchboxes. Sometimes the men portray women. Both Nakamura and Nakshima perform refined female head tilts and glances with superb comfort and skill before shifting back for an energized masculine Kabuki trio with Mishima. Yokoshi seems to be employing experimental contemporary gender play, but this too is derived from conventional Kabuki-styled *onnagata* (female impersonator) performances. As Kabuki is traditionally only performed by men, the role of the *onnagata* would not stand out as odd for a Japanese audience. But for a Western viewer, the gender play explicates a concerted effort to enact different cultural mores.

These differentiating factors of dress, physical manner, and gender performance evoke the exotic, lulling us with images of gentle women, effeminate men, and the promise of a faraway land that does not exist, while actually giving us the women and men of a much closer realm that easily could exist. In a review of the work, I noted feeling an instant nostalgia for a Japan I had never encountered "beyond the film screen."[9] The snapshot images may look like a Japan of our imagination, partly fed by a latent belief in the sublime grace of an entire culture, but in reality Yokoshi and her fellow performers are telling us an American story. Carver's tales follow two couples who spend a lot of time sitting, drinking gin, and talking about love and loss. On the book's back jacket, the scholar and critic Frank Kermode notes how Carver's writing "is so spare in manner that it takes a time before one realizes how completely a whole culture and a whole moral condition is represented by even the most seemingly slight sketch." Carver gives us an America where life is not sublime or perfect but familiar. Yokoshi gives us that America, too. In utilizing the seductive pace and intense focus of Su-odori and casting racially marked Asian bodies in the choreography, Yoko-shi manages to alter our idea of America by making its signifiers almost invisible.

Yokoshi has stated that she works to subvert any distinct reading on which the audience might settle.[10] By not attempting a literal translation of the stories into dance, she is again able to affect an intricate encounter between the unfamiliar and the common. We are not bogged down by a narrative that defines the artistic agenda, but in catching glimpses of a world that constantly shifts, we see tensions and socially ordained behavior that is both part of a recognizable adult American life and not. The purposeful ambiguity results in a work unwilling to be placed solely within the realms of traditional Japanese or Eurocentric contemporary dance. She still manages to draw these cultures into each other but then ripples them away in constant and highly subtle ways. This amalgamation of styles forces frequent re-viewings of our ideas for tradition and innovation. The shape of a couple's intimacy may not parallel a typical American structure, but the emotional undertones of desire and disgust are recognizable in culturally specific ways.

In a 2006 interview with fellow choreographer Tere O'Connor for Movement Research's *Critical Correspondence*, Yokoshi discusses her ability to achieve the interplay between experimentation and convention by playing at a "super-individualistic American role—which is uniqueness and freedom and expression matters" inside a form that is all Japanese. For her, "living in the States as a foreigner for this long, and contemplating this completely different value system constantly, everyday," has forced a constant awareness of her otherness. With *what she when she* Yokoshi employs that consciousness of her additional otherness. Now considered a foreigner in Japan (after having lived in the United States for decades), she has been granted access to restricted material:

The reason why I had access to this is because I live in the United States. I think my teacher originally thought of me as American artist, because this is exclusive art form. If I lived in Japan, I couldn't get into the school, no way. I just don't have access to it. But because I'm in the States for so many years . . . I guess it's a distance thing so, she knows I'm Japanese, of course, but the distance made her excited.[11]

Distance allows Yokoshi to do something with this material that "is pretty much taboo and impossible to use in a different context." In effect she is "hacking the system." This hacking occurs at multiple levels. In one way, the somatic role of her Japaneseness implies authenticity through a Western filter, but in actuality, as she states, "though you are from that culture, you don't practice it, at all."[12] The culture is not of a Japan that exists outside of organized rituals paying homage to history.

Yokoshi pulls apart the conflicting ideas and attitudes of her doubled Otherness to "hack" the system, turning the ambivalence of her outsider status into the avenue for a successfully blended, holistically sound work. She is able to appropriate this form in the United States where that Western filter allows us to celebrate these bodies inhabiting multiple levels of difference, their difference from a mainstream white body and their difference from the Japanese tradition. During our interview, Yokoshi recounted how Japan Society's artistic director Yoko Shioya fought against Yokoshi's 2005 New York Dance and Performance Award because she thought the critical appreciation of it was based in an ignorance and exoticism, that the dance community was rewarding Yokoshi for an incorrect belief in authenticity. I would argue that this audience was, in fact, rewarding her for her transgressions against authenticity. Their bodies create a suspension of culture, allowing for distance and objectivity at the illusion of social constructions, at, as Yokoshi states, "one's desire of a culture. Because, really, you don't call it culture. It's just your life."[13]

Yokoshi's statements repeatedly correspond with Ann Cooper Albright's championing for readings of the body that include, and value, the kind of practical consciousness a performer possesses and presents, moving the feminist discussion of the cultural construction of the female body further: "Cultural identity is not necessarily synonymous with somatic identity. Yet neither is a somatic identity any more 'real' or essential than a social one simply because it is anchored in the body. Rather the two are

interconnected in the process of living that we call experience."[14] Yokoshi
places the physical and cultural experiences of her dancers adjacent to the
physical and cultural experiences of her audience, creating a meeting of
an American writer's fictional world with the fictional world of Kabuki.
Albright's expansion of Judith Butler's concept of "becoming" to include
choreographic performance allows me to consider a noticeably different
occupation of the Asian body by reading Sam Kim's body in her solo performance, *Avatar*. In *Avatar* Kim is neither a socially constructed entity—
a tabula rasa or a passive, empty vessel into which society pours all of its
values—nor is she a wholly natural entity that exists outside of the cultural
sector. She operates in a state of bothness.

After graduating summa cum laude and Phi Beta Kappa from Barnard
College in 1995, Sam Kim began performing and making work regularly in
New York City to much critical and professional acclaim. Her work has
been commissioned and produced by all the key experimental dance venues
in the city. She, like Yokoshi, was a Movement Research artist-in-residence
and has been deeply involved with the downtown dance community in
various advocacy capacities. She has danced with many downtown NYC
luminaries and was invited to apprentice with the Bill T. Jones/Arnie Zane
Company. When discussing Kim, against such qualifiers as "Asian American," "female," and "contemporary artist," we must acknowledge the complicated nature of her own relationship to these identity constraints, which
she considers "clunky and cumbersome."[15]

It serves well to consider her work in a historical context. In an attempt
to extract herself from a historical classification of postmodern dance and
where everything an artist does is viewed within the context of historical
precedence and thus by nature a reference to the past, Kim is part of a collection of artists who have begun to consider themselves as posthistorical
to work beyond the nomenclature of current discourse. Ironically, this very
desire to redefine the present principles of art making—and how she is
perceived within this process of art making—arouses an unwitting homage
to the early struggles of Bill T. Jones. Jones, like Ping Chong, began working in the 1970s as an ambivalently racialized avant-garde choreographer in
a white art scene. A look at the significant parallels in Jones's and Kim's
lives and visions reveal the challenging terrain experimental artists of color
in America have continued to traverse.

Jones and Kim share the similar experience of growing up in largely
white communities, Jones in upstate New York and Kim in midwestern

America. Jones is one of the most highly regarded choreographers of our time. Aside from his role as executive artistic director of New York Live Arts (the organization established out of a merger of Dance Theater Workshop and the Bill T. Jones/Arnie Zane Company), he has received two Tony Awards, a 1994 MacArthur "Genius" Award, Kennedy Center Honors, and induction into the American Academy of Arts and Sciences, and he was named "An Irreplaceable Dance Treasure" by the Dance Heritage Coalition. For Jones, the role as leader of an organization he called "an outpost for the avant-garde" is a nod to his legacy of forging opportunities for artists of color through an unrelenting focus on unqualified artistic excellence and a deeply rooted resistance to marginalizing descriptors.[16]

Jones's childhood awareness of societal difference forged an early ambivalence about the desire to participate in the white social situations that required repeated denials of the African American household from which he came (and to which he would return).[17] Kim acknowledges her adolescent experience as a primary force in the development of her "own keen outsider mentality."[18] These formative experiences created a level of cultural multiplicity for both artists and played itself out in what can be viewed as a highly political choice of aesthetic, whether called postmodernist, avant-garde, contemporary, or downtown. Jones was influenced by his studies of experimental movement in the "minimalist Asian-modern dance fusion of Kei Takei and the postmodern concepts of the Judson Church dancers."[19] Yokoshi was the first resident commissioned artist in Bill T.'s new artistic home, where Kim also shows her work. The ties binding the three artists center on a shared relationship to artistic practice rather than any racially defined tethers.

Like Ping Chong's work, Jones's work has remained intellectually demanding, brutal, and beautiful, while regularly focused on a concern with social justice. Similarly, Jones too has expressed a conflicted relationship with narrow, racial, and cultural allegiances:

> I rankled at being called a "black artist." Coming of age in the '60s, I had embraced a host of values that placed a premium on freedom from social definition, and being so described seemed an attempt to diminish individuality, to reduce the possible interpretations of what I was trying to express. It seemed perpetuated by racist people. Add to this my deep feeling of alienation from both black and white culture and the implicit social tension between the white avant-garde and black performers, and this strategy became essential.[20]

However, Carl Paris questions Jones's "alienation" in his 2005 article "Will the Real Bill T. Jones Please Stand Up?" as misleading, offering that the artist never actively separated from his ethnicity but in fact used his racial identity when needed. I would claim this as Jones asserting a similar ambivalence to being pigeon-holed that the much younger Kim maintains.

For Kim, coming of age as a Korean American in the suburbs of St. Paul, Minnesota, endowed her with a profound experience of marginalization:

> I was always viewed through the lens of race first and foremost, i.e. I was a virtual cardboard cutout. This ran counter to how I saw myself: an artist with a progressive worldview who never accepted the blunt trappings of identity as sufficient terms for self-definition. However, this constant being at odds with the world forced me to cultivate a razor-sharp awareness of how others "read" identity, and gave me insight into how much of a construct identity is at core.[21]

Kim acknowledges her otherness and claims it as her own historical narrative. It is her own lifelong preoccupation, but she does not manifest it in her work in an obvious or literal manner. This has not unshackled her from a situation similar to Jones's early experience with the African American community's apathy toward his work as a result of his own objections to being called a "black artist." Kim has striven to place herself outside of racial discourse while claiming alienation from both mainstream (white) and marginalized (racially marked) cultures. The avant-garde becomes a refuge even when Kim acknowledges that whether her identity is a performed construction or a natural manifestation of culture, it does not change the way that she is perceived as an Asian American woman.

Kim's willingness to defy conventional ideas of how a proper Asian artist should exhibit herself could make her a problematic figure in a discussion of race and dance. [22] Her complicated status as an Asian American female artist can be understood if considered within a context similar to feminist critiques of the German choreographer Pina Bausch's representation of women. In some of Bausch's earliest works touring in the United States it was "generally agreed that Bausch's neutral presentation of gender violence was a failure of political obligation."[23] Feminist critics expected female artists to actively choose and act within the parameters of a recognizable political agenda. A female choreographer was expected to uphold a progressive message within her own artistic work. Marginalized communities have enacted similar responses to artists in their community who are reluctant to firmly accede to such group expectations.

Kim's 2006 solo, *Avatar*, was commissioned and presented by the Taiwanese American choreographer H. T. Chen's *Ear to the Ground*, which is a semiannual performance series held in Chinatown's Mulberry St. Theater. The context of Kim's participation in Chen's series, which primarily supports self-identified Asian American artists, reveals a particular ambivalence to the complicated structures of dance making and presentation in NYC. Based in Chinatown, H. T. Chen's Mulberry St. Theater (now Chen Dance Center) is geographically part of the downtown environment and has been the initial launching pad for many NYC dance artists, including the choreographer Muna Tseng, who cites working there as "the beginning of my consciousness as an Asian American artist."[24] Unlike his showcase series, *Newsteps*, which is open to all emerging choreographers, the *Ear to the Ground* series is not generally considered part of the downtown circuit because of its culturally specific agenda, though it has served over thirty artists since 1994. However, whether one identifies as Asian American or not, most choreographers are loath to give up commissioning money and residency time.

Chen has been a part of the experimental community, as a resident company of La Mama, and in 2009 he was honored with a NYC Mayor's Award for Arts & Culture for over thirty years of supporting the work of other artists and serving the NYC Chinese community. While his choreographic work is a blend of Western modern dance with Asian aesthetics (generally, Chinese dance vocabularies), he does not require similar observance from the artists he commissions. Kim's dance reveals no signifiers of Asia, no trappings of foreign lands or mystifying ambience. There is neither a blending of traditional dance forms nor an invocation of contemporary ones such as butoh. In fact, there is nothing to frame the work as ethnically aligned except for the frame of a small Asian woman on the tiny stage. That frame is vitally important, as if to say that it is all there is, and is all we are to face and figure. We as an audience are there with her, and her essential self is what the viewer is being privileged to appreciate.

Avatar is a solo she made, singularly, for herself in order to reveal herself in work that was "completely sincere and by sincere I mean not earnest but honest."[25] The work is about identity without succumbing to the standard structures of much identity-based solo performance.[26] *Avatar* is about the choreographer working to embody herself in performance to achieve total presence and openness in time and space with a viewing public. The choreography is not a showcase for technique but a dismantling of technique.

Avatar begins bright and loud with Kim facing the upstage right corner, her back to the audience. The feminist pop/punk band Le Tigre blasts from the speakers as Kim slowly walks backward downstage. After turning forward, she lurches forward zombie-like until she clearly shatters the front row's comfort zone. Audience members shift and giggle. She gurgles and stands, opening her jaw and shifting it side to side. A slow light cue fully illuminates the audience while Kim jumps onto the spectator risers and writhes in front of the mirrors that line the house left wall. Later, she lies on the floor and traces her name with different parts of her body. She also sits on the floor in front of the audience and tickles trails up her left arm with her right hand before tracing patterns on her torso, eventually mapping out a big heart along the front of her body. She ends by lying down on her left side at the feet of the front row, to a song by the band Deep Lust blaring from the speakers.

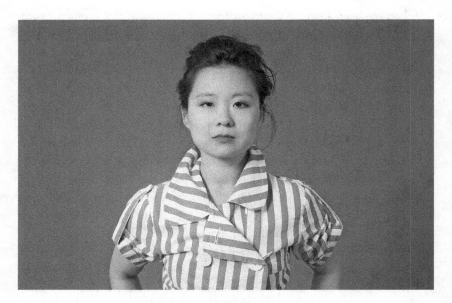

FIGURE 7.2. Sam Kim (photo by Ryan McNamara)

This works as a revelation and a challenge to the audience. Kim thrusts her body into our sightlines and commands that our attention be focused on her, on the very present, natural reality of that body. Kim brings self-conscious insolence to the stage by simply presenting herself to the audience, instead of portraying a fictional character. The dance shocks, not so much in the revelation of her slight female form but in her boisterous disregard for propriety as a woman, as a dancer, and as an Asian person. She is unapologetically acting out and acting up, demanding our consideration without decorating herself in frivolous movement, virtuosic display, or seductive beauty. This resistance against familiar notions of dance works to unsettle the audience and separates Kim from the apparently harmless spectacle that dance often offers. In effect, Kim is propelled as an agent for moving authentically and as an enemy of cultural aesthetics of ideal beauty.

She demands recognition for her own physical reality, for her beingness, which defies a typical notion of the dancer/audience exchange. The audience has paid to see and consume her, but she does not make that exchange pleasant because she presents herself as a desirable product. Her challenge to the traditions that govern the nature of a dance performance and cultural representation celebrates her differentness and refuses to disappear or rewrite physical disparity inside a nicely framed package (i.e., within an aesthetic of beauty, grace, and line). Kim insists on sincere ingestion and refuses any attempt to overcome, transcend, or transform out of the reality of an artist's physical existence. Set with an agenda to liberate her sexualized (female) and racialized body from an ethnocentric, patriarchal system that understands Asian women as foreign objects, Kim emphasizes the artifice of woman-as-object by doubling her physical presence (the female performer as subject) with her physical existence (the female body as object) on stage.

Kim blurs the clean and clear demarcations between what Rebecca Schneider called the "constructed and constructor,"[27] messing up artistic and cultural norms by unsettling the audience through a process of physical proximity and portrayals of awkward (potentially ugly) gestures (the gurgles, the zombie walks, other actions like opening her mouth wide, shifting her jaw, and rolling her tongue around the outside of her mouth). Kim's focus on the "decay of the body" works to prevent the viewer from enacting a safe reading of her youthful Asian female body.[28] Her aggressive invasion into the space of the audience demands a response because she is no longer passive and distant. As Shobana Jeyasingh writes, "When the sloe-eyed damsel moves into the semi next door she loses that most exotic of qualities—distance."[29] One might see an exotic, foreign body and equate it with racialized and gendered expectations of submission, but Kim's forceful presence moves the audience to recognize their responsibility. Kim offers the audience an opportunity for alternatives responses "even if that response is to squirm uncomfortably in one's seat."[30]

With *Avatar*, Kim enacts autobiography in what Albright considers an intersection of the artist's physical existence with performance. In autobiographical performance, choreographers "write" themselves with movement and various additional media—while recognizably located by physical indicators of identity, these bodies manage to disrupt those identities. Autobiographical performance asks audiences to consider dancers' bodies as vehicles for more than basic cultural identity. In *Avatar*, the highly internal focus and repeated facing away from the audience establishes a deep inner personalism that affects a pathway to social commonality. The audience, experiencing simultaneously conflicting responses to the confusion of both an invasion and a shunning by the performer, is forced to actively consider their own presence and role. Space is taken away, and time is given for the viewer to wallow in ambivalence as one considers how this single body can share the common experience of messy, embarrassing bodily functions, corrosion, solitary isolation, and forced social interaction. Kim reveals "the body's infirm boundaries and borders," showing it as both culturally aligned and fiercely individual.[31]

Kim's placement of her body and Yokoshi's arrangement of a cast of bodies (including her own) in a public arena both serve to contest simple representation. By foregrounding the constantly shifting nature of their performing body's cultural boundaries, they generate amalgamations that expand away from monolithic notions of cultural alliance, effectively bringing the "foreign" home by occupying the same space as recognizable "American" elements. They assemble a collection of signifiers and then, through their presentation of inescapable corporeal realities, immerse the viewer within the experience at hand.

Kim and Yokoshi operate in an artistic community that favors this engagement of the audience, respecting a range of artistic practices and equating value from process as much as with production. Public performance is still considered a culminating element, but it is increasingly viewed as one aspect in an entire comprehensive progression that includes conception, research, development, refinement, and review. It allows the various building blocks to assemble,[32] and it is where process realizes itself as product, where the tangible components of body, set, space, sound, and light bind with elusive abstract agendas to initiate a chain reaction of inspection, interpretation, and some arrangement of understanding of the individual artist and their cultural context.

Downtown NYC audiences allow for the blurring of categorical boundaries and blending of seemingly disparate forms by these artists. In fact, the downtown scene welcomes work that challenges norms in its constant push for innovation. Viewers expect aesthetic experiences that engage more than just visual stimulation and sensory pleasure. The community has cultivated a practice of understanding performance as communicative exchange, seeing performance as one part of an ongoing artistic discourse. As a curator and dance writer, Andy Horowitz expressed his ideas about contemporary dance criticism in an online essay:

> The aesthetic propositions are different. . . . If you buy a ticket to *Book Of Mormon*, the outward experience is the same as attending a show at PS122 (buy a ticket, take a seat, it starts, it ends, go home) but the demand on the audience is different. . . . The time-based, body-based performance event asks the audience to do more than passively watch, but to *engage*, to pay attention, to reflect, to think. The performance event is a proscribed durational experience located at a specific nexus of space, time and embodiment, a philosophical/aesthetic field of inquiry.[33]

The audiences for which Yokoshi and Kim perform tend to be equipped with a perceptual rigor that is a natural outgrowth of the rich menu of offerings from New York City's contemporary performance community. The sheer density of artists provides viewers with a constant immersion among viewings, preshow/postshow panel discussions, critical writing, cultivation events, and audience development series. Most of the audiences for Yokoshi's and Kim's works arrive with an understanding that the "questions that the choreographer and dancers are proposing are fundamentally different and rooted in different conditions of origin" than standard entertainment.[34]

I would mention that this difference in "conditions of origin" would include any artistic stipulation to satisfy the Asian American community's interest in increased acceptance in mainstream culture. Aside from the comments from the artists that have been included, one primary reason may be the general absence of Asian Americans attending contemporary live performance. As the choreographer Muna Tseng points out, in downtown dance, the Asian American audience is not a substantial one: "I went to see a performance by the Alvin Ailey Company up in Harlem and there was such incredible support from the community. . . . I remember thinking, it's going to be a long time until we have this kind of support for our own kin. Asians are just not very supportive of the arts, especially not contemporary arts."[35] Although a case can be made for the widespread appeal of the Ailey Company because of their use of vernacular dance forms and their highly virtuosic performances, Tseng, a collaborator and contemporary of Ping Chong, is elucidating the difficulty of presenting challenging material to aesthetically conservative communities. Against that backdrop, it is fair to assess that aligning oneself too specifically within an ethnic category can be highly detrimental to contemporary artists for the simple equation of breadth of reach, not to mention a potential limit on the scope of their work.

These two women do not make the reading of their work against an Asian American agenda straightforward. However, their artistry highlights the complexities of cultural understandings in dance. The experimental culture of the downtown New York City contemporary dance scene allows Yokoshi and Kim to engage various identities on stage. These engagements invite and challenge ideas of the Self and Other. The artists succeed (in part) because of the ways in which they choose to situate themselves inside and outside of classifying structures. This ambivalent relationship with traditional methods of presentation, structures for performance, and sociopolitical limits on racial representation offer possibilities for an expansion of what could be considered Asian American performance. Perhaps the absent audience Tseng describes above has directly formed Yokoshi and Sam into the ambivalent figures here. As Asian American audiences become conversant in avant-garde performance and begin to invest in works by Asian American artists working in experimental forms, more artists from within the Asian diaspora will come to embrace the direct identification.

Notes

1. Jennifer Dunning, "Yasuko Yokoshi Depicts Love, the Passage of Time, and the Everyday," *New York Times*, March 25, 2006; Deborah Jowitt, "Passion Distilled: A Choreographer Turns Her Postmodern Gaze on an Ancient Style," *Village Voice*, March 30, 2006.

2. Ping Chong, "The Verbal Mural," in *Tokens: The NYC Asian American Experience on Stage*, ed. Alvin Eng (New York: Asian American Writer's Workshop, 1999), 417.

3. *Jook-sing*, a derogatory Cantonese term for overseas Chinese, translates as "hollow bamboo."

4. Yasuko Yokoshi, press packet biography, 2000–2005, in author's possession, 2005.

5. Yuriko Saito, "Japanese Aesthetics," in *Encyclopedia of Aesthetics* (New York: Oxford University Press, 1998), 546–547.

6. New York Live Arts, "Resident Commissioned Artist," http://www.newyork livearts.org/event/rca_yokoshi, accessed March 30, 2012.

7. Yasuko Yokoshi, telephone interview by author, November 10, 2006.

8. Jowitt, "Passion Distilled," 2006.

9. Maura Nguyen Donohue, "*what she when she*," *Dance Insider*, March 31, 2006, http://www.danceinsider.com/f2006/f0331_2.html, accessed June 9, 2009.

10. Yokoshi, interview by author.

11. "Yasuko Yokoshi in Conversation with Tere O'Connor," *Critical Correspondence*, February 22, 2006, http://www.movementresearch.org/criticalcorrespond ence/blog/?p=648, accessed February 22, 2006.

12. Ibid.

13. Yokoshi, interview by author.

14. Ann Cooper Albright, *Choreographing Difference: The Body and Identity in Contemporary Dance* (Middleton, CT: Wesleyan University Press, 1997), 12.

15. Sam Kim, interview by author, New York City, November 21, 2006.

16. Sarah Kaufman, "Bill T. Jones/Arnie Zane Dance Company to Merge with Dance Theater Workshop," *Washington Post*, December 10, 2010.

17. Carl Paris, "Will the Real Bill T. Jones Please Stand Up?," *Drama Review* 49, no. 2 (2005): 65.

18. Kim, interview by author.

19. Paris, "Will the Real Bill T. Jones," 65.

20. Bill T. Jones with Peggy Gillespie, *Last Night on Earth* (New York: Knopf Doubleday, 1997), 164–165.

21. Kim, interview by author.

22. See Karen Shimakawa, *National Abjection: Asian American Body Onstage* (Durham, NC: Duke University Press, 2002).

23. Ann Daly, "Trends in Dance Scholarship: Feminist Theory across the Millennial Divide," *Dance Research Journal* 32, no. 1 (2000): 41.

24. Muna Tseng, "The Verbal Mural," in *Tokens: The NYC Asian American Experience on Stage*, ed. Alvin Eng (New York: Asian American Writer's Workshop, 1999), 419.

25. Maura Nguyen Donohue, "From the Body to the World," *Dance Insider*, May 23, 2006, http://www.danceinsider.com/f2006/f0523_2.html, accessed June 9, 2009.

26. For descriptions of Asian American solo performance, see Esther Kim Lee, "Between the Personal and the Universal: Asian American Solo Performance from the 1970s to the 1990s," *Journal of Asian American Studies* 6, no. 3 (2004): 289–312.

27. Rebecca Schneider, *The Explicit Body in Performance* (New York: Routledge, 1997), 36.

28. Kim, interview by author.

29. Shobana Jeyasingh, "Getting Off the Orient Express," in *Routledge Dance Studies Reader*, 2nd ed., ed. Alexandra Carter and Janet O'Shea (New York: Routledge, 2010), 182.

30. Albright, *Choreographing Difference*, 100–101.

31. Rachel C. Lee, "Where's My Parade? Margaret Cho and the Asian American Body in Space," *TDR: The Drama Review* 48, no. 2 (2004): 109.

32. Ibid.

33. Andy Horwitz, "Talking about Dance Criticism and the Changing World," *Culturebot*, July 4, 2012, http://www.culturebot.net/2012/07/13868/talking-about-dance-criticism-and-the-changing-world/, accessed July 5, 2012.

34. Ibid.

35. Tseng, "Verbal Mural," 428.

Afterword

A Conversation with Denise Uyehara

YUTIAN WONG

In 2004 Denise Uyehara and I published a conversation in *Maps of City and Body: Shedding Light on the Performances of Denise Uyehara*.[1] Informed by a decade-long discussion that began in Augusto Boal's Theatre of the Oppressed workshop in Long Beach, California, the conversation broached the vexing question of aesthetics and politics in Asian American performance. Conducted in the shadow of the 1990s when the Los Angeles riots, the movement to abolish bilingual education, and the dismantling of affirmative action in higher education shaped the discourse of Asian American identity politics, the conversation assumed a comfortable position within the Asian American performance scene that privileged work that spoke directly to the experience of marginalization and invisibility.

At the end of the twentieth century the 1990s were bookended with the 1991 Los Angeles uprising, in which a disproportionate portion of Koreatown and Korean American–owned businesses went up in flames after the acquittal of the four white Los Angeles Police Department officers who beat up Rodney King, and the 1999 arrest of Wen Ho Lee, the Taiwanese American nuclear scientist who was falsely accused of being a spy for China. In the years between 1991 and 1999, California voters passed Proposition 209 in 1996 to end raced-based affirmative action in public employment, contracting, and education.[2] In the realm of public education, and in particular higher education, supporters of Proposition 209 claimed that affirmative action policies unfairly disadvantaged white students by subjecting them to reverse discrimination. Given the difficulty of selling the concept that white men have been victimized by affirmative action, supporters of Proposition 209 named Asian Americans the true victims of affirmative action, pitting Asian American students against African American and Latino students. These events anchored the trifecta of Asian American difference as inassimilable immigrants, model minorities, and foreign enemies. Asian American performers working at the intersection of dance, physical theater, and nonlinear, text-based performance believed that live performance could enact politically transformative experiences and privileged content to override mainstream perceptions of Asian Americans as politically passive (or even apolitical) and socially conservative subjects.

The kinds of narratives featuring stories about immigrant and refugee experiences that I wrote about in *Choreographing Asian America* and that were referenced by Maura Nguyen Donohue in chapter 7, "Ambivalent Selves," dominated Asian American performance programmed in spaces such as Highways Performance Space in Santa Monica, California, the Asian American Writers' Workshop in New York City, and the Asian Arts Initiative in Philadelphia.[3] Now that a decade has passed since the publication of *Maps of City and Body*, Denise and I joked about checking in once every ten years to talk about Asian American performance. The chapters collected in this volume are in many ways the result of that conversation as the field of study of Asian American dance studies has finally come into form.

In this concluding chapter, I leave the reader with a conversation about Asian American creativity as a space in which to luxuriate while playing with the materials of art making that include form, concepts, and the distractions of everyday life that might or might not be overdetermined as Asian American. What began in the 1990s as a conversation about the possibilities of what Asian American performance could be continues here as a dialogue about the making of Asian American performance in the twenty-first century. The conversation shuttles between the vexing question of aesthetics and politics that continues to haunt the endeavor of Asian American dance studies—what we might think of as what a performance is made of versus what a performance is made about. Between aesthetics and politics is the question of inspiration as the unquantifiable element of art making that scholars often avoid because it can come across as naive, pat, wishy-washy, or intellectually lazy. In this last chapter, inspiration operates like a map tracking a series of free associations that manifest in a body of a decade's worth of work.

$\sim$

YUTIAN WONG: For much of the 1990s and early 2000s you were based in Los Angeles and were known for your works that dealt with Asian American identity and in particular Asian American gender and sexuality. Works like *Hello (Sex) Kitty: Mad Asian Bitch on Wheels* (1995) became a clarion call for politicizing queer Asian American women. Characters like the Asian Lesbian Stand Up Comedian, Vegetable Girl, and the Mad Kabuki Woman were confrontational and a radical departure from the "realistic Asian American women" that performers like Jude Narita tried to evoke in *Coming into Passion/Song for a Sansei* (1987).

The subjects of gender and sexuality were intertwined with abstracted notions of locale, bodies, and memories in *Maps of City and Body* (1999) where you juxtaposed childhood memories, friendship, and different kinds of violence that manifest themselves close to home. *Big Head* (2003) was a departure from *Hello (Sex) Kitty* and *Maps of City and Body* and staged your family's history and the internment of Japanese Americans during World War II as a form of coalition building with Arab Americans after 9/11. By 2006 *The Senkotsu (Mis)Translation Project* took on American imperialism and the military presence in Okinawa in relation to your own Okinawan heritage and the complicated relationships of colonization and diaspora between Japan, Okinawa, and the United States.

What I have seen in your work is a gradual evolution from subject matter that is deeply personal and politicizes specific bodies and identities to work that takes on larger political statements about militarism and institutional racisms. Would this be a fair way to summarize the work from this early part of your career in terms of content? Could you reflect on this shift?

DENISE UYEHARA: In my early work the performances came from a very personal space, so the content was often about very intimate subjects like sexual identity and sexual violence in the Asian American community. Since my background was in creative writing, I based many of my performances on monologues where I would stand on stage and broadcast my feelings to other people. It took a very long time for me to create work that was more interactive and not necessarily based on my own personal experience. It took me a long time to start challenging myself to work with new forms and content. Along the way, I wondered if my identity was changing. Lucy Burns once asked me, "Are you still queer?" because I had shifted away from making work specifically about women or gender. I am still a queer-identified bisexual Asian American woman even if I am making work about issues important to other communities. Lucy Burns pointed out to me that queer is being connected to larger global issues and how different communities are connected to each other.

WONG: I remember you had a map of the world on the wall of your studio, and it was full of pushpins indicating the places you had performed and all the places you wanted to perform. *Hello (Sex) Kitty* was the show that literally put you on that map. Not only did you perform the piece in progressive theater spaces and festivals interested in producing work by artists of color, but *Hello (Sex) Kitty* also made the rounds of the college touring circuit. Academic programs such as Asian American studies and women's studies and student organizations serving Asian Pacific Islanders and LGBT communities brought you to campuses around the United States. In many places you performed, you were probably the first queer-identified Asian American public figure that people in your audience had encountered. I remember when you first started teaching the Rad Asian Sisters Performance Workshops in 1997, you had so many people who wanted to be in your workshop and you had to turn people away. You were still touring *Hello (Sex) Kitty* and there was a definite sense that people were inspired by you. How did you know it was time to stop performing *Hello (Sex) Kitty?*

UYEHARA: *Hello (Sex) Kitty* was a really important show to me and audiences loved it, but eventually I realized that it was a show that would not die unless I made a conscious decision to stop performing it. At the time it filled a need to address queerness and the intersections of race, gender, and sexuality. At a certain point I felt the need to challenge myself and move on. I understood *Hello (Sex) Kitty*, I knew those characters, and I knew it was going to be hard to let them go because you feel as if you can lose the audience who want to see you as that character.

WONG: The characters were fierce, and they were funny. The Asian American Lesbian Stand Up Comedian made fun of presenters and funders who misunderstood avant-garde performance for sketch comedy routines, and the Mad Kabuki Women trounced on a stage full of vegetables in a fit of unspecified revenge. 1995 was the year that *All-American Girl*, the only American television show featuring an Asian American family, was canceled after one season, which eventually launched Margaret Cho's career in a new direction when she started touring *I'm the One That I*

Want in 1999 before it was released as a film in 2000. Many of the issues that Margaret Cho ranted about in her stand-up comedy show—body image, racial stereotypes in Hollywood film, sex—were things that you and other Asian American avant-garde artists had been addressing for years. What did you do when you decided to take your work in a different direction?

UYEHARA: Interestingly enough, I began to look back at some of the earliest performances that I created before *Hello (Sex) Kitty*. I did this to rediscover where my first impulses came from. My earliest work was interdisciplinary because I did not know any better. I did not know you had to create a show in a certain way so that you could go on tour. I did not know that it would be easier to tour a text-heavy show based on monologues or that it would be easier to receive grants if your work fit into one genre. I made work that interested me and not shows that would be profitable so I that could survive as an artist.

WONG: I am glad you brought up the issue of money and the economics of performance, and I want to come back to that later, but first can you reflect on your earliest work that you are referring to?

UYEHARA: The piece that still resonates with me today is *Headless Turtleneck Relatives* (1993), which is about my grandmother who committed suicide. My family was in shock when my grandmother committed suicide by setting herself on fire. Making the piece was a way to make sense of something that was so complicated and nonsensical at the time. When I started creating the piece my family was up in arms. They were upset that I was creating work about such a painful topic, but it was something that I needed to do. I created a piece that took me back to her last moments in life because none of us had witnessed what happened. My grandmother self-immolated in her car. It was horrific, and she left a note that said, "I've lived a wonderful life, I want to go to the spiritual world." At the time, my grandmother's note felt like such a contradiction, and I could not understand why someone would want to kill herself in this manner and then write a letter about having lived a wonderful life and wanting to go to the spiritual world.

Part of the performance was based on a dream that I had about my grandmother where she came and talked to me shortly after her death. The other part of the performance was based on my having to meditate on what it would be like to kill oneself. What came out of the tragedy was a fifteen-minute monologue, which I think of as a poem. I tell the story about my grandmother's death while sitting on a chair in front of a white easel, I rub charcoal on my hands and then I rub the charcoal on a white board behind me on the easel. When I walk away from the easel there is a negative space where she (my grandmother) or myself (the performance artist) was, but the image could be anything.

I once ended up in a strange situation where I performed in front of a room full of senior citizens and children. Nobuko Miyamoto had asked me to perform with her group on a triple bill, but I didn't know whom we were performing for. When I got there, the performance venue turned out to be a library, and just as we were about to perform, I realized the people in the audience were mostly senior citizens and children. I was really nervous and thought I was going to traumatize everybody. Afterwards the children came up to me while I was rolling up the piece of paper with the charcoal on it and asked, "What were you drawing?" I said, "Oh, what do you see?" They said, "Oh, I see the grandmother's hair," "I see the grandmother kissing the grandfather," "I see angel's wings," "I see a halo."

It was amazing to hear these kids talk about death, how they felt about it, and understand that I was expressing something about that story through a drawing. I was so relieved they weren't traumatized, but they had a truly honest interest and inquiry into what I was doing. One older man told me, "This story is larger than this room." I was struck by this comment, because at the time I didn't really know what I was doing. I just did something I needed to do, because if I didn't, I thought I was going to go crazy. I needed to have someplace to commune with my grandmother, and just be still for a moment. I needed to relive a moment where I wasn't present with her so I could say good-bye to her, or perhaps hello, because there was no open casket at the funeral or sitting by her deathbed or anything like that. *Headless Turtleneck Relatives* is still the most important piece for me. After I started performing it, I realized that everybody was telling me in their responses that there is power in the arts, and what I could do was a gift and I needed to be responsible with it. That realization is what launched my career.

WONG: What compels you to make work?

UYEHARA: I had some dramatic training and some performance art experience. But it was the first time—well, I don't want to get too warm and fuzzy metaphysical about it—that my grandmother came to me in this dream, and it felt very real. I woke up feeling like "Okay, that was just a dream," and I can rationalize it because I come from a family of scientists, but then I did not know what it was. It was so lucid that I knew it was my dream world talking to me. I really do go to that place for inspiration. I do take it very seriously even though I don't really talk about it very much since it sounds really New Age and kind of hippie. There is nothing wrong with being New Age or hippie, but it really isn't my generation. I don't really know what I would call it, but it is definitely a space that I preserve and reserve for new work where I try not to be rational, and I try to make the rest of my life very stable so that I can have those spaces to be very wild and to be in touch with things that I don't understand. I try not to overanalyze them, I just try to be there with them, be there with ancestors, or be there with people who've departed or energies or memories. That's where a lot of my work comes from.

WONG: You talk about your work in a metaphysical way in terms of bringing forth things in the world that do not make any sense. Oftentimes, Asian American performance scholars (myself included) avoid the question of inspiration given the way that Asian and Asian American artists are often pigeonholed by mainstream critics as drawing on some kind of ancient well of Asian spirituality. There is a tendency to politicize Asian American performance as much as possible, and perhaps we lose sight of where creativity or irrationality might come from.

UYEHARA: I think that is why I create work. Because there is so much that does not make sense in the world. Art is my vessel in which to hold contradictory ideas. Instead of writing political papers or becoming a politician or an activist, I chose to put my concerns about the world into an art-making practice. I hung out some with people who were social activists, and what they did and are still doing is really important, but I would run into a wall with that. With art I have found there to be more potential to move in any direction, because you use your imagination, and that was my calling.

WONG: Your work has always been engaged with political issues, so what is the wall that you are talking about when it comes to social activism?

UYEHARA: For me, I found that activism could become rhetoric. I knew that I had the potential to be very good at just talking about, for example, being Asian American. I came out in the mid-1980s when identity politics was coming into form, and you could talk about being Asian American, especially at universities. Identity politics were good for talking about race and speaking truth to power, but then this idea of truth became a way to isolate oneself. I knew I was more complex than that. I witnessed contradictions within my own community and the way that I lived. It was too convenient for me to express that through political activism. There are people who are much better at being activists, and I knew that I would fail and decided I should do what I am better at.

WONG: You relocated to Tucson, Arizona, in 2006 and have continued to be extremely prolific. *Transitions* opened in November 2011, *Archipelago* in February 2012; now you are working on *Dreams & Silhouettes/Sueños y Siluetas* [formerly called *Bus Stop Dreaming*], scheduled to open in January 2014, and you've been conceptualizing a new piece called *Dinner and a Movie*. All of these projects are very different from each other. Could you talk about communing, going back to a certain place, that moment where you felt compelled to make something? Is this what is happening in your current work?

UYEHARA: I did not realize how moving to Tucson would challenge me as an artist. The Asian American community in Arizona is small compared to California, and there isn't a critical mass of artists doing cross-disciplinary performance art, so I had to find new ways to work, and I had a different audience. There is a very polarized political scene in Tucson when the state legislature passed SB 1070, which is one of the strictest anti-immigration laws in the country. The state also banned the teaching of ethnic studies, and in particular Mexican American studies, in a K-12 public school system that is almost 50 percent Latino.

Bus Stop Dreaming (2012) was a response to SB 1070, and I wanted to create a free show. SB 1070 requires anyone who is a not a U.S. citizen to carry documentation proving they are allowed to be in the U.S. The law allows police officers to stop people in the street, and if they can't prove that they are allowed to be in the United States, they can be arrested. The law basically makes it illegal to walk around in public and not look white. I met Jason Aragon of Copwatch, which is an organization of people who act as eyewitnesses to deportations. The police or "border patrol" will randomly stop people on the street or in their car. If someone can't produce any papers on the spot proving they are in the United

States legally, the police try to get the individual to sign a paper to waive their rights and begin the deportation process.

When people in the community see this happening, they call Jason and his team of two or three other people, and they videotape the whole exchange. Aragon has horrifying footage of a Mexican or "brown" family being stopped at night in South Tucson. The family was stopped, probably for no reason, and the border patrol took the parents away and impounded the car, leaving the grandmother and children on the side of the road at night. I was stunned when I watched the footage. It reminded me of the kinds of stories you hear about Nazi Germany, where you could be stopped because of how you look, and if you don't have papers, you could be taken away and disappeared. It also reminded me about something you said to me about the Japanese American internment during WWII. You said the body is somewhere else. It's made invisible so the evidence is gone. Because of this I asked Jason and his group Pan Left to apply for a MAP Fund grant to create a site-specific work that takes place at sites of deportation in South Tucson.

We use actual footage of deportations and project them on the bodies of the performers or behind the performers at different sites where people have been stopped and taken away. *Dreams & Silhouettes/Sueños y Siluetas* was originally titled *Bus Stop Dreaming* and refers to one incident in which a woman was stopped while she was waiting at a bus stop in the middle of the day. She was scared and fled into a grocery store and hid in the women's bathroom. When she finally came out, the police arrested her and started the deportation process. The biggest challenge is getting audiences to come out and see the show. We want the community most affected by this to see the show, but they are afraid to go out at night because they are afraid of getting picked up by the police. And rightly so because that is exactly what is happening.

Early on we also called it *Bus Stop Dreaming* to humanize the people who are captured in the videos. It's about asking why people come here (to Tucson, to Arizona, to the United States) to work, and if they are undocumented what happens to them, and how can we create a space that moves beyond labels and look at people and their lives. When reporters talk to conservative people, they will say, "Now that I know somebody that is undocumented—I don't feel that those laws should apply to them." Or if you know somebody that is here "illegally" without papers, you have a different take on what should be done about undocumented people. Part of what we want to do is to try to create a kind of humanity through performance, and part of it is to heal. Mary Charlotte, the late director of Pan Left, says the community needs to heal from all of these police raids. My performances don't really solve any problems, but they open dialogue and allow people to imagine differently, I'm hoping.

WONG: Going back to something you said earlier about creating a show that you can tour in order to make money to support yourself as an artist, how does that factor into what you are doing now? After all, *Dreams* is a free show.

UYEHARA: I realized that people don't go to theaters anymore. The rest of the world is doing something else. They are not going to the theater to see dance concerts or performance art, so how can we meet people where

FIGURE 8.1. Denise Uyehara and Yvonne Montoya in *Dreams & Silhouettes: Sueños y Siluetas* (formerly *Bus Stop Dreaming*), 2012 (photo by JP Westenskow)

they are? I am tired of trying to force people to pay $15–20 to see a show. I think there is a shift in the way artists are looking at how they can create work. I was talking to Robert Karimi—he's Iranian and Guatemalan, and doing these amazing pieces about cooking and health in relation to his father's diabetes—and he said, "We don't even care about the box office anymore, we just want people to see the show. Our objective now is to just pack the house wherever we go. It is not to patronize the community, but more to just to have a different way of looking at art." But the flip side of that is that you have to find ways to create the work somewhere affordable. Even so, living in Tucson has forced me to look for grants for long-term projects. I am also looking at larger national grants. When I left Los Angeles I lost sources of local funding that I had taken for granted.

WONG: Are you gaining more national attention since you moved?

UYEHARA: Ironically, I was forced to look for larger grants at the national level because of where I am in my career and the fact that there is not a lot of state and local funding for the arts in Arizona. There are not that many national grants for multidisciplinary artists, but I had to try and get them. I had to start thinking that it was possible. I applied for the MAP Grant eight times and finally received one in partnership with Pan Left Productions and Jason Aragon and a second one for a collaborative project called the Shooting Columbus Collective, only after moving to Tucson. I think the lack of state and regional funding in Arizona forced me to rethink the type of work I was applying with. Since moving here I've received two MAP Fund Grants, the National Performance Network Creation Fund, and support from the Network of Ensemble Theaters for collaborative projects.

WONG: It sounds like moving to Tucson was in some ways disorienting, but it has also made you focus and find new ways to work.

UYEHARA: When I talk to people who are from places like California, in particular, it is really hard to come to Arizona. California has more of everything, and then you come here to Tucson, and it makes you focus more. It makes you go really basic. I ask myself, what really matters? There is not a lot of distraction, not as much to do. There are really interesting artists doing work out here, but usually there are only one or two interesting events happening on any given night, as opposed to ten in LA. It makes you focus more.

WONG: You have also been working with artists who bring a different perspective to the projects. It is not all the same people who have all seen the same thing.

UYEHARA: That was one of the challenges, actually. Being in the Southwest, you do think about "What are the communities here?" I do feel that there are these interesting parallels between Mexican American families who have been living in Arizona for eight or nine generations and Japanese American families. I went to a community forum, and most of the people present were older Mexican Americans, and it reminded me of Japanese American communities. Everyone was familiar with each other and breaking bread together because they have a long history in one place, yet they still have to deal with having one's legitimacy in the United States questioned. And that is definitely the situation here in Tucson for a lot of people. Anybody that looks Mexican can be questioned for any reason here. And I, ironically, am not the target minority group. Sometimes I think I am the only Japanese American person in Tucson.

WONG: Now that you've been away, when you go back to California, do you see Asian Americanness in a different way?

UYEHARA: I think what has happened is, when I was moving to Tucson I was changing how I felt about what community could mean. I was forced to think about that because I am not around my Asian Pacific Islander community or Queer community so readily. I definitely have found some, and there are some really good people here, but there's not the huge critical mass. You kind of have to do it for yourself. I have done some soul searching about that, not so much for me, but for my kids because I can't just do the lazy yuppie thing and enroll my kid in weekend Japanese language school, because there are none. I have to think about what identity is and what I want to purposefully expose my kids to.

And for myself as an artist, I realized that moving here has helped me to figure out some things about what my next steps are in relationship to the Asian Pacific Islander community and how to link to other communities. I started doing that before I left Los Angeles, but now I really have to do it. Working with Adam Cooper [Cooper-Terán], for example, was interesting because we were both exploring stories and myths from cultures that we were both in and outside of. He is of Yaqui descent, but he does not live on the Yaqui urban reservation. His mother told him these amazing stories of how her village was flooded by the Mexican government, but he has not been back there. As for myself, I am of Okinawan descent, but I am not living in Okinawa, yet my relatives took me to these caves to show me where they hid during the war. All of that was so much a part of who they are now, and I felt both connected to it and not connected to it. That was part of why we did the piece together. It was about asking, what are those kinds of stories and where do we find a connection without forcing the issue? It was different for me to work with Adam because we tried not to make it like "We are the world, and that is why we're the same." [*laughs*] We just decided to see what happens if we put these two stories next to each other and see how the audience responds.

We did find some connections to the idea of water, for example. I told him the reason the piece is called *Archipelago* is because I have always been fascinated with the idea of land surrounded by water, but also the opposite, which is water surrounded by land. What if we extend that metaphor to people surrounded by other populations where you are isolated? How do we make contact with those isolated groups? We talked through a lot of ideas of myth and stories and where we felt we fit in and "What is it like to walk from island to island, culturally speaking?"

There is a moment in that piece where we have these pools of light on the ground, and we take off these headdresses. He has deer antlers from a deer that his father actually shot and they ate, and I'm wearing what looks like an upside-down lotus blossom. It is a *hanagasa*, which is kind of inspired by a famous Okinawan dance called *yotsutake*. We made them completely out of white material, so we're dressed in white so we can project onto it as well. In this last scene, we take off our different regalia and put them down in these different pools of light, and as we're talking we cross from island to island, and just brush hands in the center. We pass each other as if we're kind of realizing that there is another entity there. We never were able to perform it in rehearsal because we kept laughing, because it seemed kind of hokey [*laughs*], and then when we did it in performance it made sense, it was moving. It was just acknowledging each other; it was what we needed to do. We didn't need to force it.

WONG: You are talking about a lot of basic questions about identity and the difference between being and doing. Before the premiere of *Archipelago*, someone asked you about whether or not you were appropriating Native American and specifically the Yaqui deer dance in the performance.

UYEHARA: We did not want to perform our identities. That's why Adam is not performing a deer dance. We talked about it, and he was the one that brought it up. Maybe the people from his village did the deer dance in the village square when they went back, but we don't really know. As we began to work on it, he realized, "I don't know what the dance is. I don't really feel like doing that." He was really clear about it. At the same time, he had the other things he wanted to do, including wearing deer antlers on his head, which is probably why some people assumed there was a deer dance in the show. The antlers belonged to a deer that Adam's father actually shot near their house in the northwestern part of Tucson. In some ways it is related to and resonates with the deer dance, but the connection from Adam is through his father, who shot the deer. It was not about trying to perform some kind of deer dance that would prove he was authentically "Yaqui."

I would imagine this is the same way he works with video: he takes icons and elements that are significant to him and mashes them up, and he holds them with respect and finds a way to bring that into performance or into video images. There are a lot of icons in the imagery he is using that he explained to me, but then if you were to see it, you might not know what it is. There is a scene where there is a coyote skull and an amazing fire projection on my headdress to evoke the fire deity because that is in both cultures. He brought in different elements, and I asked him what they were as we went along, so we had these discussions about it. For me too, I did not want to force my identity as Okinawan, because I feel "Am I Okinawan? I don't know" and that's really part of the piece. Instead, we worked with less text and more imagery and movement. It was a larger stroke.

There are two monologues that I do, and one is an origin story about a brother and sister who survive a great flood, and then they become the progenitors of Okinawan people. It is actually a story that is only known in the southernmost islands of Okinawa. The flood connects my story to Adam's story about the flooding of his mother's village. The other monologue is about visiting the caves of my relatives. Those are probably the two most text-based moments, and then I had to really think outside of my own box of how to perform without talking.

FIGURE 8.2. Denise Uyehara and Adam Cooper-Terán in *Archipelago*, 2012 (photo by Trevor Baker)

I earned an MFA in a dance-based program (World Arts and Cultures at UCLA), which made me think about what the body is doing in different ways. I feel like it is easy to lie to people when we are just talking. It seems like the truth, and they accept it as the truth, but it is really not necessarily the truth. I don't know if that makes sense, because all performance in a way is a lie, but I don't feel that text-based performance is expansive enough for what we are trying to do. So instead I began the piece with a dance inspired by movement from *yotsutake*. I end up trying to tap these Okinawan castanets while Adam is creating smoke with sage. At the same time there is a video projection of jets dropping bombs from above, so I'm trying to attack these jets with the castanets. I had to think differently about what I was going to do instead of talking about it.

WONG: Is it possible for you to just "be" whatever it is that you think you are?

UYEHARA: It is easy to just declare who you are, but it is actually harder to go through a process of not talking. It is more frustrating, and it is harder, but I think the results are more layered, and it carries more weight. It is really hard for me to perform without trying to explain what I am doing. It was good to work with Adam because he does not like talking at all. I was surprised the guy even took off his mask. He was wearing a white cloth around his face so you can't really see him, but by the end he took off his mask, and he spoke a little bit, and it was a nice give and take in our work. He usually does not talk at all, but he talks through his videos with that imagery. That is the challenge for me, to think how can I move more or do something else that's not narrative-based?

WONG: In October 2011 we talked quite a bit about *Transitions* (2011), your collaboration with James Luna. I understand it was a commission commemorating the LA art scene, and you were selected to reconstruct a performance art piece from the 1970s. In talking to you at the time, you were grappling with the issue of reconstruction vs. reinterpretation—really foundational questions about art making. It also marked a moment in which you were placed within a performance art lineage. Why did you choose to work with James Luna?

UYEHARA: The project was part of a Getty Foundation initiative called Pacific Standard Time, which funded a number of individual art organizations, including the Los Angeles Contemporary Exhibitions (LACE). Each of the organizations sponsored their town series. I was commissioned by LACE to create a work of their series called LA Goes Live.

I ended up creating three different pieces for *Transitions*. One was an impromptu piece about James. He is known for *The Artifact Piece* (1987), in which he lies in a Plexiglas case in the Museum of Man in San Diego. People thought he was a taxidermed Indian and came to observe him. When they realized he was alive, it was even more strange and unnerving. I performed lying down, as if we were lying down next to each other because at the time I was thinking of re-creating a piece by him. Not necessarily that piece, but one of his. It was quite interesting and successful.

The next time LACE had a symposium, I was asked to perform something again, and I was really pregnant, so I performed in a paper kimono I had made, and somehow by the end I was naked, which I didn't think I was planning to do. Then the third time it was me and James together, and it became, again, very different because LACE put together funding to bring him on board, and then it jumped it to a whole other level because by then I didn't feel like I had to re-create anything.

We looked back at a piece that he had done called *Transitions* in which he took inanimate objects out of a bag and created new rituals around them. So in a way we took things out of a proverbial bag of our own lives and identities and created a new ritual about surviving Orange County. At some point, we realized we had lived three and a half miles from each other in Orange County, California. His parents and grand-parents live in the last wooden house surrounded by 1970s housing tracks. There's a big subdivision, a wall, a freeway, and then James and his family. They are like the last Native Americans on the street, so we created this piece about surviving Orange County that became the new *Transitions*.

It was about the transition from moving from where he grew up, in a very rural Orange County, to becoming a young man and coming into his own as an artist. For me, it was about growing up a very suburban part of Orange County and becoming an artist from there. Somehow we both made it out of Orange County and formed our identities. It might be a one-time collaboration, but it was good to work with each other, and I think we learned about each other in some ways.

WONG: Can you talk about the process of re-creating the work?

UYEHARA: Yes, I decided to work with James Luna and after interviewing him, I realized I really did not want to re-create one of his pieces, and we ended up creating a performance together. We did not have a lot of time together to create the performance, but we worked some here in Tucson and once in Los Angeles at LACE.

The resulting piece ended up being modular. We alternated time on stage, and I brought in Adam Cooper to work with us at the end of our process. We all ended up going to Adam's parents' house for dinner, and James got to meet Adam's mother, who is Yaqui Indian, and his father, who is Russian, and it was a really great way to ground the work. It was kind of a three-way collaboration at the end, although Adam deferred to us as the younger artist. On the day of the performance James threw out his back. He was originally going to start the performance as the "Indian janitor," but he had to rework it so that he sat outside in a wheelchair holding a cup. We pulled it together and did the show, and it actually came together pretty well.

I had Rebecca Bushner, a visual artist based in Tucson, create a kimono for me. It had forty-foot-long arms that stretch out like giant wings. LACMA rigged it so that we could lower it toward the end of the piece, so it was like the iconic kimono hanging on the wall, and then I put it on, and we have people help me unfurl it, so the sleeves go out in each direction. I start turning, and the sleeves wraps around and around, and I kind of cocoon myself in it.

For the last part of the performance we had Adam Cooper film James and me walking around at the mall. It's supposed to be the South Coast Plaza mall in Costa Mesa, California, but we shot the footage at a mall in Tucson. Of course, it looks the same, because it's a mall. In the video, we made it look dream-like. James is wearing a roach (Mohawk head-dress), and I am wearing a kimono and a purple wig. In the film we walk through the mall to Karen Carpenter's "We've Only Just Begun." The film is projected on the wall as we finish the piece. That became our next *Transitions*. So it is very funny but also odd. I don't really know what it means. I just wanted to do it, and I was fortunate to work with some really good artists.

WONG: I've read about *Dinner and a Movie*, and it is such a poignant and nonsensical story. It is sad, funny, huge, and intimate all at the same time. What do you want to say about *Dinner and a Movie*?

UYEHARA: [*laughs*] It's really just an idea, and I was forced to put it on paper for a grant proposal. First of all, my partner, daughter, and I took a reconnaissance trip to the Federal Prison Camp, now called the Gordon Hirabayashi Recreation Area. When I first read about the camp, I thought, "Wow, maybe I should create something about that." I re-member thinking, "Does this have any relevance for people in Tucson?" because there are no Japanese Americans here. How interesting that all of a sudden I don't even know who my audience would be for this proj-ect. In Los Angeles if I did a piece like that, there is a very big Japanese community. Not that they are the audience that comes out for that, but there is an affinity and connection to it, and a history. So in Tucson there are not that many Japanese Americans.

WONG: Los Angeles is the place that people were taken away from.

UYEHARA: Yes, the memory is there.

WONG: Tucson is where people were hidden away.

UYEHARA: Internment was not even a big issue for people out here. When Gordon Hirabayashi showed up in Tucson, the federal marshal couldn't find the right paperwork and was like, "Just come back after dinner and a movie, because we can't find your papers." It wasn't a big deal, and people didn't consider Japanese Americans a threat to national security, at least not the way they did on the West Coast where there was a lot of hysteria. It took me six years to really figure out what the story has to do with current-day Tucson.

We drove past the prison camp on the way to Mt. Lemmon. Halfway up the mountain, we passed a recreation area, and I saw this campsite, but it wasn't a campsite. It was a prison camp. Immediately I thought, "I should do this performance where I walk up this mountain to this campsite." Then I thought, "No, that's crazy, I'm never going to do that. I'll never be in good enough shape to do that."

At some point I realized that the road leading to the prison camp was built by the prisoners who were held at the camp. The prisoners had to build their own prison site. Before the prison camp was built the prisoners were living in tents. It was like a low-level prison. I recently started to make the connection with other types of hidden labor, because Arizona has this very large private prison industry, and prisons have been able to utilize prison labor for private industry. Depending on which state you live in, prisoners are making things like chicken nuggets in school lunches, furniture, eyeglasses . . . and so on. I am pretty sure that Arizona participates in this and uses prison labor in agriculture. In a way it does provide people with vocational skills, but it is also exploitative. So I started thinking, is there a connection between what is happening now and Hirabayashi working at this camp? I'm not sure exactly, but that's how the pieces are speaking to me recently.

The project has to take place in the city of Tucson, because I cannot expect anyone to go up to the site on the mountain. I am thinking about re-creating the site and have people work on the piece using archaeological maps. I met a volunteer archaeologist for the National Forest Service, and we were talking about the work he had been doing to make archaeological maps of the site.

Everything about *Dinner and a Movie* is just so mundane and yet it's so ironic, because it's saying, "You really aren't enough of a security threat, but you kind of are because we're going to put you in prison, but you're not threatening enough, just go have some dinner." I decided to take this idea and see what would happen if you have people come together, labor together, break bread together, and then watch a movie together. I might have a prison intake form asking people questions about what they know about the Catalina Highway, whether you feel differently about the food one is eating if you know it was made by prisoners, would you feel differently about its quality?

There is just so much strange stuff happening in Tucson with the prison system and immigration. People need places to respond and talk about these issues. Again, there are so many talking heads and rhetoric out there already, and I would rather create a space where people can think and imagine differently about a crisis. I don't know if the two issues are completely parallel. The archaeologist felt that Hirabayashi's story and the current-day crisis about immigration are two very different things, different because [during the internment] you were a citizen already, and yet your constitutional rights are being violated, which is what Hirabayashi was contesting, but I am looking at it in more of a general way. The legitimacy of the residents who are of Japanese decent was being questioned, and at the same time—in the case of Hirabayashi—their labor was used to build infrastructure for tourism. I am still working out if this is a parallel or not, or if they even have to be. Maybe they are not. I think for me, as a Japanese American person having done a lot of work about the internment camps and relocation in Los Angeles, I think this is that next step, to make a leap and create work about other crises that are happening.

NOTES

1. Denise Uyehara, *Maps of City and Body: Shedding Light on the Performances of Denise Uyehara* (New York: Kaya/Mua, 2004).

2. Proposition 209 is a California ballot proposition also known as the California Civil Rights Initiative. The proposition borrowed the language of the Civil Rights Act of 1964 to end the consideration of race and gender in hiring decisions in public employment and admissions decisions at public universities.

3. Yutian Wong, "Club O' Noodles's *Laughter from the Children of War*," in *Choreographing Asian America* (Middletown, CT: Wesleyan University Press, 2010), 57–86.

Bibliography

Abe, George. "Life History Interview." With Art Hansen and Sojin Kim. Transcript. *Big Drum: Taiko in the United States* exhibition, Hirasaki National Resource Center, Japanese American National Museum, 369 East First Street, Los Angeles (hereafter HNRC/JANM). December 10, 2004.

Ahlgren, Angela K. "Drumming Asian America: Performing Race, Gender and Sexuality in North American Taiko." PhD diss., University of Texas at Austin, 2011.

Albright, Ann Cooper. *Choreographing Difference: The Body and Identity in Contemporary Dance*. Middletown, CT: Wesleyan University Press, 1997.

Ancheta, Angelo N. *Race, Rights, and the Asian American Experience*. New Brunswick: Rutgers University Press, 2001.

Anderson, Janet. "'Two Hands' at Annenberg." *Broad Street Review*, October 18, 2011. http://www.broadstreetreview.com/dance/two_hands_at_annenberg1. Accessed August 18, 2014.

Angry Asian Man. "Crazy for Kaba Modern." *Angry Asian Man*, March 24, 2008. http://blog.angryasianman.com/2008/03/crazy-for-kaba-modern.html. Accessed March 25, 2008.

Apeles, Teena. "From Subculture to Popular Culture: The New Rhythm Nation." *Audrey*, July 1, 2010, 30–34.

Ault, Elizabeth. "Nightmares of Neoliberalism: Performing Failure on Hell Date." *Spectator* 31, no. 2 (2011): 45–52.

Azuma, Eiichiro. *Between Two Empires: Race, History, and Transnationalism in Japanese America*. Oxford: Oxford University Press, 2005.

———. "Editor's Introduction: Yuji Ichioka and New Paradigms in Japanese American History." In *Before Internment: Essays in Prewar Japanese American History*, edited by Gordon H. Chang and Eiichiro Azuma, xvi–xvii. Stanford: Stanford University Press, 2006.

Bascara, Victor. "Cultural Politics of Redress: Reassessing the Meaning of the Civil
    Liberties Act of 1988 after 9/11." *Asian Law Journal* 10, no. 2 (2003): 101–130.
———. *Model-Minority Imperialism*. Minneapolis: University of Minnesota Press,
    2006.
Baxman, Inge. "At the Boundaries of the Archive: Movement, Rhythm, and Muscle
    Memory. A Report on the Tanzarchiv Leipzig." *Dance Chronicle* 32, no. 1 (2009):
    127–135.
Bender, Shawn Morgan. "Drumming between Tradition and Modernity: Taiko and
    Neo-folk Performance in Contemporary Japan." PhD diss., University of Cali-
    fornia, San Diego, 2003.
———. *Taiko Boom: Japanese Drumming in Place and Motion*. Berkeley: Univer-
    sity of California Press, 2012.
Benjamin, Walter. "Theses on the Philosophy of History." In *Illuminations*, trans-
    lated by Harry Zhon. New York: Harcourt, Brace & World, 1968.
Berg, Shelley C. "Sada Yacco: The American Tour, 1899–1900." *Dance Chronicle*
    16, no. 2 (1993): 147–196.
Big Drum: Taiko in the United States. Directed by Akira Boch, Sojin Kim, and
    Masaki Miyagawa. DVD. Frank H. Watase Media Arts Center, Japanese Amer-
    ican National Museum, 2005.
Bloom, Julie. "Before the Games Begin, He Has to Make Moves." *New York Times*,
    July 6, 2008.
"Bollywood Challenge." *Randy Jackson Presents America's Best Dance Crew*. MTV,
    August 30, 2009. Burbank, CA: Warner Bros.
Bolte Taylor, Jill. *My Stroke of Insight: A Brain Scientist's Personal Journey*. New
    York: Viking Penguin, 2008.
———. "My Stroke of Insight." TED Talk, video, 18:19. Filmed February 2008 at
    TED2008. http://www.ted.com/talks/jill_bolte_taylor_s_powerful_stroke_of
    _insight. Accessed April 6, 2014.
Bragin, Naomi. "Shot and Captured: Turf Dance, YAK Films, and the Oakland,
    California, R.I.P. Project." *TDR: The Drama Review* 58, no. 2 (2014): 99–114.
Brecht, Bertolt. "Alienation Effects in Chinese Acting." 1935. In *Theatre/Theory/
    Theatre*, edited by Daniel Gerould, 444–461. New York: Applause Theatre &
    Cinema Books, 2000.
Brown, Wendy. *Edgework: Critical Essays on Knowledge and Politics*. Princeton:
    Princeton University Press, 2005.
Burns, Lucy Mae San Pablo. "Splendid Dancing: Filipino 'Exceptionalism' in Taxi
    Dance Halls." *Dance Research Journal* 40, no. 2 (2008): 23–40.
Butler, Judith. *Bodies That Matter: On the Discursive Limits of "Sex."* New York:
    Routledge, 1993.

Caldwell, Helen. *Michio Ito: The Dancer and His Dances*. Berkeley: University of California Press, 1977.

Canadian Multiculturalism Act. Justice Laws website, Government of Canada. http://laws-lois.justice.gc.ca/eng/acts/C-18.7. Accessed February 15, 2015.

Canning, Charlotte. "Feminist Performance as Feminist Historiography." *Theatre Survey* 45, no. 2 (November 2004): 227–233.

Carver, Raymond. *What We Talk about When We Talk about Love*. New York: Alfred A. Knopf, 1981.

Chang, Eury. "Canada's First Generation of Butoh: Kokoro Dance Celebrates 25 Years as Contemporary Butoh Pioneer." *Ricepaper/Asian Canadian Arts and Culture* 16, no. 1 (Spring 2011): 34–37.

Chang, Jeff. *Can't Stop Won't Stop: A History of the Hip-Hop Generation*. New York: St. Martin's Press, 2005.

Charnas, Dan. *The Big Payback: The History of the Business of Hip-Hop*. New York: New American Library, 2011.

Chatterjea, Ananya. *Butting Out: Reading Resistive Choreographies through Works by Jawole Willa Jo Zollar and Chandralekha*. Middletown, CT: Wesleyan University Press, 2004.

Chen Dance Center. "Our Repertoire." http://www.chendancecenter.org/index .php/the_company/repertoire/. Accessed August 18, 2014.

Cheng, Kuang Yu. "The Transition of Nation Identity in Taiwan and the Politics of Exporting *Minzu Wudao*." In *Dance, Identity and Integration: Conference Proceedings, Congress on Research in Dance, International Dance Conference Proceedings, Taiwan, August 1–4, 2004*, edited by J. LaPointe-Crump, 78–85 Cambridge, MA: Congress on Research in Dance, 2004.

Chong, Ping. "The Verbal Mural." In *Tokens: The NYC Asian American Experience on Stage*, edited by Alvin Eng, 438. New York: Asian American Writer's Workshop, 1999.

Chua, Amy. *Battle Hymn of the Tiger Mother*. New York: Penguin Books, 2007.

Chua, Amy, and Jed Rubenfeld. *The Triple Package: How Three Traits Explain the Rise and Fall of Cultural Groups in America*. New York: Penguin Books, 2014.

Cirque Du Soleil. *Dralion*. July 19, 2013. https://preprod-www.cirquedusoleil.com /en/shows/dralion/show/about.aspx. Accessed October 13, 2015.

Co.ERASGA. "About Us." http://www.companyerasgadance.ca/en/about_us/about _the_company/. Accessed February 5, 2015.

Cowell, Mary-Jean. "Michio Ito in Hollywood: Modes and Ironies of Ethnicity." *Dance Chronicle* 24, no. 3 (2001): 263–305.

Cowell, Mary-Jean, and Satoru Shimazaki. "East and West in the Work of Michio Ito." *Dance Research Journal* 26, no. 2 (Fall 1994): 11–23.

"Crews Choice Challenge." *Randy Jackson Presents America's Best Dance Crew.* MTV, February 7, 2008. Burbank, CA: Warner Bros.

Daly, Ann. "Defining Your Brand Identity: What Business Are You In?" *Chicago Artists Resource.* http://www.chicagoartistsresource.org/articles/defining-your -brand-identity-what-business-are-you. Accessed October 14, 2015.

———. *Done into Dance: Isadora Duncan in America.* Middletown, CT: Wesleyan University Press, 2002.

———. "Trends in Dance Scholarship: Feminist Theory across the Millennial Divide." *Dance Research Journal* 32, no. 1 (2000): 39–42.

"Dance Interview: Howard Schwartz." *DancePlug,* August 8, 2008. http://www .danceplug.com/insidertips/interviews/howard-schwartz. Accessed December 8, 2011.

de Certeau, Michel. *The Practice of Everyday Life.* Translated by S. Rendall. Berkeley: University of California Press, 1988.

DeFrantz, Thomas F. "The Black Beat Made Visible: Body Power in Hip Hop Dance." In *Of the Presence of the Body: Essays on Dance and Performance Theory,* edited by Andre Lepecki, 64–81. Middletown, CT: Wesleyan University Press, 2004.

———. *Dancing Many Drums: Excavations in African American Dance.* Madison: University of Wisconsin Press, 2002.

Denhart, Andy. "Big Changes Ahead for America's Best Dance Crew." *Hitflix.com,* July 13, 2014. http://www.hitfix.com/news/big-changes-ahead-for-americas-best -dance-crew. Accessed October 15, 2015.

Diamond, Elin. "Introduction." In *Performance and Cultural Politics,* edited by Elin Diamond, 1–12. New York: Routledge, 1996.

Donohue, Maura Nguyen. "Asian Dancers, a Balancing Act." *Dance Magazine,* June 2005.

———. "From the Body to the World." *Dance Insider,* May 23, 2006. http://www .danceinsider.com/f2006/f0523_2.html. Accessed June 9, 2009.

———. *"what she when she."* *Dance Insider,* March 31, 2006. http://www.dance insider.com/f2006/f0331_2.html. Accessed June 9, 2009.

Drew, Emily M. "Pretending to Be 'Postracial': The Spectacularization of Race in Reality TV's *Survivor.*" *Television & New Media* 12, no. 4 (2011): 326–346.

Duggan, Lisa. *Twilight of Equality: Neoliberalism, Cultural Politics and the Attack on Democracy.* Boston: Beacon Press, 2004.

Dunning, Jennifer. "Yasuko Yokoshi Depicts Love, the Passage of Time, and the Everyday." *New York Times,* March 25, 2006.

"Ei Ja Na Kai—Post Taiko Jam Jam 2009." YouTube video, 2:51. From North American Taiko Conference 2009. Posted by kaukadj, August 20, 2009. https:// www.youtube.com/watch?v=c8Z7a4e5sBg. Accessed August 21, 2009.

Espiritu, Yen Le. *Asian American Panethnicity: Bridging Institutions and Identities.* Philadelphia: Temple University Press, 1992.

"Evolution of Street Dance Challenge." *Randy Jackson Presents America's Best Dance Crew.* MTV, March 20, 2008. Burbank, CA: Warner Bros.

Experimental Dance and Music (EDAM). "About EDAM." http://www.edam dance.org/pages/aboutedam.html. Accessed February 15, 2014.

Falcone, Jessica. "Garba with Attitude: Creative Nostalgia in Competitive Collegiate Gujarati American Folk Dancing." *Journal of Asian American Studies* 16, no. 1 (February 2013): 57–89.

Fatona, Andrea Monike. "'Where Outrage Meets Outrage': Racial Equity at the Canada Council for the Arts (1989–1999)." PhD diss., University of Toronto, 2011.

Fiske, John. *Reading the Popular.* New York: Routledge, 1989.

Fleetwood, Nicole R. *Troubling Vision: Performance, Visuality, and Blackness.* Chicago: University of Chicago Press, 2010.

Foo, Josey. *A Lily Lilies: Poems.* Notes on dance by Leah Stein. Callicoon, NY: Nightboat Books, 2001.

Forbidden City. Directed by Arthur Dong. 1989. San Francisco: Deep Focus Productions, 2002. DVD.

Foster, Susan L. *Reading Dancing: Bodies and Subjects in Contemporary American Dance.* Berkeley: University of California Press, 1986.

———. "Worlding Dance—An Introduction." In *Worlding Dance*, edited by Susan L. Foster, 1–13. New York: Palgrave Macmillan, 2009.

Fowler, Geoffrey. "At Lincoln Center: Shen Wei on Choreography Style." *Wall Street Journal*, July 7, 2009.

———. "East Meets West on New York's Upper West Side." *China Real Time* (blog). *Wall Street Journal*, July 2, 2009.

Francia, Luis H. *A History of the Philippines: From Indios Bravos to Filipinos.* New York: Overlook Press, 2014

Fujimoto, Yoko. "'Ei Ja Nai Ka?' Lyrics to Accompany Dance." Unpublished manuscript, 2001.

Gerdes, Ellen V. P. "Hard-Working Dance Students: Lessons from Taiwan." EdM thesis, Temple University, 2009.

———. "Shen Wei Dance Arts: Chinese Philosophy in Body Calligraphy." *Dance Chronicle* 33, no. 2 (2010): 231–250.

Giersdorf, Jens Richard. *The Body of the People: East German Dance since 1945.* Madison: University of Wisconsin Press, 2013.

Gil, José. "Paradoxical Body." *TDR: The Drama Review* 50, no. 4 (2006): 21–35.

Gonzalves, Theodore. *The Day the Dancers Stayed: Performing in the Filipino American Diaspora.* Philadelphia: Temple University Press, 2009.

Goodwin, Andrew. "Fatal Distractions: MTV Meets Postmodern Theory." In *Sound and Vision: The Music Video Reader*, edited by Simon Frith, Andrew Goodwin, and Lawrence Grossberg, 37–56. New York: Routledge, 1993.

Gordon K. Hirabayashi, Petitioner-appellant, v. United States of America. 828 F.2d 591 (9th Cir. 1987). http://law.justia.com/cases/federal/appellate-courts/F2/828 /591/368928. Accessed February 15, 2015.

Grewal, Inderpal. *Transnational America: Feminisms, Diasporas, Neoliberalisms*. Durham, NC: Duke University Press, 2005.

Grosz, Elizabeth, "Space, Time, Bodies." In *Space, Time, and Perversion: Essays on the Politics of Bodies*, 83–102. New York: Routledge, 1995.

Hanayagi, Chiyo. *Fundamentals of Japanese Dance*. Tokyo: Kodansha Shuppan Service Center, 1981.

Hay, John. "The Human Body as a Microcosmic Source of Macrocosmic Values in Calligraphy." In *Self as Body in Asian Theory and Practice*, edited by Thomas P. Kasulis, Roger T. Ames, and Wimal Dissanayake, 179–212. Albany: State University of New York Press, 1993.

Heller, Nancy. "Kun-Yang/Lin Dancers Program Marred by Repetition." *Philadelphia Inquirer*, March 25, 2013.

Hiatt, Brian. "'N Sync Descend on Times Square for In-Store Appearance." *MTV .com*, March 21, 2000. http://www.mtv.com/news/819908/n-sync-descend-on -times-square-for-in-store-appearance/. Accessed June 12, 2014.

Hirabayashi, Jay. "In Memory of Kazuo Ohno." *Ricepaper/Asian Canadian Arts and Culture* 15, no. 3 (Fall 2010): 52–53.

Hirabayashi, PJ. "Life History Interview." HNRC/JANM. January 26, 2005.

Hirabayashi, PJ, and San Jose Taiko. "Ei Ja Nai Ka?" Handout. Unpublished score (1994) distributed in the "Ei Ja Nai Ka?" workshop at the 2009 North American Taiko Conference.

Hirabayashi, Roy. "Life History Interview." With Art Hansen and Sojin Kim. Transcript. *Big Drum: Taiko in the United States* exhibition. HNRC/JANM. January 26, 2005.

Hodgins, Paul. "Acclaimed Dance Troupe Comes to Costa Mesa." *Orange County Register*, April 13, 2010.

Hoelscher, Steven. "Making Place, Making Race: Performances of Whiteness in the Jim Crow South." *Annals of the Association of American Geographers* 93, no. 3 (2003): 657–686.

Horwitz, Andy. "Talking about Dance Criticism and the Changing World." *Culturebot*, July 4, 2012. http://www.culturebot.net/2012/07/13868/talking-about -dance-criticism-and-the-changing-world/. Accessed July 5, 2012.

"Hua Hua Zhang's Visual Expressions." Annenberg Center Live, University of Pennsylvania, October 2011. http://www.annenbergcenter.org/event/hua-hua -zhangs-visual-expressions-181. Accessed October 13, 2015.

Humphrey, Doris. *The Art of Making Dances*. Edited by Barbara Pollack. New York: Grove Press, 1959.

Izumi, Masumi. "Reconsidering Ethnic Culture and Community: A Case Study on Japanese Canadian Taiko Drumming." *Journal of Asian American Studies* 4, no. 1 (2001): 35–56.

Jackson, Merilyn. "Hua Hua Zhang Puppetmaster." *Dance Journal*, December 4, 2010. http://philadelphiadance.org/blog/2010/12/04/hua-hua-zhang-puppet master/. Accessed April 1, 2014.

———. "In Search of Honest Generosity: A Backward Glance at the Dance Season." *Broad Street Review*, June 26, 2010, http://www.broadstreetreview.com /dance/the_dance_season_nine_nighlights. Accessed April 1, 2013.

———. "Kun-Yang Lin's Quest: Connecting Body to Soul." *Broad Street Review*, September 4, 2010. http://www.broadstreetreview.com/dance/kun_yang_lins _quest_connecting_body_to_soul. Accessed April 1, 2013.

———. "Spiritual Movement: 'Mandala' Is a Masterwork of Art and Stagecraft." *Philadelphia Inquirer*, February 12, 2011. http://static1.squarespace.com/static /52dec4c5e4b00bfdc05d604e/t/52eff2c8e4b03c2851db81d3/1391456968717 /20110212-phila-inquirer-review.pdf. Accessed October 13, 2015.

Jeyasingh, Shobana. "Getting Off the Orient Express." In *Routledge Dance Studies Reader*, 2nd ed., edited by Alexandra Carter and Janet O'Shea, 181–187. New York: Routledge, 2010.

Johnson, Robert. "East Meets West in Shen Wei's Brilliantly Imaginative Dance Trilogy." *Newark Star-Ledger*, July 10, 2009.

Jones, Bill T., with Peggy Gillespie. *Last Night on Earth*. New York: Knopf Doubleday, 1997.

Jones, Joni L. "Performance Ethnography: The Role of Embodiment in Cultural Authenticity." *Theatre Topics* 12, no. 1 (2002): 1–15.

Jowitt, Deborah. "Dance: Springing into Action." *Village Voice*, September 26, 2006.

———. "Dancing in Tune with the Earth." *Dance Magazine*, April 2006.

———. "Passion Distilled: A Choreographer Turns Her Postmodern Gaze on an Ancient Style." *Village Voice*, March 30, 2006.

Judging Genocide. Journeyman Pictures, video, 18:56, July 2007. http://www.jour neyman.tv/57479/short-films/judging-genocide.html. Accessed April 6, 2014.

Kasrel, Deni. "Spirited Away." *Philadelphia City Paper*, February 16, 2011.

Kaufman, Sarah. "Bill T. Jones/Arnie Zane Dance Company to Merge with Dance Theater Workshop." *Washington Post*, December 10, 2010.

———. "From China by Way of New York, a Cultural Revolution." *Washington Post*, October 24, 2005.

Kawabata, Yasunari. *The Dancing Girl of Izu and Other Stories*. Translated by J. Martin Holman. Berkeley, CA: Counterpoint Press, 1998.

Kawai, Roko. "Untitled." Parents of Murdered Children (POMC), Contra Costa/
    East Bay Chapter newsletter, February/March 2010.
Kim, Sam. *Avatar*. Ear to the Ground. Mulberry St. Theater, New York City. May
    23, 2006. Live performance.
———. Rockefeller Foundation, MAP Fund Dance Grant Application. 2006.
Kisselgoff, Anna. "Dance; With His Heart in His Imagery." *New York Times*, June
    24, 2001.
———. "An Indian at One with the Buffalo in Eiko and Koma's Spirit World."
    New York Times, November 7, 1991.
Knapp, Jennie. "Ensemble's Mix of Drumming, Dance Thrilling." *Richmond Times
    Dispatch*, March 2, 1999, D6.
Ko, Nalea J. "The Jabbawockeez Unmasked." *Pacific Citizen* (Los Angeles, CA),
    October 7–20, 2011, 9.
Kraszewski, Jon. "Country Hicks and Urban Cliques: Mediating Race, Reality, and
    Liberalism in MTV's Real World." In *Reality TV: Remaking Television Culture*,
    edited by Susan Murray and Laurie Ouelette, 179–196. New York: New York
    University Press, 2004.
Kraut, Anthea. *Choreographing the Folk: The Dance Stagings of Zora Neale Hurston*.
    Minneapolis: University of Minnesota Press, 2008.
Kübler-Ross, Elisabeth, and David Kessler. *On Grief and Grieving*. New York:
    Scribner, 2005.
Kun-Yang Lin/Dancers. "About the Company." http://kunyanglin.org/About1.htm.
    Accessed August 18, 2014.
———. *Autumn Skin: Journeys of East/West*. March 2010.
———. *Mandala Project: Returning to the Circle*. February 2011.
———. *One: Gifts from Afar*. Program, March 2013.
Kwan, SanSan. *Kinesthetic City: Dance and Movement in Chinese Urban Spaces*.
    New York: Oxford University Press, 2013.
———. "Performing a Geography of Asian America: The Chop Suey Circuit."
    TDR: The Drama Review 55, no. 1 (Spring 2011): 120–136.
Lai, Larissa. *Slanting I, Imagining We: Asian Canadian Literary Production in the
    1980s and 1990s*. Waterloo, ON: Wilfred Laurier University Press, 2014.
Lao Tzu. *Tao Te Ching: A New Translation*. Translated by Sam Hamill. Boston:
    Shambhala, 2005.
Lee, Erika, and Naoko Shibusawa. "Guest Editor's Introduction: What Is Trans-
    national Asian American History? Recent Trends and Challenges." *Journal of
    Asian American Studies* 8, no. 3 (October 2005): vii–xvii.
Lee, Esther Kim. "Between the Personal and the Universal: Asian American Solo
    Performance from the 1970s to the 1990s." *Journal of Asian American Studies* 6,
    no. 3 (2004): 289–312.

Lee, Josephine. *Performing Asian America: Race and Ethnicity on the Contemporary Stage*. Philadelphia: Temple University Press, 1997.

Lee, Rachel C. "Where's My Parade? Margaret Cho and the Asian American Body in Space." *TDR: The Drama Review* 48, no. 2 (2004): 108–132.

"Letters from Rev. Ken Metzner, TD and Helen Faller." *thINKing DANCE*, December 4, 2011. http://thinkingdance.net/articles/2011/12/05/Letters-from -Rev.-Ken-Metzner-TD-and-Helen-Faller. Accessed August 18, 2014.

Letton, Shoko. "Eiko and Koma: Dance Philosophy and Aesthetic." MA thesis, Florida State University, 2009.

Li, Xiaoping. *Voices Rising: Asian Canadian Cultural Activism*. Vancouver: University of British Columbia Press, 2007.

Lim, Sammy. "The Dance Enthusiast Asks Kun-Yang Lin about Chi, His Mandala Works, and What He Would Do If He Were Not a Dance Artist." *Dance Enthusiast*, August 2, 2014. http://www.dance-enthusiast.com/features/view/kun -yang-lin14. Accessed August 18, 2014.

Lim, Thea, comp., with Robin Akimbo, Alaska B, Michelle Cho, and Elisha Shim. "Vogue Evolution Forever Part 1: The Racialicious Roundtable on *America's Best Dance Crew*." *Racialicious—The Intersection of Race and Pop Culture* (blog), September 16, 2009. http://www.racialicious.com/2009/09/16/vogue-evolution -forever-part-1-the-racialicious-roundtable-on-americas-best-dance-crew/. Accessed May 28, 2014.

Liu, Laura. "The Place of Immigration in Studies of Geography and Race." *Social & Cultural Geography* 1, no. 2 (2000): 169–182.

Liu, Michael, et al. *The Snake Dance of Asian American Activism: Community, Vision, and Power*. Lanham, MD: Lexington Books, 2008.

"Live Auditions." *Randy Jackson Presents America's Best Dance Crew*. MTV, January 26, 2008. Burbank, CA: Warner Bros.

Lowe, Lisa. *Immigrant Acts: On Asian American Cultural Politics*. Durham, NC: Duke University Press, 1996.

Long Center for the Performing Arts. Austin, TX. Season brochure, 2009.

Macaulay, Alistair. "A Trilogy of Asia, Conceived in Motion." *New York Times*, July 10, 2009.

———. "Woody Guthrie, Choreographer's Muse: Downtown Dance Festival at Battery Park." *New York Times*, August 17, 2012.

Mazo, Joseph H. *Prime Movers: The Makers of Modern Dance in America*. Hightstown, NJ: Princeton Book Co., 2000.

McMillian, Uri. "Mammy–Memory: Staging Joice Heth, or the Curious Phenomenon of the 'Ancient Negress.'" *Women & Performance: A Journal of Feminist History* 22, no.1 (March 2012): 29–46.

Mehra, Samantha. "Heart, Soul and Spirit: An Ethnography of the Kokoro Dance Body." Paper presented at the annual meeting of the Canadian Society for

Dance Studies, St. John's, Newfoundland, June 17–21, 2008. http://www.csds
-sced.ca/English/proceedings.html#ArticlesandEssays. Accessed August 15, 2014.

Meighan, Cate. "A Rebooted 'America's Best Dance Crew' Will Return More
Than 2 Years after Being Canceled by MTV." *MusicTimes.com*, January 11, 2015.
http://www.musictimes.com/articles/24102/20150111/rebooted-americas-best
-dance-crew-return-more-than-2-years-canceled-mtv.htm. Accessed April 19,
2005.

"Michael Jackson's *Thriller*." *Randy Jackson Presents America's Best Dance Crew.*
MTV, March 6, 2008. Burbank, CA: Warner Bros.

Michio Ito Pioneering Dancer-Choreographer. Directed by Bonnie Oda Homsey.
Los Angeles: Los Angeles Dance Foundation, 2012. Film.

Miki, Roy. *In Flux: Transnational Shifts in Asian Canadian Writing.* Edmonton:
NeWest Press, 2011.

———. *Redress: Inside the Japanese Canadian Call for Justice.* Vancouver: Raincoast Books, 2004.

Minh Tran & Company. http://www.mtdance.org/. Accessed June 11, 2009.

Murphy, Jacqueline Shea. *The People Have Never Stopped Dancing: Native American Modern Dance Histories.* Minneapolis: University of Minnesota Press, 2007.

Murray, Susan, and Laurie Ouelette. "Introduction." In *Reality TV: Remaking
Television to Culture,* edited by Susan Murray and Laurie Ouelette, 1–18. New
York: New York University Press, 2004.

Nakayama, I., comp. *Japanese Voice: A Video Archive of Singing and Techniques in
the Japanese Language.* Kanan, Japan: Osaka University of Arts, AD POPOLO,
2008.

New Orleans–Based Women's Health & Justice Initiative. "Stereotypes, Myths, &
Criminalizing Policies: Regulating the Lives of Poor Women." *Incite!* (blog),
July 19, 2011. https://inciteblog.wordpress.com/2011/07/19/stereotypes-myths
-criminalizing-policies-regulating-the-lives-of-poor-women/. Accessed June 11,
2014.

New York Live Arts. Resident Commissioned Artist Program. http://newyorklive
arts.org/programs/create/resident-commissioned-artist.php. Accessed March 30,
2012.

Nguyen, Mic. "Asian America's Best Dance Crew." *Hyphen*, March 6, 2009. http://
www.hyphenmagazine.com/blog/2009/03/asian-americas-best-dance-crew.
Accessed April 2, 2009.

O'Hara, Kathleen. *A Grief Like No Other: Surviving the Violent Death of Someone
You Love.* New York: Marlowe, 2006.

Okihiro, Gary. "Acting Japanese." In *Japanese Diasporas: Unsung Pasts, Conflicting
Presents and Uncertain Futures,* edited by Nobuko Adachi, 191–201. New York:
Routledge, 2006.

Omi, Michael, and Howard Winant. *Racial Formation in the United States from the 1960s to the 1980s*. New York: Routledge, 1986.

Ouellette, Laurie, and James Hay. "Makeover Television, Governmentality and the Good Citizen." *Continuum: Journal of Media & Cultural Studies* 22, no. 4 (2008): 471–484.

Ownby, David. *Falun Gong and the Future of China*. Oxford: Oxford University Press, 2008.

Palumbo-Liu, David. "Double Trouble: The Pathology of Ethnicity Meets White Schizophrenia." In *Asian/American: Historical Crossing of a Racial Frontier*, 295–336. Stanford: Stanford University Press, 1999.

Paris, Carl. "Will the Real Bill T. Jones Please Stand Up?" *TDR: The Drama Review* 49, no. 2 (Summer 2005): 64–74.

Parreñas Shimizu, Celine. *The Hypersexuality of Race: Performing Asian/American Women on Screen and Scene*. Durham, NC: Duke University Press, 2007.

Perez, Guillermo. "Wide Vistas from Intense Movement." *Fort Lauderdale Sun Sentinel*, April 6, 2004.

Perry, Imani. *Prophets of the Hood: Politics and Poetics in Hip-Hop*. Durham, NC: Duke University Press, 2004.

Phillips, Jevon. "Making All the Right Moves." *Los Angeles Times*, August 21, 2008.

———. "'The Jabbawockeez Present MUS.I.C': Opening the Doors to Dance . . . in Las Vegas? [Updated]." *Los Angeles Times*, May 19, 2010.

"The Philo Project: Kun Yang Lin Dancers—Germany Appeal." YouTube video, 3:59. Posted by The PHILO Project, March 21, 2014. https://www.youtube.com/watch?v=0RyQzNzkLVQ#t=55. Accessed August 18, 2014.

Ping Chong & Company. "Complete Production List." http://www.pingchong.org/interdisciplinary-performance/production-archive/. Accessed March 25, 2014.

———. "History." http://www.pingchong.org/the-company/history/. Accessed March 24, 2014.

———. "Undesirable Elements." http://www.pingchong.org/undesirable-elements/. Accessed March 25, 2014.

Polnick, Terry. "Art, Truth, Politics Clash at Kennedy Center." *Washington Times*, February 7, 2013.

"Preserving Dance as a Living Legacy." Special issue, *Dance Chronicle* 34, no. 1 (2011).

Prevots, Naima. *Dancing in the Sun: Hollywood Choreographers, 1915–1937*. Ann Arbor, MI: UMI Research Press, 1987.

Price, Peter. "'Two Hands' from Hua Hua Zhang's Visual Expressions." November 5, 2011. http://thinkingdance.net/articles/2011/11/05/Two-Hands-from-Hua-Hua-Zhangs-Visual-Expressions. Accessed August 18, 2014.

Rahaim, Matthew. *Musicking Bodies: Gesture and Voice in Hindustani Music.* Middletown, CT: Wesleyan University Press, 2012.

"Representing Africa: The Changing Face of African Dance in the Bay Area." Performing Diaspora Symposium, August 10, 2013. Podcast available at http://counterpulse.org/performing-diaspora/symposium/2013-symposium/. Accessed August 10, 2014.

"Rice Terraces of the Philippine Cordilleras." UNESCO, World Heritage List. http://whc.unesco.org/en/list/722. Accessed February 5, 2015.

Richter, Kat. "Review: Be/Longing: Light/Shadow." *Dance Journal*, March 29, 2014. http://philadelphiadance.org/blog/2014/03/29/12881/. Accessed June 1, 2014.

———. "Review—ONE Gifts from Afar." *Dance Journal*, March 26, 2013. http://philadelphiadance.org/blog/2013/03/26/review-one-gifts-from-afar/. Accessed August 18, 2014.

Roberts, Dorothy. *Killing the Black Body: Race, Reproduction, and the Meaning of Liberty.* New York: Vintage, 1997.

Roginsky, Dina. "Folklore, Folklorism, and Synchronization: Preserved-Created Folklore in Israel." *Journal of Folklore Research* 44, no. 1 (2007): 41–66.

Rose, Tricia. *Black Noise: Rap Music and Black Culture in Contemporary America.* Middletown, CT: Wesleyan University Press, 1994.

———. *The Hip-Hop Wars: What We Talk about When We Talk about Hip-Hop—And Why It Matters.* New York: Basic Books, 2008.

Roxworthy, Emily. *The Spectacle of Japanese American Trauma: Racial Performativity and World War II.* Honolulu: University of Hawai'i Press, 2008.

Said, Edward. *Orientalism.* New York: Random House, 1978.

Saito, Yuriko. "Japanese Aesthetics." In *Encyclopedia of Aesthetics*, edited by Michael Kelly, 546–547. New York: Oxford University Press, 1998.

Salamone, Gina. "Shen Yun, the Show Beijing Doesn't Want You to See, Returns to New York's Lincoln Center." *New York Daily News*, March 25, 2012.

San Juan, Carolina. "Ballroom Dance as Indicator of Immigrant Identity in the Filipino Community." *Journal of American and Comparative Cultures* 24, no. 3–4 (Fall/Winter 2001): 177–181.

Savigliano, Marta Elena. *Tango and the Political Economy of Passion.* Boulder: Westview Press, 1995.

———. "Worlding Dance and Dancing Out There in the World." In *Worlding Dance*, edited by Susan L. Foster, 163–190. New York: Palgrave Macmillan, 2009.

Schechner, Richard. *Performance Studies: An Introduction.* London: Routledge, 2002.

Schiller, Nina Glick, and Georges Eugene Fouron. "Long Distance Nationalism Defined." In *Georges Woke Up Laughing: Long Distance Nationalism and the Search for Home*, 17–35. Durham, NC: Duke University Press, 2001.

Schloss, Joseph G. *Foundation: B-boys, B-girls, and Hip-Hop Culture in New York.* Oxford: Oxford University Press, 2009.

Schneider, Rebecca. *The Explicit Body in Performance.* New York: Routledge, 1997.

Segal, Lewis. "That'll Leave a Mark: Shen Wei Dancers Will Turn the Disney Hall Floor into a Painted Canvas." *Los Angeles Times*, June 20, 2007.

Seng, Theary C. *Daughter of the Killing Fields: Asrei's Story.* London: Fusion Press, 2005.

Shapiro-Phim, Toni. "Mediating Cambodian History, the Sacred, and the Earth." In *Dance, Human Rights and Social Justice: Dignity in Motion*, edited by Naomi Jackson and Toni Shapiro-Phim, 304–322. Lanham, MD: Scarecrow Press, 2008.

Sharma, Nitasha. *Hip Hop Desis: South Asian Americans, Blackness, and a Global Racial Consciousness.* Durham, NC: Duke University Press, 2010.

Sharma, Preeti. "The (T)errors of Visibility." MA thesis, University of California, Los Angeles, 2008.

Shay, Anthony. *Choreographic Politics: State Folk Dance Companies, Representation, and Power.* Middletown, CT: Wesleyan University Press, 2002.

Shea Murphy, Jacqueline. *The People Have Never Stopped Dancing: Native American Modern Dance Histories.* Minneapolis: University of Minnesota Press, 2007.

Shen Wei Dance Arts. "About Shen Wei." http://www.shenweidancearts.org/about -shenwei/. Accessed August 21, 2014.

———. *Connect Transfer II.* Program notes. December 3, 5, 6, and 7, 2009.

———. "Metropolitan Museum of Art, Temple of Dendur, 20th Annual Conference Gala Awards Dinner Performance: Shen Wei Dance Arts." YouTube video, 7:05. Posted by committee100, July 8, 2011. http://www.youtube.com/watch ?v=brmvN83E5sA. Accessed March 1, 2012.

———. "Olympics Opening Dancing Beijing 2008." YouTube video, 6:53. Posted by Jerry Widjaja, August 11, 2008. https://www.youtube.com/watch?v=7scUIT 7z23Y. Accessed October 13, 2015.

———. *Re-(Part 1).* Program notes. Kimmel Center, Philadelphia, February 15, 16, 17, 2008.

———. *Re-(I, II, III),* July 2009.

———. *Re-(Part III).* Program notes. Lincoln Center, New York, July 9, 10, 11, 2009.

"Shen Yun Dancer Profile: Alison Chen." YouTube video, 5:36. Posted by Shen Yun, December 12, 2011. https://www.youtube.com/watch?v=P18S4BLx-Vg. Accessed March 25, 2012.

"Shen Yun Dancer Profile: Chelsea Chai." YouTube video, 6:01. Posted by Shen Yun, December12,2011.https://www.youtube.com/watch?v=bARWHUOcTYc. Accessed March 25, 2012.

"Shen Yun Dancer Profile: Miranda Zhou-Galati." YouTube video, 4:36. Posted by Shen Yun, December 12, 2011. https://www.youtube.com/watch?v=NP12OZQ DMlE. Accessed March 25, 2012.

"Shen Yun Dancer Profile: Tim Wu." YouTube video, 7:09. Posted by Shen Yun, December 12, 2011. https://www.youtube.com/watch?v=H_JAAj2VJbk. Accessed March 25, 2012.

Shen Yun Performing Arts. "Reviving 5,000 Years of Civilization." http://www .shenyunperformingarts.org/about. Accessed March 25, 2012.

Shimakawa, Karen. *National Abjection: The Asian American Body Onstage*. Durham, NC: Duke University Press, 2002.

Shin, Elise. "JabbaWockeeZ Wins! America's Best Dance Crew Recap." *Asian Week*, March 27, 2008. http://www.asianweek.com/2008/03/27/americas-best-dance -crew-asian-jabbawockeez-finale-winner-week-7/. Accessed March 27, 2008.

Siegel, Lee. "Declawing the Tiger: A Spanking for Amy Chua." *New York Observer*, January 19, 2011.

———. "Rise of the Tiger Nation." *Wall Street Journal*, October 27, 2012.

Small, Christopher. *Musicking: The Meanings of Performing and Listening*. Middletown, CT: Wesleyan University Press, 1998.

Soja, Edward. *Thirdspace: Journeys to Los Angeles and Other Real-and-Imagined Places*. Oxford: Blackwell, 1996.

Srinivasan, Priya. *Sweating Saris: Indian Dance as Transnational Labor*. Philadelphia: Temple University Press, 2013.

Staub, Maria. "Shen Wei's Olympic Moves." *New York Sun*, June 9, 2008.

Takahashi, Jere. *Nisei/Sansei: Shifting Japanese Identities and Politics*. Philadelphia: Temple University Press, 1997.

Takaki, Ronald. *Strangers from a Different Shore: A History of Asian Americans*. Rev. ed. Boston: Little, Brown, 1998.

Taylor, Diana. *Archive and the Repertoire*. Durham, NC: Duke University Press, 2003.

Tchen, John Kuo Wei. *New York before Chinatown: Orientalism and the Shaping of American Culture, 1776–1882*. Baltimore: Johns Hopkins University Press, 1999.

The Tenth Dancer. Written and directed by Sally Ingleton. Brunswick, Australia: 360 Degree Films, 1993. Film.

Thiong'o, Ngugi wa. *Something Torn and New: An African Renaissance*. New York: Basic Civitas Books, 2009.

Tiongsen, Antonio, Jr. *Filipinos Represent: DJs, Racial Authenticity, and the Hip-Hop Nation*. Minneapolis: University of Minnesota Press, 2013.

Tommasini, Anthony. "Virtuosos Become a Dime a Dozen." *New York Times*, August 12, 2011.

Tsai, Tina. "Jabbawockeez, Unmasked." *Asian Week*, March 13, 2008. http://www
.asianweek.com/2008/03/13/jabbawockeez-unmasked/. Accessed March 13, 2008.

Tseng, Muna. "The Verbal Mural." In *Tokens? The NYC Asian American Experience on Stage*, edited by Alvin Eng, 419. New York: Asian American Writer's
Workshop, 1999.

Tuan, Yi-Fu. *Space and Place: The Perspective of Experience*. Minneapolis: University of Minnesota Press, 1977.

Tusler, Mark. "Sounds and Sights of Power: Ensemble Taiko Drumming (*Kumi
Daiko*) Pedagogy in California and the Conceptualization of Power." PhD diss.,
University of California, Santa Barbara, 2003.

Ty, Eleanor. *Unfastened: Globality and Asian North American Narratives*. Minneapolis: University of Minnesota Press, 2010.

Uba, George Russel. "International Ballroom Dance and the Choreographies of
Transnationalism." *Journal of Asian American Studies* 10, no. 2 (2007): 141–167.

Uyehara, Denise. "*Headless Turtleneck Relatives*: Excerpts." In *Getting Your Solo Act
Together*, edited by Michael Kearns, 75–79. Portsmouth, NH: Heinemann, 1977

———. *Hello (Sex) Kitty: Mad Asian Bitch on Wheels*. In *O Solo Homo: The New
Queer Performance*, edited by Holly Hughes and David Román 377–409. New
York, NY: Grove Press, 1998.

———. *Maps of City and Body: Shedding Light on the Performances of Denise Uyehara*. New York: Kaya/Mua, 2004.

Vu, Maveric. "Dance, Dance Evolution: Asian Americans Pop, Lock and Break
Their Way into Hip-Hop Dance Culture." *Hyphen*, no. 21 (Fall 2010). http://
www.hyphenmagazine.com/magazine/issue-21-new-legacy/dance-dance-evolu
tion. Accessed November 29, 2011.

Wang, Oliver. "Rapping and Repping Asian: Race, Authenticity, and the Asian
American MC." In *Alien Encounters: Popular Culture in Asian America*, edited
by Mimi Thi Nguyen and Thuy Linh N. Tu, 35–68. Durham, NC: Duke University Press, 2007.

———. "These Are the Breaks: Hip-Hop and AfroAsian Cultural (Dis)Connec-
tions." In *AfroAsian Encounters: Culture, History and Politics*, edited by Heike
Raphael-Hernadez and Shannon Steen. 146–164. New York: New York University Press, 2006.

Wei, William. *The Asian American Movement*. Philadelphia: Temple University
Press, 1993.

Weisz, Steven. "Review: Kun-Yang Lin/Dancers—Beyond the Bones Revisited."
Dance Journal, April 1, 2012. http://philadelphiadance.org/blog/2012/04/01
/review-kun-yang-lindancers-beyond-the-bones-revisited/. Accessed April 1, 2014.

Wilcox, Emily. "Against American Imperialism: The Forgotten Legacies of Third
World Leftism." Paper presented at the annual Congress on Research in Dance/

Society of Dance History Scholars Conference, Riverside, CA, November 14–17, 2013.

———. "Han-Tang *Zhongguo Gudianwu* and the Problem of Chineseness in Contemporary Chinese Dance: Sixty Years of Creation and Controversy." *Asian Theatre Journal* 29, no. 1 (2012): 206–232.

———. "'Selling Out' Post Mao: Dance Labor and the Ethics of Fulfillment in Reform Era China." In *Chinese Modernity and the Individual Psyche*, edited by Andrew Kipnis, 43–65. New York: Palgrave Macmillan, 2012.

Witzel, Matthias. *Understanding Trauma in Cambodia Handbook*. Translated by Yim Sotheary and Om Chariya. Edited by Theary Seng. Center for Social Development and German Development Service, 2007. http://www.matthias-witzel .com/index.php?id=21&lang=en. Accessed April 7, 2014.

Women's Health & Justice Initiative. "Stereotypes, Myths, & Criminalizing Policies: Regulating the Lives of Poor Women." *Incite!* (blog), July 19, 2011. http ://inciteblog.wordpress.com/2011/07/19/stereotypes-myths-criminalizing-poli cies-regulating-the-lives-of-poor-women/. Accessed June 11, 2014.

Wong, Deborah. "Moving: From Performance to Performative Ethnography and Back Again." In *Shadows in the Field: New Perspectives for Fieldwork in Ethnomusicology*, 2nd ed., edited by Gregory Barz and Timothy Cooley, 76–89. New York: Oxford University Press, 2008.

———. *Speak It Louder: Asian Americans Making Music*. New York: Routledge, 2004.

Wong, Sau-ling C. "Dancing in the Diaspora: Cultural Long-Distance Nationalism and the Staging of Chineseness by San Francisco's Chinese Folk Dance Association." *Journal of Transnational American Studies* 2, no. 1 (2010).

———. "Denationalism Reconsidered: Asian American Cultural Criticism at a Theoretical Crossroads." *Amerasia Journal* 21, no. 1 & 2 (1995): 1–27.

Wong, Yutian. "Artistic Utopias: Michio Ito and the Trope of the International." In *Worlding Dance*, edited by Susan L. Foster, 144–162. New York: Palgrave Macmillan, 2009.

———. *Choreographing Asian America*. Middletown, CT: Wesleyan University Press, 2010.

———. "Club O' Noodles's *Laughter from the Children of War*." In *Choreographing Asian America*, 57–86. Middletown, CT: Wesleyan University Press, 2010.

———. "Towards a New Asian American Dance Theory: Locating the Dancing Asian American Body." *Discourses in Dance* 1, no. 1 (2002): 69–90.

Woo, Michelle. "Kaba Modern Created a Dance Dance Revolution: Popping and Locking with UC Irvine's Dance Crew and the Movement It Helped to Create." *OC Weekly*, January 19, 2012. http://www.ocweekly.com/2012-01-19/culture /kaba-modern-irvine/. Accessed January 19, 2012.

Wu, Ellen D. "Asian Americans and the 'Model Minority' Myth." *Los Angeles Times*, January 23, 2014.

Wu, Kuang-Ming. "Chinese Aesthetics." In *Understanding the Chinese Mind: The Philosophical Roots*, edited by Robert E. Allinson, 236–264. New York: Oxford University Press, 1989.

Xu, Zhao. "Dancing in the Spotlight on Opening Night." *China Daily*, August 6, 2008. http://www.absolutechinatours.com/news/Dancing-in-the-spotlight-on-opening-night-503.html. Accessed August 18, 2014.

"Yasuko Yokoshi in Conversation with Tere O'Connor." *Critical Correspondence*, February 22, 2006. http://www.movementresearch.org/criticalcorrespondence/blog/?p=648. Accessed February 22, 2006.

Ying Huang. "The State of Dance Research in Taiwan, Republic of China." *Dance Research Journal* 31, no. 1 (1999): 130–136.

Yokoshi, Yasuko. Press packet biography, 2000–2005. In author's possession, 2005.

———. *what we when we*. Danspace Project, New York City. March 23, 2006. Live performance.

Yoshihari, Mari. *Musicians from a Different Shore: Asians and Asian Americans in Classical Music*. Philadelphia: Temple University Press, 2008.

Yu, Jin-Wen. "The Energy Flow of the Human Being and the Universe: Tai Ji Philosophy as an Artistic and Philosophical Foundation for the Development of Chinese Contemporary Dance." PhD diss., Temple University, 1994.

Contributors

ANGELA K. AHLGREN is an assistant professor in the Department of Theatre and Film at Bowling Green State University. She has taught at Texas A&M University and Ohio University, and she earned her PhD in performance as public practice from the University of Texas at Austin. Her forthcoming book is titled *Drumming Asian America: Taiko, Performance, and Cultural Politics*. She has also performed with the Minneapolis-based taiko group Mu Daiko and has worked as a state manager and staff member for Theater Mu/Mu Performing Arts.

ROSEMARY CANDELARIO is an assistant professor of dance at Texas Woman's University. Her forthcoming book is titled *Flowers Cracking Concrete: Eiko & Koma's Asian/American Choreographies*. She has published in the *Journal of Theatre, Dance and Performance Training, The Scholar & Feminist Online, International Journal of Screendance*, and *Asian Theatre Journal*. She earned a PhD in culture and performance from UCLA.

EURY COLIN CHANG is a Vancouver-born theater artist and scholar, currently pursuing a PhD in the Department of Theatre and Film at the University of British Columbia (UBC). His graduate research into Asian Canadian theater performance is being supported by the Social Sciences and Humanities Research Council. In 2013 he was the recipient of the Errol Durbach Graduate Scholarship in Theatre at UBC. His most recent peer-reviewed article, "Towards Reconciliation: Immigration in Marty Chan's *The Forbidden Phoenix* and David Yee's *lady in the red dress*," was published in the fall 2015 issue of *Theatre Research in Canada*. In addition

to his academic work, he serves as the artistic director of Creative Domin-
ion, a nonprofit society dedicated to the creation of new performance (www
.creativedominion.ca).

BRIAN SU-JEN CHUNG earned his PhD in American culture at the University of Michigan, Ann Arbor, and is currently an assistant professor of
ethnic studies at the University of Hawai'i at Mānoa. He is currently
preparing a book manuscript that explores how a specific vision of the
"Chinese immigrant" has been imagined and produced through the spatial
discourses and the neoliberal and biopolitical dynamics of Silicon Valley
placemaking. His research on this topic has appeared in *Verge: Studies in
Global Asias*.

MAURA NGUYEN DONOHUE is an associate professor of dance at Hunter
College, a faculty associate of the Roosevelt House Institute of Public Policy, and a founder of MND/inmixedcompany. Her commissioned choreography has been presented in New York City for the past twenty years,
and her company has toured throughout North America, Europe, and Asia.
She writes for *Culturebot*, served as guest editor for *Critical Correspondence's
University Project*, served as adviser and Asian bureau chief for the *Dance
Insider* (2000–2009), and has published in *Dance Magazine, American Theater Journal*, and *HK Dance Journal*. She serves on the New York Dance
and Performance ("Bessies") Awards Committee and the board of directors
for Movement Research. She has served on the board of directors for Dance
Theater Workshop (NYC) and Congress on Research in Dance.

ELLEN V. P. GERDES is a doctoral candidate in culture and performance
at the University of California, Los Angeles. Her current research focuses
on intersections of performance and politics in Hong Kong. She has taught
at Temple University, Drexel University, Rowan University, and Bucknell
University and has published in *Asian Theatre Journal, Cultural Studies/
Critical Methodologies*, and *Dance Chronicle*.

ROKO KAWAI is a dancer/improviser/teacher/writer. Her performance
work has explored the specificity of classical Japanese dance vis-à-vis postmodern improvisation, for which she was awarded the Pew Fellowship on
the Arts for Choreography, Japan-U.S. Friendship Commission Fellowship,

and a Leeway Transformation Award for women artists working in social justice. In 2013 she served as co-curator for the Performing Diaspora Festival in San Francisco, where she spearheaded the symposium panel "Body Destroyed/Body Remembered: Genocide, Civil War and Performance." From 2012 to 2015, she worked at the Yerba Buena Center for the Arts in San Francisco as the performing arts manager of contextual programming. She is now the senior grants officer at STAND! For Families Free of Violence, an anti–domestic violence agency in Contra Costa County.

DENISE UYEHARA is an interdisciplinary artist who investigates themes of memory and what marks the body as it travels across borders of identity. Her work has been presented in London, Helsinki, Tokyo, Vancouver, and across the United States. She is a founding member of the Sacred Naked Nature Girls and a frequent university lecturer. Awards include the MAP Fund, the Brody Arts Fund, support from the Asian Cultural Council, City of Los Angeles Cultural Affairs Department, and the Arizona Commission on the Arts. Her book *Maps of City and Body* (2003) documents her process. See www.deniseuyehara.com.

YUTIAN WONG is an associate professor in the School of Theatre and Dance at San Francisco State University and the author of *Choreographing Asian America* (2010). Other publications have appeared in *Discourses in Dance*, *Short Film Studies*, and *World(ing) Dance*, edited by Susan L. Foster (2009). Recent work on the disciplining of Asian American dance will appear in *RELAY: Theories in Motion*, coedited by Thomas F. DeFrantz and Philipa Rothfield (forthcoming).

Index

Note: *page numbers in italics refer to illustrations; those followed by "n" indicate chapter endnotes.*

STUDIES IN DANCE HISTORY

Published under the auspices of the Society of Dance History Scholars